Comrades and Christians

*Religion and political struggle in
Communist Italy*

Comrades and Christians

*Religion and political struggle in
Communist Italy*

David I. Kertzer

*Associate Professor, Department of Sociology and Anthropology
Bowdoin College*

Cambridge University Press

Cambridge
London   New York   New Rochelle
Melbourne   Sydney

Published by the Press Syndicate of the University of Cambridge
The Pitt Building, Trumpington Street, Cambridge CB2 1RP
32 East 57th Street, New York, NY 10022, USA
296 Beaconsfield Parade, Middle Park, Melbourne 3206, Australia

First published 1980

Printed in the United States of America
Typeset by Photo Graphics, Baltimore, Md.
Printed and bound by Hamilton Printing Co., Rensselear, N.Y.

Library of Congress Cataloging in Publication Data
Kertzer, David I   1948–

Comrades and Christians.

Bibliography: p.

Includes index.

1.   Communism – Italy.   2.   Partito comunista italiano
3.   Communism and Christianity – Catholic Church – Italy.
4.   Italy – Social conditions – 1945–   5.   Italy –
Politics and government – 1945–   I.   Title.
HX289.K47   334.43′0945   79–15313
ISBN 0 521 22879 4 hard covers
ISBN 0 521 29700 1 paperback

*To my parents, Morris and Julia Kertzer,
who nurtured my interest in politics,
religion, and other cultures*

There is something eternal in religion which is destined to survive all the particular symbols in which religious thought has successively enveloped itself. There can be no society which does not feel the need of upholding and reaffirming at regular intervals the collective sentiments and the collective ideas which make its unity and its personality. Now this moral remaking cannot be achieved except by the means of reunions, assemblies and meetings where the individuals, being closely united to one another, reaffirm in common their common sentiments . . .
[Durkheim 1915:427]

The problem of religion, intended in its lay rather than its confessional sense, is that of the unity, sanctified by faith, between a world view and a conforming norm of behavior; but why call this "religion" and not call it "ideology" or simply "politics"? [Gramsci 1971a:6]

Contents

Tables

xiii

Preface

To most Americans, the strength of the Italian Communist Party (PCI) is a great mystery. Associated with dark visions of totalitarianism and inevitably linked to Moscow, it is difficult for Americans to understand the appeal the Communist Party has in Italy. That almost one-third of all Italian voters cast their ballots for the PCI in 1979 is, in this perspective, a great enigma, unfathomable in the land of the Holy See.

It is my hope that reading this book on the nature of Communist Party strength in one of Italy's reddest zones will clear up this mystery, at least in part. For readers who have come across accounts of "Eurocommunism" more times than they can remember without ever learning of the lives of any "Euro-Communists" who are not members of Parliament or intellectuals of renown, this book is intended to provide a glimpse into the social fabric of Euro-Communist experience. And for those curious about the coexistence of the strongest Western Communist Party with the bastion of the Catholic Church, this book is intended as an introduction to Church–Communist relations in Italy, focusing on the way in which the national conflict is played out in one local setting.

There has certainly been no dearth of writings on the Italian political situation, particularly in the last few years since the prospect of Communist participation in the Italian government became likely. Many of these studies are misguided, some are perceptive, but rare is the report based on an appreciation of the place of the Communist Party in the lives of its members and supporters. Party platforms have been examined, Party officials interviewed, voters given questionnaires, electoral results scrutinized, but in all these the essential social context of Communist allegiance has been remote or absent.

It is an element of anthropological faith that no aspect of society can be fully understood unless it is examined in its broad social context. To understand a people's religion, for example, we must know something about their economic organization, their political system, and their kinship relations. In the same way, to understand a people's political allegiances, activities, and beliefs, it is crucial to see how these relate to other elements of the people's lives. The strength of traditional anthropological methodology lies just in this task, in acquiring a well-rounded picture of a people's day-to-day lives and seeing how various elements of their social universe affect one another.

The cornerstone of this traditional anthropological approach is participant-observation, and this book represents an attempt to demonstrate the value of participant-observation research to modern, urban study. Although a substantial number of anthropologists and others have conducted such research in the remote peasant villages of Southern and mountainous Italy, participant-observation research in the large urban centers has been rare. The reasons for this are numerous, from the traditional "peasantization" of American anthropology to the aversion to personalized, empirical research among Italian social scientists.

Indeed, the very applicability of the participant-observer, holistic approach to *urban* research has been questioned within the social sciences. The anthropologist, according to the stereotype, is at home in a small, rural community or, best of all, on a South Pacific atoll, where he can eventually come to know the entire local population on a personal basis. Although this is a pleasingly romantic portrait, it is essentially erroneous, for anthropologists have long been involved in the study of large-scale (but generally nonurban) societies; and studies of large American communities have a similarly long history.

One must admit, however, that studying Yankee City or Middletown is a rather different proposition from studying a city of half a million inhabitants, such as Bologna. Clearly it is impossible to do a participant-observation study of such a large population taken as a whole. This means that either some other method must be employed or some smaller division of the city (whether delimited by geographical or social criteria) must be selected. My choice of the latter alternative was based on the belief that participant-observation fieldwork yields a richness of human understanding unobtainable through more formal, quantitative approaches. This is not to say that such quantitative approaches are unimportant. On the contrary, the very existence of such larger-scale, empirical studies greatly enriches the results that can be obtained through smaller-scale, intensive study. Ideally, our understanding of social organization should be based on the integration of data, analysis, and perspectives obtained from a diversity of approaches.

This book is based on fieldwork I conducted from September 1971 through August 1972, with a brief return visit for six weeks in May and June of 1976. Unless otherwise noted, all events described in this book took place in 1971–2. The major portion of the fieldwork formed part of my doctoral dissertation research under the direction of Alex Weingrod at the Department of Anthropology, Brandeis

University. Of the influences leading to my choice of Italy for fieldwork, Alex was the most important. His encouragement and aid provided the main stimulus for the planning of this work, and his later advice enriched its first written incarnation, my doctoral dissertation.

I arrived in Italy armed with names of Italian social scientists and assorted intellectuals to contact, thanks to Alex Weingrod and Paolo Valesio, who I had been fortunate enough to have as an instructor of Italian language at Harvard. As a result of the networks thus opened up to me, my first few weeks in Italy were both profitable and enjoyable as I began my real education in Italian society. I would particularly like to thank Gilberto Marselli, Emma Morin, and Alessandro Pizzorno for the kindness they showed a strange anthropologist who came to them in those weeks with wild ideas about studying and living among working-class Communists.

Special thanks are due Arturo and Anna Parisi, whose aid and friendship provided a treasured part of our life in Bologna. Arturo not only helped us argue our way into an apartment, but then arranged for official sponsorship of my research by the Istituto Carlo Cattaneo, enabling me to get a visa. His aid in revising my questionnaires and in numerous other ways has contributed substantially to this study.

My research was facilitated by many others as well, including social scientists, politicians, and people of the Church. Don Antonio Toldo, director of social research for the Archdiocese of Bologna, kindly provided data from his studies of Church attendance in Bologna. I am similarly indebted to Luigi Arbizzani, then director of the Istituto Gramsci of Bologna, for his bibliographical aid in my research on the PCI. Renato Zangheri, mayor of Bologna, and Federico Castellucci, then deputy mayor in charge of municipal decentralization, generously gave of their time in agreeing to be interviewed. These individuals are but the most notable of the scores of representatives of city government, the Church, the PCI, the Christian Democrats, the Socialists, and many other organizations whose cooperation facilitated my research.

But the essential prerequisite of this study was not the aid provided by social scientists and people of renown, but rather the aid proffered by the people of Albora, the Bolognese whom I studied and from whom I learned. Communists and Catholics, Socialists, the unaffiliated, and the politically uninterested welcomed me and permitted me liberties that they were under no obligation to provide. I came as a foreigner, as an American, often asking embarrassing questions, questions local people would have enough sense not to pose, yet people not only put up with my eccentric ways, but made me feel welcome. Most noteworthy in this regard was the cooperation and encouragement I received from the Communist Party officials of Albora. Representing the party in power, they had little to gain and potentially much to lose by allowing an outsider to pry into the most sensitive of their affairs. Yet not only did they invite me to all their local membership meetings, but they invited me to their leadership strategy planning sessions and to their annual section congresses, at which the national party platform was discussed and section leadership elected. For the opportunity they provided me I remain profoundly thankful. I am only sorry that, in keeping with my attempt to protect the anonymity and confidentiality of the Alborese, I cannot thank by name those who took so much of their own time to help me carry out this study.

Fieldwork was greatly enriched by the work of Susan Dana Kertzer, my wife, who participated in almost every phase of the research. As a woman, Susan had easier access to some people and some activities than I did. In addition to such sex-role-linked research, Susan played a major role in the study of the storefront church, the topic discussed in Chapter 8. She has also read and expertly edited more drafts of the chapters of this book than either of us cares to remember.

My 1971–2 fieldwork was supported by grants from the National Institute of Mental Health and Brandeis University, and the first year of analysis was supported by a dissertation fellowship from the Woodrow Wilson National Fellowship Foundation. The book was written in 1978 while I was fortunate enough to be a Fulbright-Hays Senior Lecturer at the Department of Social Sciences at the University of Catania, Italy. I would like to thank Alberto Spreafico, chairman of the department, and Raimondo Catanzaro, the department member responsible for foreign scholars, for their kind and magnanimous help in a hundred different ways during my stay in Catania. I would also like to acknowledge with deep appreciation the thoughtful and efficient aid provided by Cipriana Scelba, Executive Director of the Commission for Cultural Exchanges Between Italy and the United States in Rome.

Various drafts of this book have been read by Alex Weingrod, David Jacobson, Arturo Parisi, Gianfranco Pasquino, and Peter Lange. This book has benefited greatly from their counsel. I thank Cesare Malservisi not only for allowing me to reproduce his ballad "Però, Però la Nona," but also for providing me with an Italian translation of the original, which is in Bolognese dialect. Gabor Brogyanyi looked over my English rendition of the song and offered some helpful suggestions. Finally, I want to thank Louise Caron for protectively and efficiently typing the manuscript, while fending off other demands on her time. Bowdoin College kindly provided funds to defray expenses connected with the preparation of the final manuscript. Some of the material constituting Chapter 6 of this book has appeared in another form in *Anthropological Quarterly* (1974) and *Journal for the Scientific Study of Religion* (1975). Likewise, portions of Chapter 7 have been published in another form in *Ethnic Encounters* (George L. Hicks and Philip E. Leis, eds., Duxbury Press, 1977).

Italians generally pigeonhole all social scientists into political categories – Communist, Socialist, Catholic – for social science is regarded as a political and polemical process. Although I agree as to the essentially political nature of social investigation, perhaps because of self-deception I do not see myself as falling very easily into any of the ready-made Italian political categories. At the same time, I am aware that aspects of this book may be used for partisan polemical purposes by either side in the Communist – Church conflict. Given the Communists' position of preeminence in Bologna and in the attention the Party receives in these pages, it is perhaps more vulnerable to criticism and attack. Here, for what little it may be worth, I would like to state my own personal political view that the PCI has been a positive force in Bologna, both in terms of organizing and acting in the interests of the working-class population and in terms of running the most efficient, livable large city in the nation. There is no American city that does not suffer in comparison to Bologna.

D.I.K.

Brunswick, Maine

Abbreviations

ARCI	Associazione Ricreativa Culturale Italiana
DC	Democrazia Cristiana
FGCI	Federazione Giovanile Comunista Italiana
LC	Lotta Continua
MSI	Movimento Sociale Italiano
PCI	Partito Comunista Italiano
PLI	Partito Liberale Italiano
PRI	Partito Republicano Italiano
PSC	Proletarian Struggle Cooperative
PSDI	Partito Socialista Democratico Italiano
PSI	Partito Socialista Italiano
PSIUP	Partito Socialista Italiano di Unità Proletaria
UDI	Unione Donne Italiane

The word "Party" capitalized refers to the Italian Communist Party (PCI).

The word "Church" capitalized refers to the Roman Catholic Church.

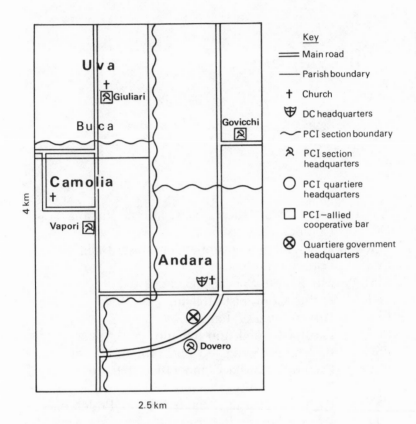

Figure 1. Schematic map of Albora

1

Introduction

Home of the Vatican, center of Roman Catholicism, Italy
may seem to the non-Italian an unlikely setting for the rise
of the largest and strongest Communist Party in a non-
Communist state. What seems a paradox to the outsider
is, of course, but a way of life to the Italian, who accom-
modates himself to the conflicting calls on his allegiance
made by the Church and the Communist Party (PCI).
From the halls of parliament to the central piazzas of
mountain villages the struggle between Church and Communist Party goes on, often in ways having little to do with
the national strictures of either institution. It has been a
battle without a victor, for, though the PCI has grown and
Church forces have declined, the competitors have established various *modi vivendi* in the hamlets, villages, and
cities throughout the nation. Just how the PCI and the
Church interact at the local level, what factors determine
this interaction, and how people respond to their calls of
support is the subject of this book, the study of the Communist Party and the Church in a Communist *quartiere*.

Though both the Church and the PCI have been described as monolithic institutions, the activities of Church
and Party in the community are not simply mirror images
of policy formulated at a higher bureaucratic level. National policy interacts with a wide range of local social

1

factors in determining the kinds of contact that people have with the Church and the PCI. At the same time, it would be foolish to try to understand Church–Party competition at the local level without reference to national institutional policies and strategies, for the local churches and Party sections are hardly autonomous. Church and Party activities in the community are the product, then, of the interaction between official organizational policies and local social and political considerations.

The two worlds

Il mondo cattolico e il mondo comunista–the Catholic world and the Communist world–are among the most common terms of political discourse in Italy.[1] Though, as will be discussed later, these labels can be misleading, they do help reveal some important questions. The Church and the Party are not simply segmental institutions calling for limited areas of allegiance; rather, they call on the individual's support in a wide variety of roles and situations. Being a good Catholic, according to the model promulgated by the hierarchy, entails behavior and beliefs that permeate a person's social life, and the allegiance called for by the Italian Communist Party is scarcely less inclusive. Both the PCI and the Church provide comprehensive systems of beliefs and behavior, systems that are mutually exclusive. This is recognized in the dual categorization of *mondo cattolico* and *mondo comunista*. The Church–Communist confrontation tends to divide people into two hostile and, to an extent, socially autonomous worlds.

Originally, the concept of the "world" was applied to the Church, referring to the web of organizations and devotees under Vatican authority. Each individual who recognized the Roman Catholic Church as God's instrument on earth was presumed, in this view, to have an all-pervading allegiance to the social and political as well as to ritual and ideological edicts of the hierarchy. Thus, for example, in the late nineteenth century politicians and journalists repeatedly speculated on what action the "Catholic world" might take: How would it vote? When would it recognize the legitimacy of the Italian government?

The usage of *il mondo cattolico* today follows this line, treating those who proclaim allegiance to the Church as a homogeneous social grouping opposed to other groupings. The various organizations affiliated with the Church, formally or informally, such as Catholic Action, the Christian Democratic party, and ACLI (the Italian Catholic Workers' Association), are conceived of as forming the institutional framework of the Catholic world.

The concept of the Communist world–*il mondo comunista*–arose as an analogue to the Catholic world concept. In the late nineteenth century, social analysts began referring to *il mondo socialista*, and the image of the Italian masses as divided between two competing worlds began to spread. After the Fascist hiatus, the Communist world became the heir to the Socialist world. Like the Catholic world, the Communist world is portrayed as having a variegated organizational structure including associations that are formally independent of the Party. The Communist world is peopled by individuals whose loyalty to the Communist cause is expressed in a wide range of social, political, and ideological spheres.

Analyses of the competition between Church and PCI have most commonly stressed people's beliefs and attempts at ideological conversion. This is a theoretical bias not shared in this study, which focuses instead on the social bases of allegiance. That the importance of social factors in determining people's allegiances has in the past been slighted may be partially attributed to the emphasis given by both Church and Party to ideological elements in their self-descriptions. Whether referring to its adherents as believers, in the case of the Church, or defining its membership in terms of belief in the programmatic tenets of the Party, in the case of the PCI, allegiance is portrayed ideologically. Moreover, both Church and Party portray their efforts to win over the unconverted as revolving around the spread of the Gospel.

The concept of the Communist world, though incorporating an important social component, has been the subject of little socially focused empirical research at the local level. In the American political literature of the 1950s, the Communist world was portrayed as the product of fanaticism–as in Hoffer's (1951) true *believer*–or in other psychological terms, reflecting the need of the alienated to belong (Almond 1954). In contrast, we will be looking at the PCI and the Church as part of the "normal" social universe; both Church and PCI are approached, a priori, as equally likely contenders in the battle for popular support. No assumption is made of the supremacy of ideological factors in this struggle; on the contrary, it will be shown that the battle is largely waged on social terrain.

The use of the two-world concept in examining this battle can be misleading if it is taken to mean that the social universe is neatly divided into two camps, one Catholic and the other Communist. Though both the Church and the PCI seek to include the greatest number of people possible in their sphere of social influence, they are only successful to varying degrees in various places. The extent to which the concept of the two worlds accurately depicts the local social organization is an empirical question, a question that is addressed in this book. On the basis of this inquiry, we will return in the concluding chapter to consider the analytical utility of the two-world concept in examining local social life in Italy.

The PCI has attempted to supplant the Church as the most influential institution among the masses, and in various places it has succeeded. From one perspective, the

PCI in the local context can be seen as a rival church, competing with the Catholic Church on social, ideological, and ritual grounds. The unity between world view and local social organization, alluded to by Gramsci in the passage cited earlier, is reflected in the Communist Party as well as in the Church.

Conflict between the Church and the PCI is structurally inevitable, for they both strive to provide a constellation of values and social groupings in a wide range of settings. That this conflict is endemic at the institutional level does not mean that individuals cannot resolve the conflict in ways not envisioned by the norms of either Church or Party. Although some people fully subscribe to the ideals of one of the competitors and lead lives of activism and others give undivided social allegiance without full acceptance of the institutional norms, many people divide their allegiances between the Party and the Church. Though the people in this latter category are aware of the conflict inherent in their dual loyalty, they are not unduly troubled by their theoretically contradictory behavior.

Images of Church–Communist conflict

In the United States the image of Italy as a Church-centered society is widespread. The local church, set in the main piazza, symbolizes the *paese*, its social and political life as well as its spiritual and emotional inspiration. The fallacy of this portrait has been demonstrated by a number of social scientists (Prandi 1957:403), including some clerical sociologists (e.g., Burgalassi 1968, 1970). For centuries resentment of the Church has been widespread, a phenomenon that unfortunately has not been well documented. Although the history of the anti-Church sentiments and activities of the rich and politically powerful in Italy has been well described, particularly for the nineteenth century, much less is known about the past anti-Church feelings of the general populace.

Though much has been written at the institutional and ideological level about Communist–Church conflict and many opinion surveys have been conducted, little progress has been made in understanding the social process as it is experienced by the people, that is, at the community level.[2] Many of the analyses of Church–PCI conflict, although they provide ammunition for political polemic, have little social scientific value. Catholic authors try to discredit the PCI by demonstrating the anti-Catholic nature of historical materialism or by pointing out instances of anti-Church activity by the Communists (see, for example, Araldi 1964; Bonicelli 1965; Boschini 1965; Cafaro 1964; Caruso 1974; De Rosa 1966; Nesti 1969; Perego 1962, 1965; Rossi 1963). Communist authors are eager to establish the compatibility of Communism with Catholicism and to identify instances of Church representatives acting in "un-Christian" ways (see, for example, Gruppi 1964; Lombardo Radice 1964a, 1972; Longo 1946; Santini 1975; Togliatti 1965). That the Church and the PCI are aware of the political value of social scientific work is indicated by the investment made by each in establishing social science research institutes. The Church sponsors the Pro Deo College in Rome and the ISAB study center in Bologna, for example, and the Party has branches of the Istituto Gramsci in Rome, Bologna, and Palermo.

American studies of the PCI and the Church in Italy have a politically tinged heritage as well, though until recently all the partisans have been on one side. Noteworthy in this context is the cold war tradition (Almond 1954; Cantril 1958), in which communism is treated as a disease and people's "susceptibility" to the malignancy is examined. Communist organization is portrayed as a social abnormality resulting from social or personal disorganization.

The pathology of people who had become Communist was examined in detail. However, the Communist Party's mode of operation within the broader social and cultural context is not dealt with, nor is the Communist Party organization analyzed on a par with any other institution of society.

This heavy anti-Communist tradition no longer dominates the American political science literature and in recent years a number of incisive studies of the PCI have been published (e.g., Tarrow 1967, 1975; Lange 1975; Stern 1975). However, none of these has been primarily concerned with the question of the conflict between the PCI and the Church, and most put little emphasis on local-level ethnographic research. This book represents an attempt to develop further these new perspectives on the role of the PCI in Italian society while raising a series of questions regarding the social bases of political and religious allegiance.

The people of Albora

Every fifteen minutes a bus leaves Bologna's majestic central piazza bound for Albora,[3] one of the fourteen *quartieri* circling the old walled city. Exiting the old city through Porta Albora, one of the gates that until the early years of this century shut the city off from the hinterland each night, a large plaque comes into view. The plaque, emblazoned on the hulking stone gateway, commemorates the *partigiani* who died while attacking a Nazi squadron in the battle of Porta Albora. The porticoes that protect Bologna's wide, tiled sidewalks from sun and rain are left behind as the two-lane via Albora makes its way into the *quartiere*.

After passing an abandoned sugar refinery and a few warehouses, the bus stops at a cluster of two- to four-story peeling ochre buildings, one of half a dozen such settlements in which most of Albora's 9,000 residents live. Old men, clad in dark wool sports jackets and wearing berets, slowly pedal by on rusted black bicycles while teen-aged boys screech past on motor scooters carefully adjusted for maximum volume. Heavy-set women, wearing bellowing house dresses, pass from the milk store to the *salumeria* to the dry goods shop doing their daily shopping while some pensioners sit at a table in front of a bar playing cards. As the bus travels further from the center of the city, scattered high-rise apartment buildings, some not yet ready for occupancy, tower over abandoned farmland, and between the ancient housing clusters, four, five, and six-story apartment buildings of postwar vintage line the street.

Albora is a zone in transition. For centuries it had been one of several agricultural outposts of the city of Bologna. Composed primarily of farmland owned by noblemen and other *padroni* who lived in the city, the area was populated by sharecroppers, agricultural day laborers, and artisans. Though the sharecroppers lived on the farms, the rest of the people lived in one or another of the named settlements in the area.

In the latter part of the nineteenth century, a growing population in the hinterland and a crisis in the agricultural sector contributed to the expansion of the city, which burst through its walls and began to envelop Albora. As with numerous similar areas on the periphery of Italy's major cities, Albora became the destination of thousands of immigrants from its surrounding hinterland, migrants escaping the poverty of farm life and seeking urban employment.

Albora became an urban dormitory, for few factories or businesses were located in the *quartiere*, and the great majority of residents commuted daily to their jobs in other parts of the city. Though rapidly dwindling in area, Albora's open fields testify to the underdevelopment of the *quartiere* relative to most other parts of the city. This underdevelopment is attributed by many Alborese to the years of fascism, for the Fascist government used the *quartiere* as its social refuse heap. When it was decided that the central train station should be more grandiose and the central city streets widened, the poor people evicted were relocated in shacks erected in Albora. Known as *la casa dei topi* ("the housing of the rats"), it provided shelter for many of the city's most destitute (the *topi* having a double referent). The city's leper colony was also located in the *quartiere*, and, worst of all, Albora was made into the staging area for the augmented rail lines, cutting up the *quartiere* and impeding traffic. In later years the Alborese Communists would explain that the *quartiere* was being punished for its strong anti-Fascist tradition.

Although the expanding middle-class population of the city largely avoided Albora, movement into and out of the *quartiere* took place at a formidable rate. Immigrants moving into the city found in Albora some of the cheapest housing available in Bologna, but many of them moved to other areas of the city once they had improved their economic position and could afford better housing. In the postwar period, this out-migration was also encouraged by the presence of public housing in other *quartieri*, and many Alborese, often after years of being on a waiting list, moved out of Albora for this reason. Thus, though the population of Bologna rose from 342,000 in 1950 to 493,000 in 1970 and some of the *quartieri* swelled dramatically in size, Albora counted about the same number of residents in 1970 as it had twenty years before (Bologna 1971).[4]

Following a national pattern of working-class settlements lying outside the centers of Italy's large cities, Albora's population is largely composed of immigrants. These immigrant come for the most part from nearby agricultural areas. As can be seen from Table 1, the places of birth of Albora's 5,956 immigrants closely resemble those of all

Table 1. *Immigrant Population by Zone of Origin*

Zone of origin	Albora[a]	Bologna
Neighboring *comuni*	15.2%	18.0%
Other *comuni* of the province of Bologna	29.8	29.2
Emilia-Romagna	25.7	22.3
Northern Italy	7.9	9.1
Central Italy	4.1	5.9
Southern Italy	8.5	8.6
Insular Italy (Sicily, Sardinia)	6.7	4.2
Foreign	2.1	2.7
Total	100.0	100.0

[a] $N = 5956$.
Source: Comune di Bologna 1971:205.

Bolognese. Half of these immigrants had lived in Bologna for at least fifteen years, again approximating the figures for the whole city (Bologna 1971:204). Yet the pattern of immigration in Bologna, as in other Northern cities, has been changing, with an increasing proportion of migrants coming from the impoverished South. In 1970, for example, 28 percent of the newcomers to Bologna taking up residence in Albora came from the South, a figure that would be even higher if unregistered immigrants were counted.

The people of Albora are overwhelmingly working class. Many men work in factories, but many also work for the railroad, in warehouses and stockyards, and as truckers and bus drivers. One study (Bellettini and Mazzaferro 1967) found that whereas 7.7 percent of Bologna's population could be considered upper class, just 1.5 percent of

Albora's population fell in that category. Likewise, Bologna as a whole had 16.9 percent middle-class white-collar workers, whereas Albora had just 5.0 percent. Of the people who work in the *quartiere*, most are artisans and small shopkeepers who employ no full-time adult help outside their family. Owning a milk store or a tobacco shop, far from denoting upward social mobility, is often seen as a way in which a woman may supplement her husband's wages.

Unlike some other parts of Italy (Cronin 1970, Chapman 1971), in Emilia there has been no strong tradition of women remaining at home while the men go out to work. The great majority of Albora's women do work, at least for a substantial part of their adult lives. Traditionally, women went out into the fields alongside their fathers or husbands, or, in the case of daughters and wives of artisans, the women worked with the men in the shop. By the 1930s the Fascist war effort opened up places for women in factories, and a number of Albora's women trace their work careers back to that experience. Today women work in small factories such as food processing plants; they work in retail stores as clerks; and many do *lavoro a domicilio*, piecework done at home. Although all these jobs are low paying, *lavoro a domicilio*, in which perhaps 10 percent of the women participate, is the most exploitative. Factory representatives bring around the work once every week or two, collecting and paying for the work done since their last visit. Whole families–women and their small children–often work long hours painting dolls, drawing watch faces, or sewing together purses. Although the work is illegal, for the employer does not make any of the obligatory worker's insurance payments, many women take the work anyway, for it allows them to stay at home with their small children.

Before World War II few Alborese owned their own homes, but in recent years there has been a sharp rise in

Table 2. *Level of Highest Educational Achievement of the Adult (over 21 years old) Population of Albora (1972)*

Level	Number in sample		Percentage	
	Women	Men	Women	Men
Illiterate	16	16	2.4	2.5
Some elementary school	326	263	48.5	40.3
Completed elementary school	244	227	36.4	34.8
Some junior high school	7	18	1.0	2.7
Completed junior high school	51	94	7.6	14.4
Some high school	1	2	0.1	0.3
High school diploma	21	28	3.1	4.3
Some university	4	0	0.6	0.0
University degree	2	4	0.3	0.6
Total	672	652	100.0	99.9

Source: Based on a random sample of 20 percent of the adult Albora population permanently resident in the *quartiere*, as provided by Bologna's official 1972 voting rolls.

home ownership, with 28 percent owning their apartments in 1971 (Bologna, 1972). Most of the high-rise apartment buildings springing up in Albora consist of apartments for sale, including a number of public housing projects geared to the needs of wealthier workers.

Until recent years formal education beyond elementary school was uncommon for the peasantry and working class of Italy, and this is reflected in Albora (see Table 2). In 1972 only 13 percent of the adult women and 22 percent of the adult men of the *quartiere* had attended school after the fifth grade, and these were largely drawn from the younger adults. Though a recent national law requires attendance until the age of fourteen, the law is not enforced. Parents in Albora regard schooling for children who could be out working as a sacrifice, though many parents have come to view the sacrifice as worthwhile. It is still rare, however, for a youth from the *quartiere* to enroll in the university. No more than a half dozen were attending university in 1972.

In the city, precise geographical boundaries of community are often difficult to draw. In Albora, as elsewhere, there are a number of different boundaries that can be drawn, depending on what criteria are used. People tend to see only the smallest aggregation of houses as constituting their neighborhood. One young man, for example, lamented that he was unable to find an apartment for himself and his wife in the same area as his parents, yet the apartment he found is but a half kilometer away. When people are asked where they live, they generally either answer *fuori Porta Albora* ("outside Porta Albora") or give the name of their particular settlement within the *quartiere*. In the past it was common for a person to employ the name of his parish as a means of geographical identification; this is much less common today.

In folk parlance, a *quartiere* refers to a neighborhood and may refer to an area having tens or having thousands of people. In Bologna, *quartiere* has been given a more precise, statutory meaning, for through municipal decentralization the city has been formally divided into eighteen *quartieri*.[5] Each of these has its own advisory council, its mayor's representative, and its municipal agency headquarters. Albora, one of the least populous and most heavily working class of these *quartieri*, is not simply a creation of arbitrary political boundary making, though, for it is set off from neighboring areas by a canal, a river, and a series of railway crossings.

Politically, Albora is a Communist stronghold, regularly giving 65 percent of its vote to the PCI. (Table 3 lists some recent election results.) The preeminence of the Com-

Table 3. *National Assembly Election Results, 1972*

Party	Albora	Province of Bologna	Italy
PCI	64.2	46.1	27.1
PSIUP	2.3	2.0	1.9
Extreme left[a]	0.9	0.9	1.4
PSI	6.5	7.8	9.6
PSDI	4.3	6.2	5.1
PRI	1.0	2.3	2.9
DC	15.7	24.7	38.7
PLI	2.1	4.7	3.9
MSI	2.9	5.4	8.7
Others	—	—	0.7
Total	99.9	100.1	100.0

[a] Includes Manifesto, Movimento Politico dei Lavoratori, and Servire Il Popolo.
Source: Bologna provincial data taken from leaflet published by Federazione Bolognese del PCI; national data taken from Spreafico 1977:122.

munist Party in the *quartiere* is also evident organizationally. The PCI has four local Party sections, each the site of daily activity, whereas of the other parties only the Christian Democrats (DC) and the Socialists (PSI) have a local section, and these are rarely used. At the time of the 1972 national election campaign, this organizational superiority was made clear: The PCI sponsored fifteen local rallies to just four for the DC, and the PCI campaign cars, equipped with loudspeakers, blared out Party campaign material for 150 hours, to about 10 hours for the comparable DC mobile (see Table 4 and Photograph 1).

Albora, a red, working-class *quartiere*, is hardly a microcosm of Italy; the use of a community study approach should not be presumed to entail a homunculus notion of

1. At an apartment building complex populated by the heavily Communist railway workers, a Socialist tries to deliver a campaign oration while his cohort tries to disperse the children.

representivity. Indeed, given the variegated sociocultural geography of Italy, it is doubtful that any locality could provide the basis for such generalization. Until little more than a century ago, Italy did not exist as a political entity; this fragmented political past has left a legacy of sociocultural and economic diversity that is still apparent. The most notable line of division separates North from South, but even within limited areas inside these zones large differences can be found. Politically, this is evident in the sharply contrasting voting patterns found in neighboring regions (see Figure 2). In the 1976 national elections, for example, Emilia-Romagna gave the PCI its highest vote

Table 4. *The 1972 Election Campaign Activities in Albora*

	PCI	DC
Rallies	15	4
Meetings of membership	18[a]	0
Loudspeaker car hours[b]	150	10
Door-to-door campaigners	50	0
Full-time professional campaigners	1	0
Party professionals campaigning part time	2	0
Pollwatchers and candidate representatives at polls	48	12
Members newly recruited	80	0
Campaign funds raised	1.5 million lire	0[c]

[a] This figure includes six meetings of the FGCI involving the campaign.

[b] Data on loudspeaker car hours are approximate, based on observation throughout the campaign period as well as on conversations with those running the loudspeaker cars.

[c] This is not to indicate that no one in Albora contributed money to the local DC campaign, but only that no such funds were raised through any locally organized efforts. What contributions there were sent directly to the provincial campaign headquarters of individual DC candidates.

(48.5 percent), but another northern region, Trentino-Alto-Adige, gave the Party its lowest vote (13.2 percent). Whereas Emilia-Romagna voted just 28.4 percent for the Christian Democrats, the neighboring region of Veneto voted 51.3 percent for the DC (Parisi and Pasquino 1977b). The study of the PCI–Church struggle in Bologna, then, is a study of the battle where the Communist Party is at its strongest. For many years Bologna was the largest city

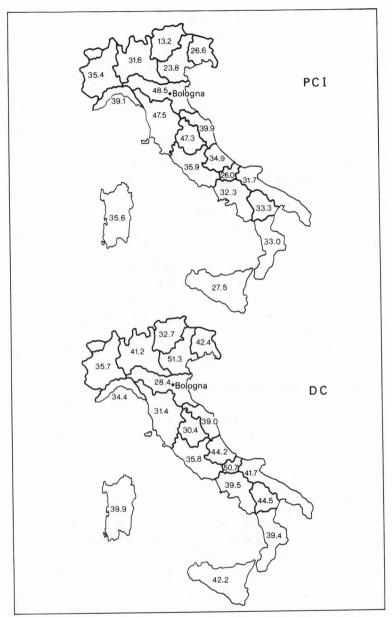

Figure 2. National election results of the PCI and the DC for the lower house, by region, 1976 (source: PCI 1977:76)

ruled by the PCI, and as such it became the Party show-
case, the symbol of Italian communism.[6]

But the city of Bologna is not our unit of analysis. The
study of a half million people is necessarily either a study
of the political elite or a social statistical smorgasboard. To
understand the ways in which the great majority of people
are involved in the political process, the people must be
studied in their local social context: the *quartiere*, the parish, the party section.

As numerous scholars have pointed out, this approach
is not without its dangers and limitations. If local activity
is conceived of as autonomous, independent of outside
forces, the sociopolitical fabric is grossly distorted. No locally focused study can ignore the larger forces that im-
pinge on local life; the PCI section cannot be understood
without reference to the Party Federation and to national
institutions, nor can the parish church be understood apart
from the ecclesiastical hierarchy. Although an inquiry into
the relationship between local-level activity and supralocal
forces is indispensable, it is clearly outside the framework
of a study such as this to examine the ways in which
decisions are reached at the higher level. Thus, for example, though we need to refer to the Second Vatican
Council to explain events in Albora, no attempt is made to
detail the genesis of the council.

Research

Fieldwork was conducted from September 1971 through
August 1972, with a six-week return visit in May and June
of 1976 (a period of emergency national elections). The
methodological cornerstone of the study was participant
observation, in courtyards, bars, athletic fields, piazzas,
parish halls, Party headquarters, and people's homes. The
goal was to get to know people of all kinds–devout Cath-

olics, militant Communists, the uncommitted, the uninterested, the skeptics, the partisans of other parties, the young and the old, the native Bolognesi and the immigrants. Though most of the participant observation took place within Albora, Alborese were followed in other socially important arenas: the markets and central piazza of Bologna, the city headquarters of the PCI, the DC, the Church and a variety of other organizations, *paesi* in the provincial countryside where people spend Sunday visiting their parents on the farm, and the Party *festa* of a commune in Tuscany with which the PCI in Albora has bonds of *gemellaggio* ("twinship"). Scores of meetings of all kinds were attended.

Interviews, both formal and informal, were held, the latter often taking place serendipitously. Tape-recorded formal interviews were limited, reserved largely for people occupying official positions–the parish priest, a Party Federation official, a deputy mayor, the local Women's League head. Interviews of people in the *quartiere* were only arranged after I had gotten to know the interviewee reasonably well. In this way I sought to go beyond public responses and to be able to verify responses through observation and by checking with other people.

Two formal questionnaires were also administered, one to the PCI officials in the *quartiere*, the other to all the people active in the local Communist Youth Group (FGCI) chapter. The former questionnaire consisted of questions regarding the socioeconomic background of the individual; the political involvement of the person's parents, spouse, and children; the way in which the individual became involved in the PCI; the Party activities he or she had undertaken; and the nature of his or her Church attendance and that of his or her parents and spouse. The youth questionnaire contained similar questions, geared toward the younger respondents.

A variety of documentary sources was also examined, including the membership records of one PCI and one DC section, the communal registration for all official residents of the *quartiere*, church censuses extending back to the mid-nineteenth century, land tenure records for the past 150 years, and a variety of Church and Party documents available in the *quartiere*, at the ISAB diocesan study center, and at the Istituto Gramsci of Bologna.

The ethnographic nature of this study contrasts with the great bulk of the Italian empirical political literature, in which three sources are most commonly relied on: aggregate statistical data (primarily election results); general attitudinal surveys; and interviews with political officials. In studying local-level politics each of these has its limitations. The attitudinal survey has been championed by some as a means of avoiding the elitism of a focus on official party pronouncements and the remarks of political leaders, while providing more depth than simple electoral results. However, a glance at the results of political surveys in Italy gives cause for concern beyond that normally occasioned by a research instrument that, by its nature, is superficial and has few controls. Since the first postwar surveys were conducted, the number of people expressing allegiance to the PCI has been substantially below the proportion who are voters and members, whereas the number subscribing in the surveys to the DC has been higher.[7] Many refuse to provide any indication of their political preference. The Barnes survey of 1968, for example, showed 15.1 percent of the respondents voting for the PCI, whereas the national PCI vote in that same year was 26.9 percent; 56.6 percent said they would vote for the DC, though only 39.1 percent did so. The 1972 follow-up survey, jointly organized by Barnes and Sani, gave similar, though somewhat less skewed, results (Sani 1975:466–7).[8] As a result of this difficulty attempts have been made to tease out political allegiance through indirect questions, a technique that testifies to researcher ingenuity but that is of questionable validity (Visentini 1974:184). In this context it is worth noting that some political scientists have begun adopting participant-observation methods (Lange 1975; Stern 1975; Evans 1976).

Conducting participant-observation fieldwork in a situation of sharp sociopolitical polarization means struggling to define a nonpartisan role in a setting in which there is no precedent for such a role. Far from viewing social science as value-free or apolitical, the Alborese (and Italians in general) see social scientists as a major part of the political landscape. When speaking of a sociologist or political scientist, the first thing the politically interested Alborese wants to know is whether he is a Communist, Socialist, or Catholic. The Communist sociologist is expected to conduct research that will benefit the Communist cause; the Catholic sociologist will benefit the interests of the Church. Needless to say, the priests of Albora are not eager to aid the work of the Communist social scientist, nor is the Party eager to welcome the Catholic social scientist into its private strategy-planning meetings.

Anthropologists have long claimed the virtue of having an outsider as a fieldworker, and in this case, as in other cases of intense political conflict, the position has some merit. As a foreigner I was permitted to occupy a role outside the system to an extent not easily accomplished by an Italian. The fact that I was not a Communist Party member did not prejudice me in the eyes of the Alborese Communists. However, an Italian who was not a PCI member would be viewed differently, as someone who was critical of the Party. As an American and as a Jew, I could attend Mass every Sunday without that being interpreted as a statement of anticommunism.

Being an American had its drawbacks, since charges of CIA international intrigue were prominently featured in the newspapers of the day. Indeed, at one section Party congress to which I was extended an invitation, a federation representative (who apparently did not know of my presence) thunderously proclaimed in his remarks that "CIA agents are everywhere." Somewhat more original was the conclusion of a middle-aged woman, who had read in a magazine that 2,000 Israeli spies constituted the best espionage force in the world. Since it seemed too coincidental that Albora's first Jew should arrive just as she read the article, she deduced that I was one of the 2,000.

The spy problem was less a concern than the continual necessity of exercising caution in alternating between involvement in Communist Party and Church activities. People in Albora do not leave a discussion at the Party section headquarters to keep an appointment with the priest. Though I made clear my conception of my research role to everyone, it was uncomfortable for the Alborese as well as for me to share in the private discussion of one side and immediately go to speak with people from the other side.

Some examples may be instructive. While my wife and I were attending a DC campaign rally in the parish hall, sitting with thirty-five other people but a few feet from the DC national congressman who was speaking, we all heard the sound of screeching tires. Within a few seconds the door opened and Silvana Manni, a seventeen-year-old girl, entered. Known to almost all present as the daughter of one of the leading Communists in Albora, Silvana was among the organizers of the *quartiere* Young Communist chapter. Though the deputy continued speaking, most eyes were on her as she spotted us and made her way to our seats. When she reached us she loudly asked what we were doing at a DC meeting. Quickly observing that there was no hole in the floor for me to crawl through, I responded that I wanted to learn more about the DC's platform. At that, Silvana, for the first and only time in her life, gave both my wife and me a big kiss and walked out of the hall. As the horns blared and tires screeched, I pretended to concentrate on the deputy's speech.

A mirror image of this scene took place the next month, as the election ballots were being counted. Standing with the leaders of a local Party section outside the cooperative bar, we awaited the results of each electoral seat being brought to us by Party couriers. I was given the task of computing the percentages for each seat as the tallies came in. In the midst of this activity, driving by in his Fiat 500, don Giorgio spotted me among the Party faithful. Stopping the car, the young assistant parish priest beckoned me with a cheerful greeting and, as I stood next to his car a few feet from the onlooking and now quiet Party officials, he asked how I was doing, what was new. When I rejoined the comrades five minutes later no one mentioned my conversation.

Potentially the most damaging incident for my research stemmed from events outside the *quartiere*. When, in early 1972, the United States began mining Haiphong harbor, Italians joined much of the rest of the world in loud indignation. As an American I felt particularly responsible for the action of the U.S. government and felt it was incumbent on me to do what I could. The problem with my taking political action, given my research situation, was that Vietnam was very much a domestic political issue in Italy, one of the major themes used by the PCI to try to discredit the DC, since the Christian Democratic government had supported the American war effort. Indeed, in lambasting the DC, one of the arguments made by the PCI was that even the American people were against the war. For me to start issuing public pronouncements about the criminality of the U.S. war effort would serve as PCI ammunition against the DC and the Church.

Feeling that my first responsibility was to protest the

war, I helped organize the contingent of *Americani contro la guerra* for a massive province-wide antiwar demonstration in downtown Bologna. The demonstration was sponsored by a variety of organizations, including the PCI, and we handed out a leaflet we had prepared denouncing the U.S. war policy. The demonstration took place outside Albora and, in its aftermath, I received no indication that any of the *quartiere* Church faithful had seen me there. In any case, the event had wide enough sponsorship that I felt I could explain my participation, for I had in the past taken issue with the prowar position of some of the Church faithful in Albora. Two weeks later, however, during the national election campaign, a PCI rally was held in the midst of the *quartiere*; the theme of the rally was victory for the liberation forces in Vietnam. A hundred people gathered for the evening rally and, shortly after the *quartiere* Party head opened the program, two of the Party officials came to ask me to speak. As the rally was amidst a cluster of new high-rise buildings blaring the proceedings into everyone's apartment, I was not eager to speak. I did not want to get involved in local partisan politics and I was worried about what such participation might do to my carefully cultivated relations with the people of the Church. Citing my discomfort at public speaking in Italian, I tried to decline, but one of the Party officials pulled a copy of our antiwar leaflet from his pocket, calling on me simply to read my declaration. This was a request I could hardly refuse, so, my implied denunciation of DC policy echoing through the hallways, I spoke to an enthusiastic crowd. To what extent word of this activity spread among the Church loyalists in Albora I never found out. Though I never noticed any effect from my talk that night, I think it could easily have made my work among the Church people difficult, and for several days after the rally, I waited for the worst to happen. Doing what seems morally and politically right is not necessarily doing what is best for fieldwork research. Weighing the various factors makes for an unpleasant kind of calculus.

This, then, is a study of the competition between the Roman Catholic Church and the Communist Party in a working-class *quartiere* in the heart of Italy's *cintura rossa* ("Red Belt").[9] The focus is on how this drama is played out among a limited number of people, and the hope is that a sense of people's daily lives is imparted as well as a better understanding of the nature of Church–Party struggle. This is the story of the efforts of the Church and the PCI to win and to maintain the allegiance of the Italian people. It is a case study of what LaPalombara (1965:291) aptly calls the "basic postwar political struggle" in Italy.

2

Communist World

At 10 P.M. on the Friday before national elections a group of teen-agers from Albora entered the central train station. As they approached the tracks through the underground passageway the clamor of hundreds of voices met them. The chorus became clear as they climbed to the platform:

Bandiera rossa la trionferà!	The red flag will be triumphant!
Bandiera rossa la trionferà!	The red flag will be triumphant!
Bandiera rossa la trionferà!	The red flag will be triumphant!
Evviva il comunismo e la libertà!	Long live communism and liberty!

Swarming over the 100-meter stretch between the two trains at the platform were several hundred youths of the Young Communist Federation alongside scores of men from the Communist Party railroad workers' section. They had gathered to greet the trainloads of Southerners who were coming home from their workplaces in France, Switzerland, and Germany to vote. A new chant began:

Occupazione sì!	Jobs yes!
Emigrazione no!	Emigration no!

2. Southern Italian migrant workers living in Switzerland and Germany stop at the Bologna train station on their way home to vote in the 1972 national election. They display the PCI symbols distributed to them by the members of Bologna's Communist Youth Group (FGCI) and Communist railway workers.

The youths distributed PCI electoral literature, red banners, and plastic juice bottles, as PCI posters were rapidly plastered over the windows and sides of the trains by the immigrant workers. When the train lurched forward, every window was jammed with immigrants, joining the youths and railroad workers in a final thundering chant:

Sette maggio   May seventh
Vota comunista!   Vote communist!

Momentarily another train pulled in and the scene was reenacted; a stream of red-clad trains flowed south from Bologna that night (see Photograph 2).

On Sunday morning, as on every Sunday morning for the past fifteen years, Canari got up early. A short, lean man, forty-three years old, he had until recently owned a small furniture-cleaning shop in a neighboring *quartiere*, working long hours but making little money. Recently he left the shop and found an eight-hours-a-day position in an odd-job cooperative downtown. Like all the other members of the cooperative, Canari is a Communist, and this Sunday he was headed for the Vapori PCI section of Albora, two blocks from his apartment. Although on the ruling committee of the Vapori section, Canari rarely spoke at meetings of the membership, for he felt uncomfortable about public speaking. Having never gone beyond elementary school, he did not feel he knew as much as some of the more educated comrades. Yet he was one of the most indefatigable section activists, known especially for heading the Sunday distribution of *L'Unità*, the daily Communist Party newspaper. At the section headquarters, located above the bar of the Proletarian Struggle Cooperative, Canari counted the few hundred newspapers that would be distributed in their zone that morning and divided them into piles for each of the ten or twelve people who would be going door to door selling them.

Canari, on this election day, inserted a pink mock ballot in each paper with the hammer and sickle of the PCI marked clearly with an "X." He recalled the meeting the section held two months before in the room next door. In the wake of a parliamentary crisis, national elections had been called a year before they were due. After the provincial PCI federation met to propose its candidates, all sections were meeting to discuss the federation's choices. Forty-one of Vapori's 418 members attended, with Mario Pini, a provincial deputy, representing the federation. Nine of those present were women, ranging in age from sixteen to seventy, and the men too included young as well as old, a few farmers, but mostly urban workers. At the table at the front of the hall, Pini sat next to Girona, who represented the section's ruling committee. After a brief introduction by Girona, Pini began to speak. He recounted the seriousness of the political crisis and then addressed the matter of PCI candidates.

First of all, I should stress the fact that we are dealing with proposals, not candidates. What criteria were used in deciding on these proposals? First, the person must have dedicated his life to the political struggle of our Party, and also his personal life must be beyond reproach. Second, the national Party policy is that on the average a comrade should not serve in Parliament for more than two terms, no more than ten years. We need a broadly balanced list of candidates-workers, farmers, intellectuals, small businessmen, and artisans. They must also be people who are known and respected by the base of our Party, our members. That's why we have section meetings like this, so that all the comrades can have a voice in deciding who the candidates will be.

Pini then proceeded to discuss the list of suggested PCI candidates from the Bologna district, citing the reasons why incumbents were being proposed again or dropped. What Canari remembered most vividly from the meeting was the discussion of Torro, a current member of Parliament whom the Party wanted to replace, although he was just in his first term of office. Torro was a young worker who had risen through Party and union ranks, and, Pini explained, the Party felt he could be more effective in organizing factory workers. Following Pini's remarks, a comrade voiced concern about Torro's replacement on the ballot, and said that the same opinion had been expressed at the municipal enployees section meeting he had attended the night before. There had even been some talk that Torro was not happy with the decision. Following this, another man added that Torro was a good man, a worker, and he would like an explanation too.

After a whispered consultation with he chairman, Pini responded:

I can understand your concern. In fact, I, too, was at another meeting last night at which the same question was raised. The truth is Torro was the first to suggest that he be replaced. He said he felt ill at ease in Parliament and felt that he could not compete with all the well-educated spokesmen there. Of course, we don't believe this is true, for a worker is an equal to anyone, and we told him that. I went to school for eighteen years and have been a professor for thirty, but the best school I ever went to, the place where I learned the most, was the Party section. However, since Torro continued to have these feelings, it was agreed that another worker should take his place.

Canari had already heard of the Torro issue, for a comrade from the Dovero section in Albora, which had met two nights before, had told him about the discussion between the Party federation representative and one of the members on Torro's noncandidacy. Canari smiled a little as he looked at the list of Party candidates published on the Bologna page of today's *L'Unità*; Torro's name was near the top.

From avanguardia to partito di massa

Albora, of course, has not always been a Communist *quartiere*. Although the PCI was founded in 1921, splintering from the Socialist party in a revolutionary burst sparked by the Russian Revolution, it shortly thereafter was outlawed by the new Fascist government and its leaders were exiled or imprisoned. Until the Fascist military defeat of 1943, the clandestine Party organization had no more than 6,000 members (Poggi 1968:29). In Albora it is unlikely that there were more than two dozen Party members, organized for security in cells of three, so that each member knew only two others.

From a handful of members in mid-1943, the Party grew astronomically; three years later over 2 million people had taken out PCI membership (Poggi 1968:311). Likewise, in Bologna the Communists soared from a tiny minority to a relative majority almost overnight. A number of factors contributed to this growth—a long-standing Socialist tradition, the ravages of fascism and Nazi occupation, and the preeminent role played (from 1943 to 1945) by the Communists in organizing the *Resistenza*, the anti-Fascist resistance movement in Northern Italy.

With the defeat of fascism, a vision of a Communist Italy, a workers' state, grew among the peasant and proletarian population of much of the North. Yet, as the people's revolutionary fervor grew, the Party began to redefine its role as a proletarian revolutionary force. When Palmiro Togliatti, head of the PCI, returned to Italy from his Moscow sanctuary, he enunciated a new concept of the Party. Lenin's party of the revolutionary elite (Lenin 1929) was spurned and the Party was broadened to include the masses. This decision was based on a new faith in the electoral process as a means of winning power and on a profound pessimism about the prospects of a successful revolution. The problem Togliatti faced was not of fomenting insurrection but of controlling the revolutionary impulses of the old Communist cadres (Tarrow 1967:107). Among Togliatti's most quoted remarks from this period was his warning:

Our party today must become a great mass party; and this is why I say to the old comrades, who have the tendency to remain a restricted group of those remaining pure and faithful to the ideals and the thoughts of the Party, we say to them: "You are mistaken, you will be a leading nucleus only insofar as you are capable of making our party into a great organization which has in its ranks all the elements necessary to establish contacts with all the categories of the Italian people. Only in this way can we lead them all toward the objective we propose." [Togliatti 1944:83].

Despite the move away from the Leninist party ideal, the PCI insisted on its continued revolutionary character: "The decisive function of the Communist Party as a revolutionary force has been neither impaired nor attenuated. On the contrary, its tasks of direction, of being the instrument of the struggle for hegemony of the working-class, have grown" (PCI 1970a:7–8).

This transformation of the PCI from a party of the revolutionary vanguard to a mass party had two important consequences. First, it meant that the bulk of Party members would not be Party militants. With the influx of hundreds of thousands of people into its ranks, the ideal of "every member a militant" became a practical impossibility. This, in turn, promoted the rise of a bureaucratic elite within the Party, administering the huge mass of non-activists and setting Party policy (Sivini 1972b).

Second, the Party acquired an increasingly electoral focus (Galli 1958:271).[1] The strategy of armed insurrection was disavowed and the Marxist concept of the dictatorship of the proletariat was ultimately repudiated. The parliamentary system of "bourgeois democracy," so often the target of Marxist attack, was embraced to the extent that the Party's public goal included a multiparty system of government ruled by parliamentary coalition. The identification of the state with the Party was gone: "The building of this socialist society must be based on the secular, non-ideological nature of the state, which must guarantee religious freedom, freedom of culture, of science, of the arts, of information, expression and the circulation of ideas, including the presence of various political formations and a plurality of parties" (PCI 1970c:50).

With over a million and a half members, the PCI has achieved its goal of being a mass party, though its membership has not been evenly distributed throughout the country.[2] Almost half of the entire national membership is found in the Red Belt, composed of the regions of Emilia-Romagna, Toscana, Marche, and Umbria. Although Party strength, particularly electorally, has been growing throughout the country, Bologna remains the most heavily Communist of the large cities.[3] In the period 1968–76 almost 14 percent of the Bologna population were PCI members, compared to 2 percent in Milan and Turin (Barbagli and Corbetta 1978:18). Bologna is also notable in having a large proportion of female members (over 40 percent, compared to the national figure of about 25 percent). The national Party membership is heavily working class; in 1974 58.1 percent of the economically active members were industrial workers and 17.2 percent were agricultural workers (including day laborers, farm renters, and small farm owners). White-collar workers and intellectuals make up but a small fraction of the membership, though they are well represented in leadership positions (Barbagli and Corbetta 1978:27).[4] Looked at from a different point of view (and using 1968 data), in Italy's Red Belt 17 percent of all industrial workers, 29 percent of all agricultural laborers, 28 percent of the sharecroppers, and 16 percent of the artisans were Party members (Barbagli and Corbetta 1978:24).

Following the principle of democratic centralism, the Party is organized on three levels—local, provincial, and national—the members of each level electing the members of the next higher level through general assemblies. Originally the normal local unit of organization was the factory cell, but with the expansion of the membership and the increasingly electoral focus, residence-based sections became the predominant mode of local organization, encompassing 95 percent of the membership by 1960 (Sivini 1972b:147–8).

The middle level of PCI organization consists of the 113 federations, generally coincident with the provinces. The province of Bologna, because of its large membership and Party strength, has been divided into two federations, one based in the city of Bologna, the other in Imola. This is the level at which professional Party functionaries are first found. The Bologna Federation, for example, perhaps the strongest in the nation, employs approximately 100 functionaries and occupies a vast office complex (Evans 1967:111). Most local Party activities are coordinated at the federation level, with section heads or coordinators of several sections regularly meeting at the federation to plan new local-level campaigns. Many of these campaigns originate at the national level; the federations adapt them to local conditions.

The members of the national Central Committee of the PCI are elected at a triennial national Congress; delegates to this Party Congress are elected at the federation triennial congresses. All basic policy decisions of the PCI are made at the national level, though in theory these are based on debates held in the sections throughout the country.

Local party organization

During the last two years of the war, Albora was occupied by Nazi soldiers, who established an antiaircraft installation in the heart of the *quartiere*. Moving the people into their cellars, the Nazis took up residence in the homes of the Alborese. At the same time, Mussolini established the "Republican" government, drafting all available men to continue the fight against the Allied forces. Many men escaped from conscription by fleeing into the hills surrounding Bologna, where women and children sought refuge from Allied bombardments and hunger. A number of the Alborese in the hills joined the Communist-dominated partisan forces at this time. Upon Liberation, in 1945, the local partisans rounded up several Alborese Fascists and brought them to the tribunal established in downtown Bologna. After quick trials, some of these were executed and others let go; many of the most notorious local Fascists, those involved in assassinating Albora's anti-Fascist martyrs in the 1920s, fled the city.

After two decades in which no political organizing outside the Fascist party was permitted, the Alborese and their fellow countrymen faced the task of forming a popularly elected government and electing delegates to a constitutional assembly. The Communists and Socialists leaped into the political void, as the heroes of the *Resistenza* and the hope for the future. Though the Party was following an electoral route to power, it aimed for social hegemony, not simply electoral support. The Communist cause would advance through a diffuse social medium, as Togliatti proclaimed in 1944:

In both urban neighborhoods and rural villages, the Communist sections must become centers of working-class life, centers where all comrades, sympathizers, and independents should go, knowing that they will find there a party and an organization which is interested in their problems and which will give them guidance. They should know that they will find someone who can direct them, who can give them counsel and, if necessary, can provide them with a good time. [in Poggi 1968:32–3]

The section, in Albora and elsewhere, became the center for recruitment into the Party, for political socialization of new members, and for the extension of the Party into local daily life (Amendola 1958:14; Cossutta 1967:6). Virtually all areas of social life were encompassed in the work of the section. As the theses of the Ninth Party Congress (PCI

1960:105) proclaimed: "Every artificial separation between political struggle, ideological work and cultural activity must be eliminated."

In effecting this strategy of interpenetration of Party and popular social life in the *quartiere*, the four local sections were established on the premises of cooperative *circoli*, the major locales of adult male socializing in Albora.[5] Originally founded in the early years of the century as part of a growing Socialist and cooperative movement and expropriated by the Fascists in the 1920s, the cooperatives were brought under PCI control through election of officers active in the local Party. By identifying itself with these social centers, the Party established a power base at the heart of the working-class community (see Photograph 3).

Executive power of the section resides in the section committee, the members of which are elected by the general membership at the annual section congress. The committee members, in turn, elect from their number a secretary, who is the top executive of the section. In the early postwar years, when political information was scarce and talk of imminent workers' rule abounded, a large proportion of the Party membership in Albora attended local meetings. In recent years, however, this proportion has dwindled, and now only a minority of members attend a single meeting during the course of the year. The throng of PCI members, then, although crucial in expressing popular solidarity around the Party, plays little role in formulating Party policy or in carrying out formal Party activity on a day-to-day basis.

The section committees in Albora are composed of from five to thirteen members. Though formally nominated and elected by the section membership at the annual assembly, the members of the section committees are in fact selected by the incumbent section secretary in consultation with other Party officials. Nominations may be made from the

3. At a cooperative bar (*circolo*) in a rural corner of Albora, some residents listen to the amplified speech of a local Communist leader during the 1972 national election campaign.

floor, but few nominees are selected in this way, and, though the members must approve all nominees, a nominee of the nominating committee is never voted down. Yet this is not a matter of an autocratic secretary intimidating the membership into obedience. Rather, it is a consensus system in which those who are competing to enter the higher echelons are few and largely self-selected and in which confidence in the decision of the secretary and other influentials is widespread. The members of the section committee are expected to do what all Party members are theoretically supposed to do, that is, to be willing to spend a good part of their leisure time working for the Party.

Although there are section committee members who do very little Party work during their tenure, they are usually not renominated the following year.

The section committee, which meets once per week, is in charge of the administration of the section, with the various administrative duties being divided among its members. For example, one member is in charge of membership, another is in charge of section finances. Certain ongoing activities of the section, such as the weekly distribution of *L'Unità*, are directed by a member of the section committee who is responsible for organizing a committee of section members to share the work.

Though Party activity in Albora is carried out through the four sections of the *quartiere*, it is largely under the control of a higher level of the Party bureaucracy: the federation. Local membership campaigns, antiwar demonstrations, and the various other activities sponsored by the sections are carried out in conformity with plans made at the federation level.

The *quartiere* coordinator, overseeing Albora's four sections, provides the primary means by which, on a day-to-day basis, the federation is able to exert its influence over Party activities in Albora.[6] The authority of the coordinator, indeed, is vested in him not by the statutes of the Party but by his status as representative of the federation in the *quartiere*. He participates in the various meetings of the federation, he remains in constant touch with the decisions made by the ruling circle of the federation, and he has easy access to various federation officials. It is his job to see that Party policy and programs, as elaborated by the federation, are carried out in the sections of the *quartiere*. He is accountable not to the local sections, but directly to the federation. His is an appointive office; his selection is subject to the approval of the local Party leaders, but he is not independently elected by them.

Once a week the coordinator calls a meeting of the four section secretaries of Albora. At these meetings the coordinator outlines which federation programs should be instituted in the *quartiere* and what goals should be set, and he reports on the responses he has received from the federation regarding the various requests made by the sections for resources. All these are then discussed, deciding which programs can be initiated in the *quartiere*, what goals are possible, and what the sections need from the federation in terms of speakers, literature, and other support. The section secretaries report to the coordinator on the sections' ongoing activities, such as membership drives, and a discussion of the problems encountered is held.

For bureaucratic matters the coordinator is presumed able to supervise the local activities for the federation. However, when controversial policy matters are to be discussed locally, the federation usually sends a Party intellectual or specially trained official to "orient" the discussion. For example, when the touchy question of the India–Pakistan conflict arose, the federation sent one of its preeminent intellectuals to speak. Similarly, when the national Party triennial platform was up for local discussion, another top Party intellectual was called on to lead the sessions.

Allied organizations

Using one hand to guide her decrepit black bicycle through the puddles and balancing her umbrella with the other, sixty-two-year-old Evelina Candela rides through the streets of Albora waving greetings to the women she passes and bringing her basket filled with copies of *Noi Donne*, a left-wing women's weekly magazine. Almost every day Evelina goes out into the *quartiere*, chatting with the women about their families or launching into a rapid-fire political discourse. Evelina is viewed by the women of Albora with affection and respect, a working-class woman who is one of their own.

It has now been almost thirty years since Evelina first entered the ranks of *Unione Donne Italiane* (UDI), the Italian Women's League, which publishes *Noi Donne*. She recalled her first contact in 1945:

The secretary of UDI here, on some pretext or other, sent me a little girl to ask if I wanted this paper *Noi Donne*, and I said yes without hesitating at all. Then she sent word through the little girl that she'd like me to drop by her home, only a hundred meters away, next time I went shopping. So I went to her place and she said: "Oh, listen, I wanted to ask if you'd become a member of UDI." "Beh! of course, why not?" That's where the contact was first made. Then later, they said: "Take out membership in the PCI too." "Well," I said, "Why all this shyness . . . eh?" She responded: "But we didn't think you were a Communist." Well, I felt beh! then all this time you thought of me differently. But the mistake was also mine, because if I had these sentiments I should have gone to them, but I didn't do it, maybe because I was too timid.

Unione Donne Italiane is one of several national organizations having chapters in Albora. Although formally independent of any party, these organizations are, in Albora at least, controlled by the PCI. Ranging from sports clubs to grocery cooperatives, these organizations serve to bring the people of Albora into the social sphere of the Communist world, putting them in contact with Communist Party members, and securing their participation in activities which are seen as important by the Party, but which cannot be undertaken as easily or as well by the PCI organization itself.

Albora is not unlike other localities in this respect. The relationship of the Party section with local associations is spelled out in the PCI statute defining the section's duties:

"It must promote, direct and coordinate the activity of the Communists in every field of mass political action, in the economic, cultural, and associational centers of life in its jurisdiction" (Art. 11, PCI 1975:15–12). Party members are all called on to participate in these varied organizations (PCI 1960:112–13) to improve the Party's contact with the people: "We cannot know the problems of the people, we cannot give them solutions, if we are not a *mass* Party, present everywhere in the popular classes, firmly tied to them through capillary action, and if we do not participate in, and give our interpretation of, all aspects of popular life" (PCI 1964:67). It is hoped that through these formally autonomous organizations the Party can more easily approach and win over new members and allies, while avoiding social isolation (Poggi 1968:68). The more varied the social organizational structure under its tutelage, the more influential the Party will be. As one Party leader pointed out:

The section . . . cannot take on itself the duties of the union, the cooperative, or the cultural club. The section is not everything; on the contrary, when it becomes the only "trench," when it does not succeed in joining up with other associational instruments, it becomes increasingly difficult to create a unitary political mass movement, to develop our influence. [Natta 1967:19]

Unione Donne Italiane was formed in Rome in 1944 by a coalition of left-wing forces in anticipation of the postwar enfranchisement of women. The fact that women would be voting for the first time in Italy created concern on the Left, for women were seen as politically conservative, heavily influenced by the Church.[7] Thus from its inception UDI became an antagonist of the women's organizations sponsored by the Church. Championing such issues as equal rights at work for men and women, divorce and abortion legislation, and public day-care centers for children, UDI has embraced a Socialist model of national development. Heavily influenced by the PCI at the national level, with a Socialist minority, UDI's areas of highest membership correspond with those of the PCI, reaching an apex in the Red Belt (Manoukian 1968:220–2). Although UDI officials frequently assert that the league is *apartitica*, open to women who favor a variety of "democratic" parties, the ties with the PCI are close. In Bologna the UDI provincial federation president ran as a PCI candidate for Congress in 1972.

PCI influence in Albora's UDI organization is clear. Each of UDI's three sections in Albora is housed in one of the Party headquarters, with only the smallest PCI section in Albora not having its own UDI chapter. The most active local UDI section, that connected with the Vapori PCI section, has 180 members and six officers. The UDI section head is a member of the Vapori PCI section committee. The treasurer, in addition to being a member of the PCI section committee, is also one of the Party's nine *quartiere* counselors for Albora. Two of the other UDI officers are sisters, each married to a Vapori section secretary, one past and one present. The fifth UDI officer is a nonactivist PCI member, and the sixth is a member of the Socialist party.

UDI activity is conducted almost entirely by these six women, who have divided their area into neighborhoods, each woman, to the extent possible, responsible for the one in which she lives. Each week these women visit scores of homes, selling *Noi Donne* and chatting with the women of Albora. Three times a year the women go to virtually every home, once for the UDI membership drive, once on International Women's Day, and once to sell the UDI calendar. On these occasions social contact is established with the newcomers to the *quartiere:* a kind of Communist

Welcome Wagon. This is often the first direct contact the immigrant has with the Communist world of Albora, introducing her to a framework of women's social solidarity outside the social and ideological domination of the Church.

Of the local organizations informally tied to the Party in Albora, the most important are the *circoli*, the cooperative clubs, centers of adult male socializing. An example is provided by the Proletarian Struggle Cooperative (PSC), which was first formed around the turn of the century by a group of local Socialists who hoped to organize low-cost housing for the Alborese. Taken over in the 1920s by the Fascists, it became the seat of Fascist party activity and governance in the *quartiere* during the years of Mussolini's rule. On Liberation, a struggle between Socialists and Communists began for leadership of the cooperative, with the Communists finally wresting full control in the 1950s.

Now far surpassing the Camolia church, its primary rival as the community center, the PSC provides billiard and card tables, pinball machines, a television, and even a wine cellar for its patrons to use. Though there are a half dozen other, privately owned bars in the area, none approaches the facilities or the popularity of the PSC. In any given week hundreds of men frequent the PSC, with up to 60 people there in the evenings and on weekends. Inside the bar are copies of *L'Unità* and the various publications of the commune, as well as the publications of the different Communist-allied organizations that use the PSC for their headquarters, including groups of pensioners, sportsmen, and labor organizations.

In recent years the PSC has proposed a massive cooperative housing project in Albora that would tear down all the unfit living quarters in the area and provide apartments at low cost.[8] As a result, hundreds of Alborese have paid the modest dues to join the PSC, and every few months a meeting is held at which the deputy mayor in charge of housing speaks of the progress of the plans.

The Communist control of the PSC is manifest in a number of ways, most notably in the identity of the officers. In the past fifteen years there have been three presidents of the PSC, all of whom had been local Party officeholders. The current president was a PCI *quartiere* counselor, as was the immediate past president. Their predecessor is also a PCI officeholder, whose wife is a member of the PCI section committee. The physical signs of Communist influence are also striking. The cooperative provides rooms at nominal cost for the headquarters of the Vapori PCI section, the Young Communists' section, and various other PCI-allied organizations. On the outside wall of the PSC hangs the PCI section flag, alongside a posted copy of *L'Unità*.

Unlike these other organizations, the *Federazione Giovanile Comunista Italiana* (FGCI), the Italian Communist Youth Federation, is formally tied to the Party. As stated in its statutes, the FGCI was established to train future leaders of the Party (art. 1, FGCI 1957:9). Although few of its members actually go on to be Party leaders, the FGCI, catering primarily to those fourteen to nineteen years old, does serve to bring youths into the Communist world at an early age. No other party has a youth group in Albora, nor does the Church, since its Catholic Action youth group expired years ago because of a dearth of participants.

The youths involved in the FGCI in Albora not only are provided with instruction in Party dogma but, more important, become part of a social group centered at the local Party headquarters. In addition, many of the Party leaders come from FGCI ranks: The two top PCI leaders in Albora are in fact past presidents of FGCI chapters in the *quartiere*.

. Membership in the FGCI in Albora reached its high point of 200 in the early postwar years but then shrank, until by the mid-1960s the organization was inactive. In 1968, the year of the student rebellions in Italy and elsewhere in Europe, the Party sought to resurrect the FGCI as an instrument for combating the new left-wing groups arising among the youths of the country.[9] This process was reflected in Albora. In response to the arrival of one such autonomous left-wing *gruppetto*, which attempted to organize people in the poorest zone of the city, the PCI reinvigorated the FGCI. This was accomplished through the efforts of two of the most active PCI officials, each of whom had a teen-aged daughter. These girls were themselves good friends, and they organized a meeting of other friends; the FGCI was thus reconstituted through a preexisting social network. As this network was centered in the area of the Vapori section, the FGCI headquarters was established there (see Photograph 4). Subsequently, a *quartiere*-wide FGCI headquarters was established alongside the PCI *quartiere* headquarters. By 1972 there were sixty members officially enrolled in Albora's chapter.

The FGCI not only serves to bring the Party into the social lives of the youths of the *quartiere* but also aids the Party in repudiating the common charge that the PCI is becoming tired, bureaucratic, and corrupt with power and age. It is the responsibility of the FGCI to dwell on the idealistic and humanitarian themes of the Party. For example, the FGCI was given primary responsibility by the Party in Albora (and by the PCI Federation) to carry out the anti–Vietnam War campaign. By going door to door bearing Communist leaflets, the youths provide a public image of the Party as young and active, a task seen by the Party as particularly important in attracting the youth vote.

The supervision of the FGCI by the Party is the responsibility of the *quartiere* coordinator. He attends all formal

FGCI meetings and is responsible for ensuring that the youths restrain their proverbial overexuberance, avoiding excesses that could prove embarrassing in light of the conciliatory national Party position. Although certain illegal activity is condoned as part of the FGCI's role as the militant cutting edge of the Party, other such activity is forbidden. When the FGCI youths posted unsigned antimilitarist posters near the local army base, and when they wrote anti–Vietnam War slogans with spray paint on the walls of the *quartiere*, the Party coordinator looked the other way. However, when some of the FGCI youths painted anti-Church slogans (e.g., "Houses Not Churches"; "No to the Referendum") on the walls of an Albora church one night, they were severely chastised.

Of the several other PCI-allied organizations in Albora, brief note should be made of two: the COOP, a retail food cooperative having two outlets and 800 members in the *quartiere*, and ARCI, a recreational and "cultural" association whose numbers are also in the hundreds. Most officeholders of both groups are PCI activists. The president of Albora's COOP is a member of the Vapori section committee, and the two driving forces behind ARCI are both local Party officials.

Whether it is a matter of the COOP sponsoring annual trips to Yugoslavia or of ARCI sponsoring anti-Fascist films and anti-DC songfests, the allied organizations provide a broad web of reinforcement for the PCI as well as a wealth of social outlets for the Alborese under the aegis of the Communist world. Though some of the organizations may lie dormant, they are ready to be mobilized when needed by the Party.[10]

Together these organizations monopolize associational activity in Albora: recreational,[11] "cultural," pensioners', *partigiani*, and women's. They are intended both for members and nonmembers of the Party. For the members they

4. Two members of the FGCI in the Vapori FGCI headquarters. Portraits are of Togliatti, Lenin, and Gramsci.

provide a social means of solidifying the Party's influence. The authority and prestige of the Party are reinforced through the "independent" associations in which Party positions are extolled and the various local Party officers' high status is validated.

For non-Party members the associations are also crucial; they serve both to recruit people to membership and to envelop them in the Communist world. By maintaining a series of organizations through which the Alborese can satisfy their social and political wants, the PCI discourages people from going to any outside institution, such as the Church or the national government, for aid.

The party membership

Taking out membership in the PCI is to the Communist world what weekly mass attendance is to the Catholic world. But the meaning of Communist Party membership in Albora cannot be grasped by reading official Party norms regarding membership, nor by employing analyses of Communist Party members proffered in the traditional anti-Communist tradition of American political science. Party membership in Albora is neither a sign of a life devoted to proletarian struggle nor a sign of personal dissatisfaction or protest. Perhaps the most striking feature of PCI membership in Albora is its size, with approximately 1,800 members[12] in a population of about 6,200 adults, making Albora one of the most heavily Communist zones in Italy. Although such a huge mass of members obviously reflects a strong Party organization, it paradoxically also reflects an abandonment of the statutory role of the Party nember. As Party membership in Albora increasingly becomes identified with membership in the working-class collectivity, membership has become a badge of social identity rather than an expression of political militancy.[13]

Table 5. *Membership in Albora by Party Section, 1971*

Section	Membership
Dovero	641
Vapori	418
Govicchi	232
Giuliari	157
Total	1448

Source: PCI Federazione di Bologna 1971.

Most Party members living in Albora belong to one of the four sections located in the *quartiere*. The others, most notably railroad workers and government employees, belong to sections based at their place of employment. The geographical boundaries of the sections follow preexisting social boundaries and do not evenly divide the population. The 1971 membership figures for Albora's four sections are provided in Table 5.[14] In 1972, as a result of the mobilization for the national electoral campaign, membership rose to 1,550 in the four sections of the *quartiere*. The unequal distribution of members among the sections, it should be noted, is due not to differences in Communist strength in the various parts of Albora but to differences in general population size within the jurisdiction of the various sections.

An examination of the Vapori section[15] reveals that 40 percent of the members are women,[16] thus approaching the figure for the Bologna Federation of 42 percent. Most of the women members have husbands who are also members. Those who do not are regarded by the Alborese as requiring some explanation; for example, the husband has

Table 6. *Occupation of Male Members of PCI Vapori Section, 1972*

Number	Occupation	Percentage
128	Worker[a]	55.4
57	Pensioner	24.7
10	Artisan	4.3
8	Shopkeeper	3.4
7	White-collar worker	3.0
7	Farmer (own land)	3.0
4	Clerk	1.7
2	Sharecropper	0.9
2	Peddler	0.9
2	Student	0.9
1	Farmer	0.4
1	Farm laborer	0.4
1	Teacher	0.4
1	Invalid	0.4
231		99.8

[a] These occupational categories were composed by the local Party officials. The category *operaio* (worker) is somewhat ambiguous, but groups together people who do manual labor and whose occupations are of relatively low status. This includes factory production-line workers, glass cutters, furniture cleaners, and the like, who work for others and are paid by the hour.
Source: Section membership files.

a job that might be endangered if he were known to be a PCI member. For reasons to be discussed later, no explanation is considered necessary for a PCI man whose wife is not a member.

The members of the Vapori section are characterized by occupation in Table 6 and 7, divided by sex. As shown in

Table 7. *Occupation of Female Members of PCI Vapori Section*, 1972

Number	Occupation	Percentage
71	Housewife	47.7
33	Pensioner	22.1
20	Worker	13.4
5	Farmer (own land)	3.4
4	Farmer	2.7
3	White-collar worker	2.0
3	Artisan	2.0
2	Apprentice	1.3
2	Teacher	1.3
1	Piecework at home*a*	0.7
1	Shopkeeper	0.7
1	Nurse	0.7
1	Midwife	0.7
1	Agricultural worker	0.7
1	Invalid	0.7
149		100.1

a This official figure is a gross underestimate.
Source: Section membership files.

Table 6, the men are overwhelmingly workers and pensioners (retirement generally coming at age sixty-five for men and sixty for women). Of the economically active members, 74 percent are workers and only 10 percent have white-collar status. Occupationally, the section's membership reflects the general population of the *quartiere*, though the pensioners are overrepresented, white-collar workers are somewhat underrepresented, and professionals are absent.

Almost half of the women have listed themselves as housewives and 22 percent as pensioners. Yet these figures are

Table 8. *Date of Birth of the Members of PCI Vapori Section, 1972*

Date of birth	Number
Before 1900	28
1900–04	21
1905–09	26
1910–14	37
1915–19	34
1920–24	48
1925–29	40
1930–34	33
1935–39	30
1940–44	26
1945–49	42
1950–54	12
Total	377[a]

[a] Total of section members for whom data were available.
Source: Section membership files.

somewhat misleading, for many women doing *lavoro a domicilio* have listed themselves as "housewives." Still, excluding the pensioners, over 37 percent of the women in the section are employed outside of the home and, in general, their occupations reflect the occupational structure of the women of Albora.

Membership in the Communist Party is not, as some might suppose, a temporary segment of the individual's life cycle, a product of youthful idealism or activism. As can be seen in Table 8, membership is quite uniformly distributed throughout the various age groupings. The paucity of members born in the 1940–4 period may be attributable to

Table 9. *Year in Which Members First Joined the Party:*
Vapori Section, 1972

Year	Number	Year	Number
1921	2	1957	3
1933	2	1958	9
1937	1	1959	3
1943	10	1960	4
1944	2	1961	0
1945	148	1962	7
1946	10	1963	6
1947	4	1964	4
1948	10	1965	6
1949	5	1966	6
1950	10	1967	6
1951	3	1968	7
1952	4	1969	14
1953	3	1970	10
1954	6	1971	15
1955	8	1972	7[a]
1956	5	Total	340[b]

[a] As of July 1972.
[b] Total of section members for whom data were available.
Source: Section membership files.

a drop in the birth rate at the height of the war. The small
number of members in the 1950–4 group reflects the fact
that, although people can become members at age eighteen, many do not do so until a somewhat older age.

The contention that Party membership in Albora is a
social identity taken for life is supported by data on date of
joining the PCI (Table 9). In reviewing these data, it should
be borne in mind that Party membership must be renewed
each year; renewal is not automatic.[17] As seen in these
figures, recruitment to the Party has not been a gradual

process; rather, almost half of all section members joined the Party in the year of Liberation, 1945, the year in which the Vapori section was founded. Considering that just 215 of the section's members were old enough (eighteen) to join the Party in 1945, the fact that 165 of them had done so by that date is striking.

The massive influx of membership in the postwar years brought about a drastic change in the role of the Party member, although the Leninist conception of Party membership has not, in its entirety, been officially abandoned. Through broadening its membership base, the Party has continually sought to make itself the center of a social infrastructure for the working class. The primary medium for extending its influence has been through identification with working-class social life, rather than through abstract ideological appeals.

It is instructive to glance at Duverger's well-known typology of Communist parties as totalitarian, for he imputes an ideological priority to Communist Party membership that cannot be sustained in the Albora case:

The totalitarian party forms the mainspring of the life of its members, the fundamental belief which directs all their activities, the moral basis of their existence: to leave it is to abandon one's reasons for living, to break with the whole of oneself, to make a void and a desert within one, for the party fills all. Think of the wretchedness of the medieval Christian when he was excommunicated: the Communist or Fascist party member is in like state when he is condemned to be purged. [Duverger 1964:122]

Like the rest of the anti-Communist literature of the cold war period, this distorts more than it enlightens. Our interest in it here, though, stems from its assertions that a system of beliefs (in the Party) serves as a basis for social groupings, an assertion of dubious merit; it is more accurate to see the groupings and activities as primary and the beliefs as derivative. To leave the Party is not "to break with the whole of oneself, to make a void and a desert within one." Rather, it is to break with the relevant others; it is primarily a social loss. Duverger's analogy of the medieval Christian is most appropriate here, for excommunication in such a feudal society meant social alienation. The break was not with the "whole of oneself," but with the rest of society.

The search for new Party members in Albora is largely based on the goal of getting as many people as possible to join the Party. The search is not to find individuals interested in Marxist ideology, nor to find leaders of the working class. Almost all the pressures on the section secretaries and section committees from the federation are focused on section membership numbers. Each week during the annual membership campaigns, the federation publishes the results of the campaign in terms of numerical gains. Little attention is paid to the ideological outlook of the new recruits. A healthy section is one that is gaining members; a section losing members is a section in trouble.

The tactic suggested by the federation for conducting the membership drive is the following: "For a rapid and vast recruitment it is proposed that all the section committee members and all the activist comrades approach, house by house, the democrats, the sympathizers, the laborers and propose that they join the Party" (PCI–Federazione di Bologna 1971). This advice is only partially carried out in the *quartiere*. First of all, the formal membership campaign is conducted primarily by members of the section committee. Few others express any interest in participating in the drive. Second, recruitment is a much more informal process than is described here. One section secretary describes it as follows:

We go a little by whom we are acquainted with; we don't go to all the houses, though it ought to be like that, but we bring the membership campaign material together with the newspaper [Sunday's *L'Unità*]. It's true we don't bring the material for the membership and recruitment around sufficiently. But I'd say that hardly any sections actually go search out new members enough.

Another Party official, Albora's first *quartiere* coordinator, describes Albora's Party recruitment drives more positively: "Usually it's organized toward those we think voted for us, toward those whom, from conversations, we feel are closer to us than others. Its not left to spontaneity; it's the fruit of hard work."

As may be gathered from these remarks, Party members in Albora are recruited through informal social networks, rather than through strictly political contact. The section committee members generate a list of people whom they think are sympathetic to the Party, and this list is divided according to which section committee member or activist is most friendly with the prospective recruit. The question of his becoming a Party member is more likely to be brought up at the cooperative bar than in a doorway discussion of Party literature.

Why people choose to join the Party is an elusive question. If a Party member is asked why he joined the PCI he almost invariably gives an ideological reason for his membership. This is in line with Party norms: A person joins the PCI because he believes the PCI has the best political program of any party. The PCI is the party of the working class, opposed to the various parties representing the capitalists.

The theme of the PCI as guardian of the interests of the working class is a powerful one in Albora. Though much attention is devoted by the Party to general humanitarian themes, these seem to have minor impact on the bulk of the section membership. This is tacitly admitted by the Party. For example, Vietnam was seen by Party officials both at the federation and local levels as primarily a youth issue. Indeed, the backbone of the appeal to the young first-time voters in 1972 was the image of the PCI as *the* Italian antiimperialist party, and in Albora the highlight of the young Communist campaign effort was a march and rally around the theme "Peace for Vietnam." The appeal to the older voters, however, was on pragmatic and programmatic grounds: higher pensions and salaries, better schools, better public health care.

Aside from factors of social solidarity, the overwhelming PCI vote in Albora can be attributed to the successful efforts of the Party in convincing the people that the PCI best represents their interests and can best effect a program based on these interests. The Party has been a staunch defender of the union movement. Moreover, in its quarter century of rule in Bologna, the PCI administration has provided the best service to working-class people of any large city in the country. Its administrations have been free from the corruption so characteristic of Italian political life, and its internal unity, its stability and effectiveness have contrasted sharply with the factionalism and *malgoverno* of the other major parties.

The reason the Alborese join the PCI in such large numbers is more complex. One key is provided by a local Party leader, who explains the effectiveness of the Party recruiters as follows: "They speak with the people, they speak with the people, however, as equals, because it's a worker who speaks to another worker. And there's no reason not to believe him because you know he's a good person and therefore why shouldn't you believe him?" Again, the medium is the message. The membership appeal is made by a social equal, by a peer with whom the individual is in daily contact. Furthermore, the recruiter represents a larger group of peers who value membership in the Party. Becoming a member of the Party means becoming closer to that peer group, evoking its approval. Indeed, almost all the individuals with the highest prestige in the *quartiere* are associated with the Party and have either acquired or ratified that prestige through Party activity. To become a member of the section is to lay claim to the recognition and approval of these local dignitaries. Merely voting for the PCI need be no more than a purely personal act; joining the Party is an eminently social act.

Turning the question around, it might be asked why so many people vote PCI but do not join the Party. There are a number of contributing factors here. A person may vote for the PCI as the best of a bad choice, having reservations about aspects of the Party's policy or organization. He may be embedded in a social network that includes domains– such as kinsmen or workmates–where Communist membership is socially stigmatic. One of the most common reasons people give for voting PCI without becoming Party members is fear of losing jobs or of not being able to find employment. For those who hold or who are looking for nationally sponsored jobs, the fear of anti-Communist discrimination is especially acute. Added to this is a more diffuse fear, one held particularly by those who lived through the Fascist years: If one becomes a Party member his name may be entered on police lists, leaving him vulnerable in a political future over which he has little control.

Another reason PCI voters give for not becoming Party members is a desire to avoid the statutory responsibilities that members have. A section secretary spoke of this:

there are some workers, both young and not so young, who don't become members for fear of being made to do some activity. They're with you in their vote and also in their ideas–in general demonstrations, strikes in the factories and so on–they share them in full, but if you think of making them do some work– forget it.

The same reason is reflected in the remarks of a woman of the *quartiere* on the lack of participation in PCI activities:

That's just how people are here, myself and my husband included. Everyone thinks the Party is doing the right thing, but everyone figures he should let someone else do the work. You take this zone here: of 1000 votes 900 go to the PCI, yet hardly anyone is active in Party activities. You have 900 who go out to vote Communist, and 100 DC. Carlo and I don't take part in any activities, but you don't see us running off to vote for the priests.

It would, however, be difficult to distinguish between PCI members and nonmembers in Albora on the basis of the participation of the former in Party activities and the nonparticipation of the latter. Many of Albora's PCI members shun formal Party activity, despite the Party statutes, which state that:

Every member of the party has the duty of: (a) participating regularly in the meetings and assemblies; being active in his local organization; realizing, in his own field of activity, the politics of the party and the decisions of the directing bodies; giving the maximum contribution to the political elaboration and to the initiatives and work of the party; (b) continually increasing his own knowledge of the political line of the party and his own capacity to effect it; reading, sustaining and distributing the newspaper and the publications of the party; acquiring and deepening (excepting the provision of art. 2)[18] his knowledge of Marxism-Leninism and applying its teachings to the solution of concrete questions; being active in the mass organizations; winning new adherents to the program and action of the party; doing, by work and example, continual work of ideological and political orientation and contributing to the conquest of new militants through a permanent action. [Art. 5, PCI Statuto, 1975:11]

These precepts reveal a Leninist heritage, the concept of the Party member as a professional revolutionary who carries out the work of the Party in every sphere of his

social life. This concept of the member as full-time revolutionary seems out of place in the Alborese context. Wit-
ness the PCI statute prescribing the moral example to be
set by all members:

Every member of the Communist Party ought to understand
that his companions at work and at school, his neighbors, his
acquaintances and his relatives all look upon him as a combattant
for a better world, for a more just and sane society. Thus he
must constantly concern himself with setting an example in his
private life, with his conduct toward his own family, his neighbors, his companions at work, with his moral behavior, his hon-
esty, and the spirit of human and social solidarity which demonstrates these. [Art. 55, PCI Statuto 1975:46]

The fact is that in Albora PCI members are not seen as
moral or political examplars. It is even difficult to imagine
how one-third of the *quartiere* could be so conceived over
a thirty-year period.

Women are the weakest segment of PCI membership in
Albora. Although they compose about 40 percent of the
local membership, there are few women who take part in
ongoing Party activities. The role of the woman in Albora
is in the home, whether the woman be Catholic or Communist. Although the PCI literature speaks of the liberation of the Italian woman, little is actually done in the
quartiere to go beyond this rhetoric. There is certainly no
expectation locally that a man, by joining the Party, will
thereby change his traditional views of male superiority.
Women are expected not only to earn money but also to
take care of the children and the apartment and always to
have meals ready for their husbands. Few are the Communist men who would not resent their wives being lax in
any of these duties because they were working for the
Party. Indeed, one of the few women activists in Albora
arose at the section's annual assembly to demand that the

men stop making their wives shine their shoes and let them go out at night to Party meetings. Also revealing was the election campaign rally held in the central piazza of Bologna one night, addressed specifically to the problems of women. Only 10 percent of the people assembled were female. Most Alborese consider women to be naturally uninterested in politics. At one meeting a PCI woman activist complained of her experience in trying to get women to join the Party. Time and again, she said, the comrades' wives refuse to speak to her about joining the PCI, asserting that their husbands take care of those affairs.

Although women are less active in Party affairs than are men, the fact is that few of the members, male or female, engage in their section's ongoing activities. Meetings rarely draw more than 5 percent of the section's members and a meeting drawing more than a fifth of the membership is now virtually unheard of. An analysis of the attendance at the section's annual congresses, the most important membership meeting of the year, at which officers are elected and the Party program discussed, exemplifies this low level of membership participation in the section's formal activities. Despite the massive publicity given to the congresses and the importance assigned to them by Party norms and the local leadership, attendance was low at all four of Albora's sections. The Vapori section, with a membership of over 400, had just 30 members present at its assembly, and the Govicchi section, with over 200 members, had but 15 in attendance. The figures at the other section assemblies were comparable, with about 8 percent of the membership in attendance. These figures, although low, are not out of line with attendance patterns elsewhere in Bologna,[19]

Rather than reflecting a commitment to political activism, membership in the PCI in Albora reflects a local social context in which worker solidarity is reflected through

Party membership.[20] PCI membership is a key to in-group status, a conclusion derived from such encounters as one described in my field notes, a visit to a Sicilian barber eight years resident in Albora:

I went to Antonio's for a haircut in the morning. He told me that he was a PCI member, something he had not mentioned to me before. He smiled as he told me, somewhat proudly, that all of his friends were Communists. He added that one must have courage and not be afraid. Antonio said that he became a PCI member as soon as he moved to Albora and that his wife had also become a member. I asked him if he takes part in any Party activity. He responded with a quick no, saying he was just a member, he didn't do anything politically.

In this case the influence of social environment on the decision to join the Party is clear. Antonio had never considered joining the PCI in his Sicilian hometown, where Party membership was considered socially hazardous. Arriving in Albora, he found that all the local notables were Party members and that through Party membership he could be more easily accepted into the community. In joining the Party, however, he recognized no obligation to be active in Party affairs and rarely attended any of his section's activities. Being a PCI member meant expressing his solidarity with the other Party members of Albora.

It should be obvious at this point that the practice of Communist Party membership in Albora contradicts a number of the best-known models of Communist membership. Here the evidence from Albora accords with much of the most recent political science literature in repudiating such previously prominent theses as Duverger's categorization of the PCI as a "totalitarian party." Duverger defined the totalitarian party by contrasting it with the "restricted party":

Amongst all the communities to which individuals belong, restricted parties occupy only a secondary place; on the other hand

totalitarian parties take first place: party solidarity takes prece-
dence over all other bonds, instead of being subordinate to many
others. For a Communist, country, family, wife, friends are all
subordinated to the interest of the Party; for a liberal or conservative the party ranks far below them. Hence the general
characteristics of the totalitarian party: homogeneous, exclusive,
and sacrosanct. Restricted parties are heterogeneous; that is to
say they are composed of members whose ideas and points of
view are not absolutely identical in all their details. [1964:120]

This categorization is clearly inappropriate for the Alborese
PCI. Allegiance to the Party is not generally perceived as
calling for the subordination of allegiance to the family or
to friends. Indeed, membership in the Party is often identified with peer group and family solidarity; Party membership does not isolate the individual from his friends, it
unites him with them. The implication that the Party is
based on the rigid sharing of a body of doctrine is similarly
erroneous. Membership in the Party is a mark of social
identity, not a sign of full acceptance or even knowledge
of Party dogma.

Duverger's analysis contains within it its own negation,
or, viewed more positively, its own salvation, for despite
the mentalistic bias of his thesis, he notes:

It has been suggested that Communism should be called a "secular religion": the term applies equally well to Fascism and to all
totalitarian parties. And the religious character does not come
only from their structure–very like that of a church–or from
their totalitarianism (by nature a religion is totalitarian, for it
forms an all-embracing system explaining the universe), it depends even more on the truly sacred nature of the bonds of
solidarity. [1964:122]

The integralism of the Party, like the integralism of the
Church, is based less on intellectual attachment than on
social allegiance. The comprehensive nature of people's
ties with Party or Church, that which constitutes the Com-

munist or the Catholic world, is socially grounded, in what Duverger terms the "truly sacred nature of the bonds of solidarity."

These findings reinforce the conclusions of Tarrow (1967b:52) in his critique of Duverger: "the role and structure of marxist parties cannot be derived abstractly. . . . " In the Italian case, paradoxically, it is just where the Party is strongest that the level of membership participation and militancy is weakest. Identification with the Party in these areas, as part of the individual's overall social identity, has its ideological component, but there is little reason to believe that this component accounts for Party allegiance. In this regard, Gori's comments on PCI membership in Florence are revealing:

If there seem to be few incentives [for the Party members] to participate, reasons for abandoning the Party in which, for the most part, they no longer participate are virtually nonexistent. At root here there is a stable and ingrained identification of the mass of members with the Party; this appears to be the principal, if not the only, reason for the continued survival of the PCI's hold on the masses. [1975:273]

This identification of the masses with the PCI, freed from the analysis in terms of fanatical belief that characterized the American social science literature through the early 1960s, has in recent years been most commonly discussed in terms of "subculture." We leave further discussion of this literature and the theoretical questions raised there to our critique of the subculture concept in Chapter 10.

Party activist

Alberto Finelli grew up on a poor farm in the province of Bologna, just a few kilometers from the city. Though his parents were not Communists, they gave refuge to two *partigiani* in their farmhouse. Alberto was only four years old when, tipped off by an informer, the Nazi soldiers descended on their house. Unable to find the well-hidden *partigiani*, the Nazis seized all the farm stock–pigs, cows, and all–and, for good measure, took Alberto's oldest brother off to Buchenwald. Though this brother ultimately escaped the concentration camp and made his way home, Alberto's middle brother, just five years old at the time, was so traumatized by the Nazi visitation that, says Alberto, he has had a speech impediment ever since.

In the early postwar period the Finellis moved to Albora and Alberto joined the *Pionieri*–the youth group sponsored by Communists and Socialists for pre-teenagers–and, before long, he became head of the 200-member group in the *quartiere*. During this period he also was sent to Sunday catechism at the Andara church, which he attended regularly until one day the priest demanded that all the children give him their *Pionieri* membership cards. Taking the card from the first child, don Luigi tore it up. Except for family funerals and weddings, Alberto has not been in a church since then.

Leaving school at the age of fourteen to help support his family, Albero got a job as a porter in the downtown market. In a few years he became head of FGCI for Albora and began attending Party leadership training sessions at federation headquarters. Graduating from the FGCI, he became secretary of his section, and when the position of Party *quartiere* coordinator became available in 1970, both local activists and federation officials agreed that he would be the best candidate. As his status within the Party rose, his status among his workmates at the central market also increased, and his opinion on a wide variety of political issues was sought. Thirty-two years old, still unmarried and living with his parents in very modest circumstances in an ancient building in Albora, Alberto spent all his spare time working for the Party. Though he enjoyed the companion-

Table 10. *Occupations of PCI Officeholders in Albora*

Occupation	Number
Worker	16
White-collar	7
Shopkeeper	1
Housewife	4
Pensioner	3
Student	2
Total	33

Table 11. *PCI Officeholders in Albora–Father's Occupation*[a]

Occupation	Number
Worker	18
Farmer	3
Farmhand	4
Artisan	3
White-collar	2
Shopkeeper	2
Unemployed	1[b]
Total	33

[a] The question was phrased as follows: "What was your father's prevalent occupation when you were a youth (ten to eighteen years old)?"
[b] This number does not include all those who indicated that their father was unemployed from time to time.

Table 12. *PCI Officeholders in Albora–Education*

		Age	
Highest grade attended	Number	19–30	31–
Elementary school	12	1	11
Junior high school	13	6	7
High school	7	6	1
University	1	1	0
Total	33	14	19

Table 13. *Date of Birth of PCI Officeholders in Albora*

Birth date	Number
1900–04	1
1905–09	2
1910–14	0
1915–19	2
1920–24	5
1925–29	2
1930–34	2
1935–39	4
1940–44	4
1945–49	5
1950–54	6
Total	33

ship of his mates at the market, it was becoming increasingly difficult to come home from a long day of heavy physical labor to a long round of Party activity. As a result, a job was found for him as a custodian in a municipally run school, a position that, though physically much easier, was less enjoyable since the high school students did not

Table 14. *Birthplace of Albora PCI Officeholders*

Place of birth	Number
City of Bologna	18
Province of Bologna	10
Emilia-Romagna	3
Rest of Italy	2
Total	33

Table 15. *PCI Officeholders in Albora – Length of Residence in Bologna*

Length of residence	Number
From birth	19
40–44 years	1
35–39	1
30–34	3
25–29	1
20–24	1
15–19	1
10–14	2
5–9	3
0–4	1
Total	33

hold him in the same esteem that his colleagues at the market had. However, through dedication and relentless hard work, Alberto rose further in the Party, by 1975 taking a full-time position as a union organizer.

Among the mass of Party members in Albora there are about forty-five or fifty who can be properly termed the activist core of the Party. The activists are those who most

Table 16. *PCI Officeholders – Length of Residence in Albora*

Length of residence	Number
From birth	10
45–49 years	1
40–44	0
35–39	1
30–34	5
25–29	0
20–24	2
15–19	1
10–14	2
5–9	4
0–4	5
Total	31[a]

[a] Two individuals, not resident in Albora, have been excluded from this table. One works in Albora and on that basis joined the section in the *quartiere* although he lives in an adjoining *quartiere*. The other was brought into the PCI by an Albora activist who works with him. Although having no statutory basis, the individual joined his friend's section in Albora.

closely fulfill the standard of PCI membership enunciated in the Party statutes.[21] The activist core largely consists of forty people occupying the forty-four principal PCI posts in Albora: thirty-four section committee members, nine *quartiere* counselors, and one *quartiere* coordinator. Of these forty, ten are women.[22] Yet some of the officeholders are largely inactive, whereas there are several individuals

Table 17. *PCI Officeholders – Age at Which
they Moved to Albora*

Age at time of move	Number
0–9 years old	6
10–19	5
20–29	4
30–39	2
40–49	2
50+	1
Total	20

who, though holding no Party office, are engaged in almost daily Party work.

Although strongly working class in composition, the local activist core does have a proportionately larger middle-class contingent than does the membership of Albora (see Table 10).[23] Strikingly, of the nine PCI *quartiere* counselors, only one can be termed working class, with seven middle class and one of intermediate status. Apparently, in the one public arena of debate with other parties, the PCI is anxious to put forth its most eloquent and best-educated spokesmen. It is also true that some of the working-class Party members feel insecure about public speaking, even at Party meetings. The middle-class activists, however, come largely from working-class families, as can be seen in Table 11.[24] The officeholders in general are better educated than the membership, almost two-thirds having junior high school degrees or beyond, compared with a mere 16 percent of Albora's general population (see Table 12). Of the younger officeholders (nineteen to thirty years old), half have completed high school.

Although two of the four local section secretaries trace their membership back to the 1940's and have been in

Table 18. *PCI Officeholders in Albora–Church Attendance*

Frequency	Officeholder	Spouse	Father	Mother
Every Sunday	0	0	1	3
Once in a while	0	0	2	4
Only on a big holiday (like Christmas)	2	3	6	8
Never	28	15	23	16
Total	30[a]	18	32	31

[a] Three individuals failed to answer this question, apparently because they were hesitant to admit to occasionally attending church mass outside of the *quartiere*.

office for many years, the activist core overall is rather young, having a mean age of thirty-seven, considerably below that of the general membership (see Table 13).[25] The leadership group is also notable for the high proportion of its number born in the city and province of Bologna and those having firm social roots in Albora itself (see Table 14). Over half of the officials either were born in Albora or had lived there for over thirty years (see Tables 15 and 16). Only five of thirty-three had moved to Albora after their thirtieth birthday (see Table 17).

The dissociation of the party activists from the Church is evident in their nonattendance at mass. Of the officeholders who provided information on church attendance, twenty-eight maintained that they *never* went to church, and the remaining two only admitted to attending church on Christmas and Easter. Of the eighteen married officials responding, fifteen claimed their spouses never went to church, and the remaining three claimed their spouses (all female) went only on the major holidays. Of interest also is the fact that of the fathers of the officeholders, twenty-three were said never to have attended mass, and half the

Table 19. *Political Affiliation of Parents of PCI Officeholders in Albora*

Both parents PCI members	17
Father PCI member, not mother	2
Mother PCI member, not father	2
Both parents PSI members	1
Father PSI member, not mother	1
Neither parent member of any party	9
Total	32

Source: Questionnaire administered to Albora PCI officeholders, 1972.

mothers of the officeholders were said not to have attended mass (see Table 18).

Finally, the parents of the activists were themselves either members of the PCI or the PSI or belonged to no party at all. To what extent the parents followed their activist children into the Party is not known, but it is clear that Party activists were rarely converts from families strongly allied to the Church.

3

Catholic World

It was the day before All Saints' Day and the 9:30 A.M. Camolia church mass was crowded. Like most churches in the area, the building had a deceptively plain, dull orange exterior. Inside the dark church, though, the walls were ornately decorated, with a series of small altars lining the sides, candelabra set in front of images of the Madonna and the saints. The eight rows of wooden pews, seating four people on either side of the central aisle, were filled, people spilling over into the three extra rows of movable chairs at the rear of the hall, and into the side aisles and back of the church. As at all 9:30 masses, the first few rows were taken up by young children, boys on the left and girls on the right, shepherded by two seventeen-year-old catechists who stood in the central aisle throughout the mass to oversee their charges. The rows behind them were entirely taken up by women, women of all ages. Along the back stood five middle-aged men, dressed in dark suits, together with some late-arriving women. In the seats on either side of the altar sat ten young men (sixteen to twenty-four years old). In all there were fifty children and at least sixty adults.

Although don Mario was not in the habit of convoking meetings of his parishioners, the planning of the upcoming decennial *festa* of the Camolia parish seemed to demand a special effort to begin drumming up popular interest. Coming but once every decade, it had the potential of being the most important event for the church for the next several years. So, despite fears that few people would attend, don Mario announced the meetings at Sunday mass and circulated a flyer notifying people of the four meetings, one meeting for each of the four different neighborhoods in the parish.

Vincenzo and Maria Pelti, twenty-five-year-old newlyweds, arrived for the meeting at 9:15 P.M. They entered the church hall, just across a dirt expanse from the church building itself, between the church and the convent–nursery school. Although freshly painted, the large room was in disrepair. At one end was the stage, rarely used now but once the center of church dramatic productions. Two wood stoves provided the heat; the center of the hall was occupied by table tennis and billiard tables and a variety of other games. Don Mario was already there. A man of fifty, he was dressed, as always, in his black robe and white collar. His assistant, don Giorgio, was also present, wearing black pants and a black shirt. Just twenty-seven years old, don Giorgio had come to Camolia fresh from the seminary four years before.

Just two other parishioners came for the meeting, forty-five-year-old brothers-in-law, and a little circle of folding chairs was formed around a wood stove. Don Mario chaired the meeting, which often became animated with the simultaneous remarks of don Mario, Vincenzo, and one of the brothers-in-law. Don Mario noted that each year, with their procession for the Madonna, they were getting more and more complaints from motorists about blocking the road. There was a problem of logistics. Vincenzo interjected that personally he didn't think much of the idea of having processions: "They're an anachronism, but at least if you are going to have one, you should try to do something that will strengthen the church. I don't see why it should be the task of the priests to urge people to put little lamps outside their homes, spending all the energy of the church on such things." This suggestion brought immediate responses from the middle-aged men and don Mario. Don Mario observed that the *festa* was not just a time for prayer but was a time for joy, and he noted that there was nothing wrong with making it a festive occasion. Or as the middle-aged man put it: *La bellezza non fa mai una cosa brutta*, ("a little beauty never hurt anything").

Turning to the schedule, don Mario suggested holding the *festa* on Tuesday, Wednesday, and Thursday evenings, but after Vincenzo noted that Thursday night was when the television quiz show *Rischiatutto* was shown, an alternative plan of Friday through Sunday evening was settled on, don Mario noting that otherwise they might *rischiar tutto* ("risk everything").

For over three centuries the area now known as Albora was divided in half by a boundary separating the parish of Camolia from that of Andara.[1] The churches, renovated seventeenth-century structures, used to be the hub of a number of smaller chapels now in disuse. Although today frequented by only a minority of the Alborese, the churches until recent years were the preeminent local institutions, the major centers of community life. The churches had faced competition, though. First there was the unification movement in the mid-nineteenth century, which found the Church on the losing side of the *Risorgimento*, attacked by the new Italian patriots. Then there was the Socialist movement, complete with Socialist cooperatives, providing organizations independent of, and hostile to, the Church, and then, in the Fascist years, a plethora of Fascist organizations tied the people of Albora into a world separate from the Church.

Like most of his colleagues, don Claudio, Camolia's parish priest, had been sympathetic to Mussolini and the Fascist government, a sympathy that was expressed from the pulpit. At all local Fascist celebrations, the priests of Camolia and Andara were called on to give the benediction. While the evils of socialism were denounced from the pulpit, the priests of Albora blessed the local Fascist troops on their way to Christianize the savages of Africa. Had don Claudio and his Andara counterpart broken with the Fascists on the outset of World War II, the Church in Albora might have been much stronger in the postwar years.

Today the priests of Albora find themselves socially isolated, woefully outnumbered in a Communist stronghold. The only community activity in which they take part outside of the church is the weekly religious lessons held at the local public schools, as mandated by the agreement between the Italian government and the Vatican. The priests do not participate in any secularly sponsored community activities. There is no civic charity for which they campaign, no community school board on which they sit, nor any local municipal body in which they take part.

For many years the priests of Albora had been esteemed power brokers; indeed they were among the few literate people in the area. If people needed money, food, housing, or a job, they went to the priest. Today there are other sources of charity and brokerage in Albora, though some parishioners still come to the priests for used clothing for their children, or for a *raccomandazione*, a letter of reference to give to a prospective employer. In one case, for example, the Camolia priest spent two afternoons on the telephone, trying to aid a poor family of immigrants. The man had been arrested and jailed on a charge of assault, and the wife and four small children were being evicted from their apartment for nonpayment of the $25 rent. The landlord was a parishioner, and don Giorgio tried to persuade him not to evict the poor family.

Although these powers of the local clergy are limited, many Alborese are nevertheless eager to remain on good terms with the priests. A letter of recommendation may be written for a parishioner who does not often frequent mass, but it would not be written for someone who openly challenges the authority of the Church as defined by the priests. There are other brokerage systems available to the people of Albora, most notably that provided by the Communist Party itself, but in certain key areas – procuring employment and housing, dealing with the schools – the Church may be more effective than the Party.

The absence of any formal Church-connected voluntary associations in Albora is testimony to the organizational weakness of the Church. Not only are there no longer any Catholic Action groups in the *quartiere*, there is not even a laity council, although Church policy specifies that each parish should have one. Although some parishioners have urged the priests of Camolia and Andara to organize church councils, neither parish priest has shown any inclination to do so. One reason for their reluctance is that they feel they are the experts in running the church and that the present arrangement – in which all authority lies in their hands – is optimal. As attendance at the meetings called to organize the Church procession indicates, most of the parishioners share the belief that the church should be run by the priests and that lay involvement in church organization is superfluous. Second, the parish priests are wary of organizing a laity council that, through its numerical weakness, could publicly confirm the Church's organizational inferiority to the Communist world.

At present, besides the DC, there is only one stable social grouping connected with the churches of Albora, the Friday night discussion group of Camolia. Though lacking any formal organization, this group of about twenty male youths, aged eighteen to twenty-eight, meets regularly at the Camolia church.[2] Starting from a nucleus of youths formerly enrolled in Camolia's Catholic Action[3] boy's division and accustomed to spending Friday nights at the church, the group includes virtually all the churchgoers in that age range as well as occasional visitors who are friends of the core members. The youths gather at the church, they say, because "aside from hanging around the streets or the bars, the church is the only place to go." The parish priest, who attends the sessions, tries to give some religious content to the discussions, though the talk often leads to discussion of more manifestly political matters. The group, though operating on a small scale, has the capacity to bring individuals into the Catholic world. An example is provided by the twenty-three-year-old youth, apolitical himself, but the son of a Communist unionized father, who was brought into the Friday night group by friends at the bar he frequented. He became friendly with the young priest of Camolia and within a couple of years was carrying a statue of the Madonna through the streets of Albora in the annual church procession.

Thus whereas the PCI has numerous means of bringing newcomers into the sphere of PCI influence, the Church has few such means. The Church, moreover, provides no formal structure for local leadership in contrast to the dozens of leadership positions available in the PCI in the *quartiere*. In addition, although both Church and PCI are formally run on strict hierarchical principles, the PCI hierarchy demonstrates much greater interest in, and expends much more manpower and money on, Albora than does the Church hierarchy. The churchgoer may never get to speak with any official more senior in the Church hierarchy than his parish priest, but anyone regularly attending local PCI meetings is given the opportunity to speak informally with many such officials. The integralism commonly associated with the Church, and reflected in the concept of the Catholic world, is in fact more fully developed in Albora in the Communist Party and the Communist world. The Communist world provides an organizational structure capable of providing for a wide range of extrafamily social life; the Church is no longer so well equipped.

Christian democracy

Forty-five people, making this the largest Albora DC gathering in a number of years, sat in the Andara parish hall under a large crucifix. Two-thirds of the crowd were men, almost all wearing tie and jacket; most of the women were elderly. Don Stefano, clad in his black robe, guided people to available seats. At 9:30 P.M., when the speaker arrived, everyone stood up, remaining on their feet for a half minute in respectful silence until the speaker motioned them to sit down.

As Nerini, the sharply dressed young section head explained, their scheduled speaker, the Honorable Balti, was at the last minute held up in Rome, but fortunately they were able to prevail on Balti's brother, an influential member of the provincial federation, to come in his place. Nerini's words boomed over the darkness outside, for they had set up large loudspeakers in the church yard to broadcast the proceedings toward the high-rise apartment buildings nearby.

Balti, the head of a large bank in Bologna, spoke for ninety minutes, eighty of which were devoted to a scathing denunciation of the PCI. The subject of the Russian invasion of Czechoslovakia was raised at least a half dozen times, sprinkled judiciously through the oration. The PCI,

Balti pronounced, poses the greatest threat possible to our country. If the PCI should gain entrance to the government, Italy will follow the path of Russia and the other Communist countries ruled by a dictatorship.

On the subject of his own party, Balti noted that it was under DC leadership that Italy has been rebuilt, a miracle of reconstruction, from the ruins of the war.

We have built the best system of thruways in Europe and we have made great progress in speeding the development of the South, though admittedly we have a long way to go. And the DC is also the party that stands for Catholic values. It has been the DC that has fought against the introduction of divorce into Italy. Why, divorce is just a means of legitimizing immorality. If a person doesn't have the maturity to take the responsibility of marriage for life, then he shouldn't be getting married in the first place. Italy did not want this horrendous law, and now that the people have called for a referendum, we will have our chance to choose. This divorce law is, indeed, just one element in the deterioration of Catholic values at the hands of the left wing. We now see the phenomenon of the proliferation of public nursery schools. Well, I tell you, I think mothers are more than just animals, the child needs the nurturance only his mother can provide.

Since its establishment in the last years of World War II, the *Democrazia Cristiana*, the Christian Democratic party, has been the principal political expression of the Catholic world.[4] Although the DC has been Italy's ruling party since the Republic was founded, compared to the Communist Party, the DC in Albora is infinitesimal, pitifully inadequate organizationally to compete with the PCI. Yet it is the DC, in conjunction with the two old churches of Albora, that provides the primary challenge to Communist political ascendancy in the *quartiere*.

The DC's weakness may be traced to a number of factors, including the tenuousness of the Church's hold on popular allegiance in Albora. Furthermore, because it has not controlled the local government, the DC has not been in its customary position of dispensing municipal patronage. Finally, the primary opposition to the DC, the Communist Party, has been well organized and able to attack the *Democrazia Cristiana* on ideological and programmatic grounds as well as through its social presence. By joining the DC, the Alborese subjects himself to the epithet "enemy of the working class", a powerful stigma in this unionized and class-conscious *quartiere*.

The national bonds between the Church and the DC have been close, though they are closer in some parts of the country than others (see Caciagli 1977). The DC has often been referred to as a "party of Catholics" and an "instrument of the Church" (Manoukian 1968:20), though this latter characterization should not be taken to imply that the party is not the instrument of a number of other interest groups as well. The leadership of the DC has primarily been trained not through any party youth organization, but rather through the youth organizations of the Church. In 1965 it was estimated that over 80 percent of the parliamentary representatives of the party came from the ranks of Catholic Action and the organization of Catholic University Students (Sartori 1965:81).

Although the DC claims formal independence from the Church, it recognizes that its mass appeal is dependent on its identification with the Church. This was particularly true in the early postwar years, before the DC had built up its patronage power through establishment of *sottogoverno*. But in many localities throughout the country the Church continues to act as the local recruiting arm for DC support. For many of the DC supporters, then, DC allegiance derives from allegiance to the Church, the local-level struggle for the allegiance of the people being waged between the Church and the PCI rather than directly between the DC and the PCI.[5] Thus the two parties are not organizationally parallel:

While in fact the PCI is the center, and its allied organizations and movements depend for their instructions and, often, for their own moving energy on the Party, the DC is merely one of the expressions of the Catholic world. The organizational, executive and electoral cadres which have come to the DC from Catholic Action and from the clergy have been crucial for its existence, not to say for its success. [Alberoni 1967:28]

Although the attachment of the Communist to the Party is theoretically comprehensive, no comparable attachment is expected between the DC partisan and his party, as Poggi (1968:238) observes: "the ideal bond between DC member and the organization, on the statutory level, concerns only the political sphere. If the member is a practicing Catholic, his bond is global, his primary identification, his source of ideological inspiration, his point of reference, is the Church . . ." Lacking a committed base of its own, the DC at the local level has often been at the mercy of the clergy and Church organizations (Kogan 1966:71–2).

It should not be concluded from this portrait of DC dependence on the Church that the DC is totally unlike the other parties. DC leaders and power brokers can be analyzed in the same terms as their counterparts in other parties. It is noteworthy in this regard that, in contrast to the formal monolithic organization of the Church, the *Democrazia Cristiana* has over a dozen officially recognized factions. And although each of these is given an ideological cast, the factions are less a product of ideological diversity than a mechanism for seeking power.[6] In this context the competing factions manipulate the symbols of the Church to help their own cause.

Organizationally, the DC consists of three principal levels: the base, the province, and the nation. The base is organized by sections, and the organizational weakness of the party is evident in the lack of regular section activity throughout much of the country. Except for election time, activity in the DC is predominantly found at the provincial and national levels. As one of the top party leaders lamented: "Most of the time the section is merely a local station for receiving directives and propagandistic slogans, a slot for the collection of letters of recommendation and requests for jobs" (Fanfani, quoted in Poggi 1968:242n).

In Bologna, where the DC is particularly weak, there are twenty-two party sections, with approximately 1,500 members. One of these sections is found in Albora, headquartered at the Andara church, where it has been housed since its founding shortly after the war.[7] Its days of greatest activity were, in fact, those postwar days when the Church was most active in the anti-Communist crusade. Though its membership size remains the same at forty, there is little party activity in Albora these days.

The weakness of the DC in Albora is evident not only from its dearth of members but also from its leadership. Most strikingly, neither of the two top leaders of Albora's DC still lives in the *quartiere*. They continue as leaders of the section despite the specific DC statute that assigns all members to sections based on their place of residence (in keeping with the parish model, and in contrast with the more flexible PCI model [DC 1968:6]). The man who has headed the Albora section for the past few years now lives 25 miles away, having been transferred by his employer. He continues to serve not only as section head, but also as head of the DC delegation to the *quartiere* council. The former head of Albora's DC section now lives in another *quartiere* of Bologna, having moved from Albora in order to find more luxurious housing than was available in the *quartiere*. This man, Tassi, at sixty-five twice the age of the present head, shares the effective power in the organization with the new section head. Tassi is the man best known to the provincial DC leaders, and the person they most often contact when they want the Albora section to do something.[8] Tassi opens up the Albora DC headquarters one night per week for an hour, this constituting the normal weekly load of DC sectional activity in Albora. During this hour Tassi converses with one or two other DC members who drop by and he goes through the accumulated mail.

The ties of Albora's DC section to the Church in the *quartiere* are apparent to all Alborese. Despite the political changes in the Italian Church under Pope John XXIII, the Church in Albora, and particularly the Andara church, continues to back the DC publicly. Though national Church notables are no longer so open in their support of the DC, generally choosing subtler modes of encouraging allegiance, the Andara church could hardly be more open and public in its championing of the DC cause (see Photograph 5).

The DC section is housed in comfortable and spacious quarters in a church-owned building, paying no rent. All its public meetings are held in either the Andara or the Camolia parish halls. The Andara parish hall, adjacent to the DC headquarters, is most often used for this purpose, when it is not in use as the classroom for the church's catechism classes. It is plainly furnished, with a large crucifix hung at the center of the wall.

Recruitment of membership to the DC section is carried out through the local churches. When asked how he decided whom to approach about joining the party, the section head identified two criteria: those who regularly attend mass and those who are known to be anti-Communist. In fact, the categories are largely overlapping. An examination of the membership of the DC section bears this out, for all thirty-nine members are regular churchgoers. In addition, the DC sympathizers who attend election cam-

5. The DC mobile is parked at the Albora DC headquarters while preparations are being made for a campaign rally on the church's front doorstep.

paign meetings are virtually all people who attend mass every Sunday. Given the sympathy of the majority of the Alborese for the Communists, the DC leaders do not attempt to approach people randomly about the virtues of DC membership. Only the church milieu offers a safe environment for such discussion and a presumption of a sympathetic response. A man who frequents the church is presumed to be favorable to the DC; one who does not is presumed to be hostile. All the leaders of the DC in the *quartiere* are also lay leaders of the two churches, and all had been lay activists in the Church before they undertook positions of responsibility in the DC section.

Popular participation

The indicator most often used by the Church to determine the number of parishioners loyal to the Catholic world is weekly mass attendance. This follows from the Church precept that to be an observant Catholic one must attend mass every week. In the eyes of the priests of Albora, as well as the general population, a fairly sharp line distinguishes those who attend mass weekly from those who do not. To be firmly in the Communist world one cannot attend mass with any regularity; to be firmly in the Catholic world one must attend mass regularly.

An examination of Sunday mass attendance in Albora reveals both the small proportion of Alborese who attend mass and the overwhelmingly feminine composition of the congregation.[9] On any given Sunday only about 15 percent of the people attending mass are adult men, about 60 percent are adult women, and 25 percent are children and youths (under twenty-one years old). The phenomenon of a greater female participation in mass is by no means confined to Albora, characterizing Italy as a whole (Burgalassi 1968:25). However, the lopsidedness of the split in Albora is noteworthy. Whereas the general pattern is more on the order of a 3:2 ratio of women to men at mass in Italy, in Albora we find a ratio of about 4:1.

According to Bologna Church studies, Albora ranks next to last among the eighteen *quartieri* in percentage of population attending Sunday masses. In a survey conducted in 1959 it was found that just 9.1 percent of the Alborese went to any of the ten masses given by the two parishes. A survey a decade later, employing weak methodological procedures,[10] concluded that 11.3 percent of the Alborese attended mass at the Alborese parishes on an average Sunday in the winter and 9.6 percent in the summer (Toldo 1969:29). Observations made in 1971–2 were substantially in agreement with these figures, showing under 10 percent of the Alborese attending Sunday mass in the *quartiere*. Bologna (and Emilia-Romagna generally) is known throughout the country as a weak point of the Church, and these figures bear this out. The even weaker showing of the Church in Albora may be largely accounted for by the class composition of the *quartiere* (Toldo 1960:163).

Aside from Church ritual occasions, popular participation in the Catholic world in Albora is largely limited to participation in the *quartiere* DC section. This remains the only institution of the Catholic world in Albora that is not directly under priestly control and leadership. In other words, although the people can assume that the churches will continue to operate with or without their own efforts, this is not true of the DC, which cannot be run solely by the priests.

The membership of the DC is atypical of the Albora population not only in being composed entirely of churchgoers, but also in having relatively high socioeconomic status. The overwhelmingly proletarian character of both the *quartiere* as a whole and of the PCI membership is not shared by the DC membership. Seven of the thirty em-

Table 20. *Occupation of male members of Albora DC section*[a]

Professionals and elite	4
Engineer	
Accountant	
Bank director	
Industrial entrepreneur	
Governmental and paragovernmental employees	8[b]
Federal government employees	4
Local governmental agencies	2
Paragovernmental agencies	2
Other white-collar workers	1
Working-class occupations	13
Worker	5
Employee, industry	2
Employee, commerce	2
Employee, theater	1
Employee, artisan	1
Employee, transport	1
Employee, hospital	1
Pensioners	3
Total	29

[a] These data come from the official records of the Albora DC section, giving occupation as listed by the member. In many cases these data are not entirely clear, but an attempt has been made here to group them into categories on the basis of information in the official files and on informal checking on individuals. Least certain is the working-class occupations grouping. Some of the individuals in this category may belong to the white-collar category, and thus the working-class representation in the DC section may be inflated here.

[b] Tassi, the effective co-director of the Albora DC, is not listed here as he is formally registered in the DC section in his own *quartiere*, following DC statute. His inclusion would add to the governmental and paragovernmental employees category by one.

Table 21. *Occupation of female members of Albora DC section*

Housewives	5
Federal employees	1
White-collar worker	1
Working-class occupations	2
Pensioners	1
Total	10

ployed members of the section occupy positions that are clearly of upper- or middle-class status, and it can be estimated that in all between a third and a half of Albora's DC members hold white-collar or professional positions.[11] This contrasts sharply with the less than 10 percent of the general population and the PCI membership having such high socioeconomic status. Yet the DC is by no means an exclusively elite grouping, for a good part of its membership is working class (see Tables 20 and 21).

The median age of the DC members is forty-six and, in contrast to the PCI (with its allied FGCI), none of the members is under twenty-five years old (see Table 22). Only ten of the thirty-nine DC members are women, despite the fact that nationwide the DC has in the past received the majority of its vote from women (Cavazzani 1972:187) and the great majority of churchgoers in Albora are women. This absence of women in the DC reflects Church norms on the woman's role. Significantly, all ten women members are relatives of male members. Their membership appears to be derivative of the membership of their male relative. A woman joins the DC in Albora only if her closest male relative is a DC member. Of the ten women members, eight are wives of members, one is the unmarried daughter of two section members, and the tenth

Table 22. *Date of birth of Albora DC members*

Date of birth	Number
Before 1900	3
1900–04	1
1905–09	2
1910–14	4
1915–19	6
1920–24	2
1925–29	3
1930–34	3
1935–39	8
1940–44	4
1945–49	2
Total	38[a]

Age	Number
Over 70 years	4
51–70	14
36–50	7
25–35	13
Median age	46

[a] Data on date of birth available for thirty-eight or thirty-nine Albora DC members.
Source: Albora DC membership files.

is an elderly widow whose son is a member. None of the women is a section officer and women virtually never speak at section meetings.

The amount of time expended by the general membership in party activities is minute, with DC meetings in Albora often being scheduled no more than once a year for membership drive purposes. As in most DC sections in the country, Albora DC activity is confined largely to election campaign time; in the periods between local and national electoral struggles the local organization is dormant. The only DC meeting scheduled in Albora in 1971, the annual membership reenrollment meeting, was in fact canceled. Interelectoral activity is largely confined to section administrative work carried out by the few activists and to the party work done in connection with the *quartiere* council. DC membership is a badge of allegiance to the Catholic world, not a sign of active participation in the political struggle of the Church.

The gap between the Church's conception of its proper role in Italian society and its actual practice in Albora is immense. The integralist conception of society under the tutelage of the Church, the realization of the Catholic world concept, is found only in vestigial form. Few are the people who obey even the elementary precept of regular mass attendance, let alone the encapsulation of social and political life in the various branches of the Catholic world. Of the few people who do go beyond weekly mass attendance, offering a firmer commitment to the Catholic world, most are socioeconomic "misfits" in the community. Although the Church continues to have some influence over the majority of Alborese,[12] it no longer provides the organizational structure of the community. The Church has become but one of the competitors for the allegiance of the people.

The activist core

The number of those in Albora who can be termed activists of the Catholic world is small. In comparison with the Communist world, indeed, there is little for the Catholic activist to be active in. Not only is there a dearth of related voluntary associations, but the organizational principle of the Church itself tends to discourage any proliferation of decision makers or planners. This reflects the basic division among Catholic activists, that between the clergy and the laymen, a difference in kind of authority rather than merely in degree, a differentiation not found in the local Communist hierarchy.

An activist core of the Church, in the sense of a lay leadership, can be discerned, and it is composed entirely of adult males. The men to whom the priests turn for advice and aid hold no official church office and belong to no formal church association. However, every Sunday between masses the priests confer with a group of these men, and the men drop by the priest's quarters individually during the week, following up assignments or asking what they can do to be of aid. These are all men who can be counted on by the priests to take part in all public church activities and to be available to help out in time of need. They are also the only parishioners who are in contact with the Church hierarchy outside the *quartiere*, for they attend leadership training courses in downtown Bologna at the diocesan headquarters and, through these activities as well as through the duties they perform for the priests, they come to know a variety of diocesan officials. In all, there are perhaps fourteen of these individuals, evenly divided between the two parishes. All attend mass weekly and all regularly speak with the parish priest informally. Because interlocking of the membership of the Church and the DC activists is virtually complete, they can be considered together. The fact of this congruence can best be established through an examination of the six top DC activists.

Nerini, the head of the DC section, had been active in the Camolia church since he was a child; his father is one of the few railroad workers in Albora who regularly attends mass. Nerini was active in Catholic Action activities in the

quartiere and in the diocese and is considered by the Camolia priests as perhaps their most outstanding parishioner, always available to give them a hand. Though he
now lives over 40 kilometers away, he continues to attend
the Saturday evening mass at Camolia with his parents
every week, where he is often honored by being called on
to read from the Bible. Indeed, in 1972 he was chosen to
share the altar with the archbishop at the parish Confirmation ceremonies. Wearing the ceremonial white robe,
he read from the New Testament.

If asked to name his two most faithful young parishioners, the Camolia priest would undoubtedly name Nerini
and Pelti. The Peltis are the most loyal of any extended
family in the parish. Not only have Pelti's parents been
regular churchgoers, but so have his two uncles and their
families, and the family of his sister and brother-in-law.
They have all continually made themselves available to
don Mario for tasks that range from producing the church
drama to teaching catechism. Many Alborese identify
young Pelti as the most active person in the parish, with
one woman claiming that he was "born in the Camolia
church."

Pelti has been the key member of the nucleus of youths
that meets Friday nights at the Camolia church. He often
drops by the Church during the week to see what he can
do for the priests and never fails to attend Sunday mass
and take communion. He served as one of the few male
catechists for the church before going into the army, and
he also attended lay leadership sessions given at the Bologna diocesan headquarters.

Pelti had always supported the DC, as did both his parents and all his local relatives, and over the years he worked
for the Party in various capacities, primarily during election
campaigns, performing such tasks as poll watching. He did
not join the DC when he came of age, he said, because he

disagreed with some of its policies. Pelti was sympathetic toward the political center to center-left of the DC, and he disagreed with some of the right-wing DC leaders. He finally decided to join after being approached by his good friend from the Camolia church, Nerini, and by his father's old friend, Tassi, the two heads of Albora's DC section. They told him of the need in the *quartiere* for DC activists, of their problems in finding a good DC councilor for the *quartiere*, and reminded him that the DC is the only political defender the Church has. Both Pelti and his new bride then joined the Albora DC section, and he immediately was named to be a *quartiere* councilor. In the 1972 Camolia decennial procession, the only two adults clad in white robes, marching with the visiting priests, were the two local leaders of the DC: Nerini and Pelti.

The story of the other four DC leaders is the story of the top lay leadership of the Andara church. Tassi, the former DC section head, is perhaps the foremost confidant of the Andara parish priest. He is the man the priest turns to for political information and for aid in influencing public agencies. Like all the DC leadership, Tassi attends Sunday mass every week. Gilli and Botti probably spend more time at the Andara church than anyone except the priest. Both retired, they perform a variety of often menial chores, such as cleaning up the church after a wedding.

Querze, like two of the other top DC activists, lives outside Albora. He lived in Albora briefly, and it was at that time that he became involved in the Andara church. However, he had been a Church activist before moving to the *quartiere* and had become friendly with Pelti a decade before when they were both involved in the same Catholic Action leadership training program held at the diocesan headquarters.

A survey of the socioeconomic status of the DC leadership is also revealing. Four of the six, the four still in the workforce, have employment giving them middle- to upper-class status: one a national agency top executive, one a branch bank director, one an engineer, and one a white-collar worker. This leads to the question of whether there are material advantages to be gained from Church and DC activism. Indeed, the rewards to Church activists can be considerable, regardless of whether any individual's activism is based on such considerations. The Church activist is in the best position to benefit from the influence wielded by the parish priest in procuring jobs and other services. The priest not only will write a letter of reference for such an individual but may also actively solicit employment for him. Poggi's remark in his study of activists in Italian Catholic Action is instructive here:

The most relevant material rewards are those only indirectly connected with the experience of leadership – for example, a leader's chances of professional success or career advancement are unquestionably improved by the credit gained through services rendered for the hierarchy, irrelevant as those services may be to the merit of one's own professional performance or to the proper requirements of one's business. A man who has served his stint generously as an ACI leader, probably without making a penny out of that activity and in fact generously giving of his time and energy, can confidently expect to find later that this has much strengthened his hand, particularly in that unofficial spoils system Italians call *sottogoverno*. [1967:92–3]

These side benefits, moreover, are not limited merely to the activist core. An examination of the jobs now held by Albora's DC section members reveals that of the thirty members in the workforce, nine hold governmental or paragovernmental jobs. These range from maintenance worker positions to high executive posts. Others hold positions with organizations such as Catholic hospitals, which, although not governmental, have strong, well-known ties with the Church and the DC. In all, it appears that approximately one-half of the employed members of the Albora DC section hold jobs that Church and DC influence could have helped them to obtain.

The actual process by which this influence was applied in individual cases is difficult to document, given the secretive nature of the process, but the presumptive evidence is strong. The cases of two of the young Church–DC activists are illustrative. Nerini, the present head of Albora's DC section, is from a working-class family but, encouraged by the parish priest, he completed high school. Active in the Church and then in the DC, Nerini got a good job in a bank with strong local and national ties to the DC and the Church. He rose quickly through the bank bureaucracy and, shortly after becoming head of the Albora DC section, was appointed to be a director of a branch office of the bank, despite the fact that he was still only in his late twenties and had no college education. The ties between the DC and Nerini's employer were made explicit during the 1972 election campaign, when, as described earlier, one of Bologna's DC deputies was detained in Rome and, at the last minute, sent his brother to speak in his place. The brother, introduced by Nerini, is the head of the Bolognese regional division of the bank that employs Nerini. Nerini and the bank director appeared to be most friendly.

Pelti provides a similar case of finding employment that, though not officially a political position, was made possible through Church–DC connections. Pelti attended vocational high school, where he was trained in electronics. On finishing high school and the army, he quickly found a job in this field. Soon thereafter he was placed in a job with the federal gas company as a white-collar worker. However, the job was over 50 miles away from home and paid no more than his local electronics job. His hope was that once having gotten into the paragovernmental bureaucracy, he could ultimately obtain a transfer to Bologna. Meanwhile, people in Albora gossiped that the parish priest of Camolia had gotten him the job. Within a few months, Pelti was approached by Tassi and Nerini about joining Albora's DC section and becoming a DC *quartiere* councilor. Within two months of Pelti's decision to become a DC member and activist, he was transferred to a post in Bologna that paid him a 50 percent higher salary. Tassi, the former Albora DC head and the man who approached him about DC membership, is a regional director of the national gas company.

4

The Anti-Communist Crusade

It was just four weeks before national elections and posted on the bulletin board marked "Parish Life" in the front hall of the Andara church was a sign:

DC RALLY
THIS FRIDAY 8:30 P.M.
PARISH HALL
THE HONORABLE BERSANI WILL SPEAK
EVERYONE SHOULD COME

Nearby, Gilli and his fourteen-year-old son were sweeping up the sanctuary. Now a pensioner, Gilli, who lives just a few meters from the church, has been a member of the parish for fifteen years. Though he was born in Veneto, he has lived most of his life in the province of Bologna.

Gilli was upset, as he had just read of the death of a FIAT executive in Argentina, killed when police attacked the left-wing group that had kidnapped him. "That's what you get when you allow too much liberty," he said (shrugging off the retort that Argentina was a military dictatorship). He continued:

Italy has the same problem, too much freedom. The result: kids burning everything and having strikes in the school. What Italy needs is a stronger government. And then there's the PCI. They try to put on a mask of moderation, but if the Communists ever

came to power they'd turn the country into another Russia. In
Russia no one has a car. You aren't free to go where you want.
Bologna may be very Communist now, but it wasn't always that
way; it used to be Fascist. They just changed their shirts.

Across the *quartiere*, at the Camolia church, don Giorgio
was describing socialism as a cancerous growth, eating
away at the country:

The trouble with Italy is that there are too many parties. Many
of the people who vote for the left just vote that way as a form
of protest; they'd vote for another party if they could have any
faith in it. Right now, the government is so weak that even
though the police know all about these extreme left- and right-
wing groups that are going around blowing things up, they can't
do anything; their hands are tied. As for Bologna, it's ruled by a
red mafia. It's basically the same thing as the right-wing mafia
in the South. You have to go to them and pay their price if you
want anything done in this city.

To understand the attitudes of Albora's Church loyalists
toward the PCI and to understand the attitudes of the
Communists toward the Church, it is important to have
some idea of the history of Church–Communist relations
in Italy. Obviously, the way in which local Church adherents view the Communist Party and the kinds of political
actions they take are conditioned by the policy and pronouncements of the Church hierarchy. Equally obvious is
the fact that local Party activity and the attitudes and actions of the Party faithful are conditioned by national Party
policy regarding the Church. The people, though, not only
reflect in their attitudes and actions the positions of
Church and Party currently in force, but the whole history
of Church dealings with communism (and socialism before
that) and Party dealings with the Church. To provide a
hypothetical illustration, if the Church or the Party were
to shift from a vehement position of denunciation towards

its competitor to a policy of cooperation, it would be unrealistic to expect the mass of followers of each institution simply to follow, jettisoning all effects of previous institutional performance and policy.

For these reasons we delve in this chapter into the history of Church policy toward the Communist Party, from its origins in the nineteenth century to its most recent formulation. As this history has been the subject of a number of comprehensive studies, my purpose in this chapter is not to break new historical ground but rather to provide the necessary historical background to examine the current strategy of the Church vis-à-vis the Communists at both national and local levels. In Chapter 5, dealing with the evolution of Communist Party policy toward the Church, more detail is provided, both because nonpolemical, incisive histories of the Party's Church policy are lacking and because the Party's policies have undergone more intricate changes than have the policies of the Church.

For centuries ecclesiastical authorities have considered the Church not only the gateway to the supernatural realm but the bulwark of the temporal realm as well. Not only spiritual life but social and political life are grounded in the teachings of the Church, teachings that admit of no higher authority.

The Church's formal justification for political intervention is based on the protection of the Church and the supremacy of its norms and values over those of conflicting secular institutions. As Manoukian observes: "The lack of distinction between religious action and political action for the Church is attributable to the Church's duty of affirming and safeguarding the supreme, metapolitical principles against other principles which imply either religious indifferentism or the effective devaluation of religion and its institutions" (1968:329–30). Although the temporal suprem-

acy of the Church has been historically eroded, the principles on which it is based have not been fundamentally
changed. The document of the Second Vatican Council
on the Apostolate of the Laity echoes the ideal of Church
temporal hegemony. The spiritual authority of the Church
is not ultimately distinguishable from its temporal authority:

Christ's redemptive work, while of itself directed toward the
salvation of men, involves also the renewal of the whole temporal
order. Hence the mission of the Church is not only to bring to
men the message and grace of Christ but also to penetrate and
perfect the temporal sphere with the spirit of the gospel. In
fulfilling this mission of the Church, the laity, therefore, exercise
their apostolate both in the Church and in the world, in both
the spiritual and the temporal orders. These realms, although
distinct, are so connected in the one plan of God that He himself
intends in Christ to appropriate the whole universe into a new
creation, initially here on earth, fully on the last day. In both
orders, the layman, being simultaneously a believer and a citizen, should be constantly led by the same Christian conscience.
[in Abbott 1966:495–6]

The temporal hegemonic ideal of the Church in Italian
politics has come to be known as "integralism," the banner
under which the battle to preserve the Papal States was
fought in the mid-nineteenth century, and the banner
under which the Church anti-Communist crusade has
been waged in the twentieth. Kogan provides a succinct
definition of the integralist ideal, the ideology embodied in
the conception of the Catholic world:

Catholic integralism may be described briefly as a movement
aiming to have all human activities, especially political and social
activities, impregnated by a Catholic inspiration. It seeks to
achieve a Catholic social order that would minimize and, in the
long run, eliminate all social and political movements based on

different inspirations, such as Marxism, liberalism, secular humanism. It is antipluralist in its ultimate objectives . . . [1966:84n]

The idea that the Church should be separated from the state, that the Church should be excluded from an active political role, is not one that has ever taken deep root in the Italian Church organization. Before the French Revolution there was little self-consciousness about the issue: Church and state were one, in a feudal relationship that had continued for centuries.

The *Risorgimento*, the unification of Italy in the 1860s, was propelled by the new bourgeoisie, revolting against the feudal system. As the Church occupied a pivotal role in the feudal structure, it became a primary antagonist of the unification movement (Candeloro 1953:4). In Bologna, as in many other areas of the Papal States, liberation came with the expulsion of the Vatican's legate, the lowering of the papal banner and its substitution by the tricolored national flag on top of the central palace (Arbizzani 1961:12).

Despite its military losses, the Church held fast to its political claims. In 1864, for example, in one of the most important documents of the period, Pope Pius IX issued a Syllabus of the Errors of Our Time, condemning those who claimed the Church did not have the right to use force and to exercise temporal power. The syllabus castigated the position that the "Church is to be separated from the State, and the State from the Church" (quoted in Candeloro 1953:104–5). Refusing to recognize the legitimacy of the new Italian nation, the pope called on all Catholics to boycott the government by refusing to vote or run for office. Anti-Church sentiment flourished, dividing the country into two camps, as described by De Rosa, a historian sympathetic to the Church:

in these years two histories, two cults of Italian life were formed and coexisted: on one side the secular life, it too having its rites and heroes, with its scientific and often blasphemous exaltations; on the other side a life of unique piety, a reaction to the most polemical and violent aspects of the militant irreligiosity; a life of piety . . . which was organized in the open, in the piazza, under the eyes of the distrustful police and the object of sneers by the free-thinkers and the vulgarly anti-papal plebes. [1970:53]

Events in the latter part of the nineteenth century led to a change in this sociopolitical division. The Church ultimately recognized its defeat and both the Church hierarchy and the bourgeois stalwarts of the Liberal state saw that they had a greater, common enemy: the Socialist movement, which was rapidly spreading throughout Europe. The culmination of this *rapprochement* came in 1913, with the establishment of the Gentiloni Pact, which freed those loyal to the Church to participate in governmental affairs, to vote and run for office. The anti-Socialist secular forces were particularly eager to enlist this participation, for they feared the effects of the newly enacted universal male suffrage legislation and saw the Church as the only institution having sufficient strength among the masses to counteract the Socialist appeal.

In the aftermath of World War I the Church entered into the political arena more directly, through the formation of the *Partito Popolare Italiano* (PPI), headed by don Sturzo, former director of Catholic Action and highly trusted by the Vatican. Though not formally tied to the Church, the PPI was clearly formed to be the arm of the Church in national politics.

Born at the same time as Italian fascism, the PPI was short-lived. Its demise can be attributed to the Church hierarchy conclusion that fascism could more effectively deal with socialism, the Church's primary enemy, than could any government coalition in which the PPI could participate. In 1923 the secretary of state of the Vatican sent a letter to the Italian bishops, calling on all the clergy to avoid favoring any party in the upcoming elections, a move that was seen as a clear sign of the withdrawal of Church support from the PPI. Later, Mussolini sought the recognition and the approval of the Church to provide his regime a legitimacy, both internally and internationally, that he dearly needed. The climax of Church–Fascist cooperation was reached in 1929, with the signing of the *Concordato* by Mussolini and the Vatican, making Catholicism the only recognized religion of the nation. With the signing of these agreements, Mussolini was hailed by the Church as the greatest political figure in modern Italian history, as the restorer "not only of the social order, but of the religious and moral values as well" (Jemolo 1965:241). The political effects of this support were soon made more tangible with the plebiscitary elections in 1929, in which the president of the national *Azione Cattolica* called on the association's members to support the Fascist regime. A year later the secretary of the Fascist party was given an audience by the pope, an honor never before extended to any political party in Italy. As Mack Smith (1969:443) noted: "while the Pope boldly protested at Mussolini's more strident heresies, no government in modern Italian history had received anything like so much ecclesiastical approbation. Thousands of sermons exhorted the faithful to be loyal to their great leader . . ." It was not until the onset of World War II that the Church became disenchanted with Mussolini, for the Vatican was not happy about Mussolini's alliance with Nazi Germany. Yet the Church hierarchy certainly encouraged no resistance to the Fascist regime. The great fear was still that of socialism:

With all that was written by Catholic pens against Fascism one could fill a small bookshelf of a bookstore; with all that was written in the same period against communism, a library . . . In communism everything is condemned, doctrines, methods, facts, persons: no distinction is admitted; it is not permitted for

a Catholic to be communist . . . in Fascism the condemnation
is only of given doctrinal points, never of the movement, never
of persons . . . [Jemolo 1965:283]

Communism: the postwar threat to Church supremacy

Entering a relatively open political system after twenty
years of fascism, the Italian Church at the end of the war
was in an advantageous position for organizing the upcoming political struggle. Only the Church had been allowed
to preserve its own organizations (though not all of them)
during the Fascist years, and it alone had been able openly
to conduct leadership training. The Church organization
itself, of course, provided far more of an organizational
base than any other party could then hope to have. The
Church hierarchy decided, as it had after the previous war,
that it would be best to have a political party that, although
under Church influence, was not formally dependent on
the Church hierarchy. The new Church party, the *Democrazia Cristiana*, had as its head one of the leaders from the
old PPI, Alcide DeGasperi.

The Church lost no time throwing itself into the Italian
political struggle, for they feared that the Socialists and
Communists might win control of the new government.
The choice, as the Church hierarchy portrayed it, was
between the forces of good and evil. Catholics must rally
around the Church, as the Bishop of Reggio Emilia exhorted in 1952: "In an historic hour as grave as is ours,
there is not much to discuss; only one thing is necessary,
that all Catholics without exception unite their forces,
making just one tight, closed bloc, obedient to the authority of the Church, stopping the most terrible enemy Christianity has ever had from advancing any further" (in Prandi

1968:57). The vote was not to be seen simply as a civil act, but as a religious duty. As the Archbishop of Vasto said in 1953, the choice was not merely between differing political views, but between "God or Satan, Christ or Antichrist, civilization or barbarism, liberty or slavery" (in Prandi 1968:56). The entire Church apparatus was mobilized in the electoral campaigns of these postwar years.

The most extreme action in this anti-Communist drive was taken by the Church in 1949, when the Vatican issued a decree, the Avviso Sacro, excommunicating all Communists, the text of which follows:

AVVISO SACRO

FA PECCATO MORTALE E NON PUÒ ESSERE ASSOLTO:
1) Chi è iscritto al Partito Comunista.
2) Chi ne fa propaganda in qualsiasi modo.
3) Chi vota per esso o per i suoi candidati.
4) Chi scrive, legge o diffonde la stampa comunista.
5) Chi rimane nelle organizzazioni comuniste: Camera del lavoro, Federterra, Fronte della gioventù, C.G.I.L., U.D.I., A.P.I., ecc.

È SCOMUNICATO E APOSTATA
Chi, iscritto al partito Comunista, ne accetta la dottrina atea e anticristiana; chi la difende e chi la diffonde (Dalla scomunica può assolvere solo la S. Sede).
Queste sanzioni sono estese anche a quei partiti che fanno causa comune con il comunismo.

(Decreto del S. Ufficio – 28 Giugno 1949).

N.B. Chi in Confessione tace tali colpe fa sacrilegio; può invece essere assolto chi, sinceramente pentito, rinuncia alle sue false posizioni.

Il Signore illumini e richiami tutti i fedeli alla difesa della Fede e all'unità della Chiesa, essendo in pericolo la loro eterna salvezza.

[reproduced in *Almanacco PCI* 1978a:85]

This controversial document banned Catholics from joining the Communist Party and forbade them from reading any communist publications. Excommunication was

meted out for those who "profess the doctrine of materialist, antichristian communism, and above all for those
who defend it or who propagandize for it . . ." The document stated that Communism is materialist and anti-Chris-
tian, and that "though the leaders of Communism sometimes claim that they are not fighting religion, in fact in
their theory and in their action they show themselves to
be hostile to God, to the true religion and to the Church
of Jesus Christ" (in Perego 1962:82). This decree created a
great deal of confusion for it was not clear just who was to
be excommunicated – all Communist voters, just members, or only Party activists. Numerous priests did refuse
the various Church rites to PCI members, and this often
led to bitter conflicts. The decree was interpreted by many
local clerics to refer not to PCI members and propagan-
dizers, but to those Communist intellectuals well versed in
dialectical materialism. By and large the excommunication
order was a dead letter by the time it was finally revoked
under Pope John XXIII.

The anti-Communist activity of the Church's lay organizations can best be illustrated by the case of Catholic
Action. Through Catholic Action, youths and adults, men
and women were charged with acting as representatives of
the Church in society, with the Church being the authoritative guide concerning proper action in all fields. As a
comprehensive study of the Catholic world in Italy has
concluded:

The laity of Catholic Action do not want to be separated from
society in a kind of limbo, rather they participate with the conviction that Christianity, which the Church teaches them, provides a context of principles fit to interpret and to guide all
aspects of human activity. Thus, it is up to them to promote the
affirmation of Christian principles in private and public morals,
in the social and economic order. Catholic Action does this
primarily by uniting its adherents and creating, through its or-

ganization, a capillary presence in every sector of social life. [Manoukian 1968:333]

In this way, *Azione Cattolica* was enlisted in the anti-Communist struggle. The potency of the rhetoric in this appeal can be illustrated by a passage from a 1958 article in the Young Women's magazine dealing with the upcoming national elections:

Politics is a crossing of the ways on which man's journey unfolds . . . If we look at it in the proper way, politics is love of God expressing itself as love of men according to a social perspective . . . love, nothing else . . . We must obey the commandment of love. For this reason you will go and vote. You will make the sign of a cross over another cross [a cross is the voting symbol of the DC]. Prepare yourself through your prayers for this fundamental duty . . . The sign of the cross upon another cross will measure the extent to which Christianity has grown in your soul, over and beyond your preference, over and beyond your sympathies for individual persons, over and beyond your personal interests. [in Poggi 1967:147]

Bologna

In Bologna the Church found itself in a particularly weak position, for anticlericalism was an ancient tradition. Don Toldo, director of Bologna's diocesan study center, emphasizes the effects of the *Risorgimento*:

Little by little, the churches became deserted, the priests were ejected from civil life and confined to their vestries (when they were not publicly insulted and jeered), and the few Catholics remaining loyal were often subjected to oppression, abused in every way. Indifference and apathy came first, and then hostility and aversion toward the Church and toward religion. [1960:23]

Though the Church's problems in Bologna predated the advent of socialism, it was the Socialists and later the Communists who were to be singled out as the greatest threats to Church influence. Bologna's archbishop during World War I, for example, lamented the inability of the Church to throttle the Socialist movement: "If at the end of the last century the Socialists conquered our region, they were able to do it because of the lack of Catholics in the social arena. Elsewhere, in Lombardy and Veneto where the Catholics were equal to the task, things went differently" (quoted in Toldo 1960:25).

After World War II the Church in Bologna entered into a multipronged assault on Communist Party strength, involving both direct anti-Communist tactics and indirect methods of winning people over to the Catholic world. Included among these latter, indirect tactics was the reemphasis on the traditional Church procession and the efficient use of Church-allied organizations such as ACLI (Toldo 1960:29, 165).

Roaming the piazzas and streets of Bologna in these years were the priests of the "flying squadron," invading PCI rallies to hand out anti-Communist literature and to denounce the Red speakers (Toschi 1964). The pastoral publications of the diocese were hardly less strident, as may be seen from a typical declaration by the bishops of the region, published in a 1953 diocesan bulletin:

At stake today are the greatest and most supreme spiritual interests: liberty, and thus the possibility of religious life in Italy. Uselessly, they try to make us believe that Catholic faith and Catholic life can coexist with *atheist* marxism. In reality, you yourself can verify by looking around you that wherever Communism prevails, to that extent is the Church attacked, scorn for the priesthood sown, the Vicar of Christ reviled, and the population estranged from religious practice. [*Bollettino Diocesano* 1953:76]

Cardinal Lercaro, head of the archdiocese, masterminded this anti-Communist drive, organizing a DC mayoral candidacy, and sharply attacking the "opinion that one can be a Communist and remain Catholic."

The brief years of John XXIII's papacy, and particularly the Second Vatican Council, brought about a diminution of the Church anti-Communist crusade, yet the long-term effects of this movement have not been dramatic.[1] Instructive here is the case of Cardinal Lercaro, one of Italy's high priests of anticommunism, who returned from the Second Vatican Council to champion a *rapprochement* with the Communists. Made an honorary citizen of Bologna by the Communist city government he had previously reviled, Lercaro had less success with the Church hierarchy, who saw to it that he was retired from his position as head of the archdiocese.

Nor have the priests of Albora's old parishes demonstrated any sympathy to the "new spirit" of Pope John. The pastor of Camolia, don Mario, systematically returns unopened all mailings sent to him by "progressive" DC candidates. When the DC rally at the Camolia church during the 1972 election campaign was being planned, it was hardly coincidental that the speaker invited was Bologna's most renowned anti-Communist crusader of the DC's right wing.

It is Andara's priest, don Stefano, who is the more active anti-Communist campaigner of the two, however, and it is his behavior that is most often condemned by the local Communists, who portray him as the incarnation of all that is wrong with the Italian clergy. Don Stefano actively participated in the planning and execution of all DC activity within his parish, arriving at meetings early to confer with the local DC officials and to see that church facilities were properly set up. When a guest speaker is scheduled, most frequently a DC deputy during election campaigns, don Stefano retires to his quarters, making a dramatic entrance after the talk has begun. Invariably, the speaker stops to welcome him warmly. Nor is don Stefano hesitant to speak at such meetings, offering, in addition to his steady stream of affirmatory comments during the speeches, various suggestions for DC tactics.

The Second Vatican Council was not entirely without long-term effect in Albora, as it stimulated a movement of left-wing priests in Italy that, though small in numbers, became a magnet for young people attached to the Church but repelled by the political and social policies of the Church hierarchy, especially the Church support of the DC. The case of one such priest, who entered Albora in 1971, is discussed in Chapter 8.

By the 1970s, then, communism was still seen by those in authority in the Church, as well as by the majority of lower clergymen, as the Church's principal enemy in Italy. In pronouncement after pronouncement, the hierarchy rejected the notion that a faithful Catholic could support the PCI. The battle was joined, and though the Church received many setbacks – from the failure of its excommunication gambit to the popular referendum defeat of its antidivorce policy – it was not prepared to cede its claim to being the guiding spiritual and social force of the Italian nation.

5

Communist Policy
Toward the Church

Luciano Porri sat with his feet on his desk. Born forty-five years before on the Alborese farm where his parents labored, Porri's life centers around the Party. Heading the *quartiere's* FGCI, working full time as a union organizer, being the *aggiunto del sindaco* (the mayor's representative for Albora), and now chairing the Party's delegation to the *quartiere* council, Porri is known to all in the federation as a hard worker and strident orator for the Party. Now having a full-time position in the federation, Porri reminisced about the early postwar years in Albora, recalling the time when the pioneers were founded, the children's league, organized *per sottrarli dalle grinfie dei preti*, "to take the children from the clutches of the priests".

Asked whether he meant that a person had to choose between being a Catholic or being a Communist, Porri tried to clarify the situation:

The fact is membership in the Party doesn't imply acceptance of the principles of Marxism. If you read the statutes of the Party we say that even Catholics can be members, and we have some Catholics who are Party members, who go to mass. In fact, we have tens of thousands of Catholics in the Party, and I consider them to be true Catholics. The truth is that since we voted for the famous Article 7 of the Constitution retaining the Church's status as the official religion of the state and since in our statutes we don't have any problems with Catholics becoming Party members, we have been attacked in Emilia-Romagna by the Republicans, the Social Democrats, and the Socialists for having betrayed the anticlerical cause, for being closer to the priests than they are. But the point is that if you want to bring about socialism, you either do it with the Catholics or you don't do it at all. The Socialist state that we want to construct in Italy is a society we want to build together with the Catholics, a state in which Catholics feel they are members with rights the same as we Communists. This is the original nature of our policy.

Since its foundation, the PCI has recognized the Catholic Church as a major obstacle to winning the support of the working class and, particularly, the peasantry.[1] The establishment of Party hegemony over the peasants and proletarians was seen, in good part, as a struggle to overcome the pervasive social and ideological influence of the Church. As Gramsci (1971a:87) wrote: "A conception of the world cannot permeate all of society and become 'faith' until it demonstrates itself capable of substituting the previous conceptions and faiths."[2]

According to Gramsci, the Party's intellectual founding father, the church is essentially a political creature, a political force on the decline.[3] Although it was once a political power that reigned uncontested, it had been reduced to "one party among others" (Gramsci 1971b:311). From a position of cultural, social, and political predominance, Catholicism, in terms of religious beliefs, had been reduced largely to a "superstition of farmers, of the sickly, of the aged and of women" (1971b:312). In accordance with Marx's conception of religion, Gramsci saw Catholicism as a primitive belief system that would inexorably die as the Socialist world view became known. The Church, realizing that its power was on the wane among the masses, had created for the first time mass membership organizations (e.g., *Azione Cattolica*) to combat the "overcoming by the masses of the religious conception of the world" (1971b:303).

In essence, then, the Church is seen by Gramsci, as it was by Marx, as a political force, providing a particular world view for the masses that in turns wins (to a greater or lesser extent) their allegiance. The political interests of the Church should be seen as the determinant of its theological pronouncements rather than vice versa. Thus the social ethics of Catholicism can be seen as a product of its wordly interests:

In order to fully understand the position of the Church in modern society, it is necessary to understand that it is disposed to struggle only in order to defend its own particular corporate liberties (of Church as Church, ecclesiastical organization), that is, the privileges which it claims are bound to its divine essence; for this defense the Church excludes no means, neither armed insurrection, nor individual assassination, nor the call to foreign invasion . . . For "despotism," the Church intends the intervention of secular state authority in limiting or suppressing its privileges – and not much else: it recognizes any authority *de facto*, and as long as it does not touch its privileges, it legitimates it; if indeed its privileges increase, it exalts it and proclaims it to be providential. [1971b:312–13]

Evident in this analysis is Gramsci's preoccupation with Fascist Italy and the Church support of Mussolini. The Church provided the crutch the initially weak Fascist government needed, and in exchange formed a rulers' pact for the mutual monopoly of the nation's education and "culture" (Gramsci 1967:79).

Gramsci's vision, like that of Marx and Engels, is of a future where socialism will supplant Catholicism.[4] He clearly does not foresee coexistence. A political party, such as the Communist Party, represents a different way of conceiving the world from that provided by the various forms of religion (1971b:214). The Socialist world view will liberate man from the intellectual shackles of the religious perspective: "The philosophy of praxis is the historical conception of reality which is liberated from every residue of transcendance and of theology, even in their last speculative incarnation" (1971a:227).

In Gramsci's writings on religion there is no question of relativism. Socialism is superior to Catholicism (and religion in general) in both an intellectual and an evolutionary sense. Socialism and Catholicism are antagonistic social theories: "The position of the philosophy of praxis is antithetical to Catholic philosophy: the philosophy of praxis does not maintain the "simple people" in their primitive philosophy of common sense, but rather leads them to a superior conception of life" (1971a:12). Any position holding that socialism and Catholicism are reconcilable, that one can be both a Socialist and Catholic at the same time, stems from a gross misunderstanding of Marxist theory:

To retain that the philosophy of praxis is not a structure of thought completely autonomous and independent, in antagonism with all the traditional philosophies and religions, signifies in reality not to have cut the ties with the old world, if not to have simply misunderstood. The philosophy of praxis does not need heterogeneous supports; it itself is so robust and rich with new truths that the old world resorts to it in order to furnish its own arsenal with the most modern and effective arms. [1971a:186]

The PCI fought its battle on two levels. On one, it sought to win over the masses to communism by discrediting the Church. On the other, it sought to erase any fears among the people that it was anti-Catholic. Behind this double-pronged strategy was the conviction that if it took an openly anti-Catholic position in dealing with the masses, those people who were still influenced by the Church not only would reject the PCI but might become openly hostile to it. The ideological training would come only after the individual had broken his ties with the Church to the extent of joining the Party. The public assurances of the Communists' tolerance toward the Church began even before the PCI was formally constituted, as we find in the newspaper of the Communist faction in Turin, headed by Gramsci himself: "'Communism,' we repeat in a loud voice, 'does not want to suffocate religious liberty.' Rather, it wants to guarantee it, 'all of it,' and in the fullest way . . . In the international Communist society the Church, and all the Churches, will have true, absolute liberty" (*Ordine Nuovo* 1920). Although this quotation gives a good idea of one element of the early PCI strategy concerning the Church, Togliatti's[5] remarks are typical of the other:

The Church is, for its organic structure, for all the ideals that it defends, and for the ultimate scope reflected in all its activities, the most anti-democratic power in the world. The system of government on which the ecclesiastical hierarchy is based is an absolutely authoritarian system. Even adapting itself to the capitalist world the Church has not lost this character. If, before the war and after it, it appeared at times to make concessions to democratic ideology, this involved only a maneuver carried out to control the revolutionary wave, to maintain contact with the masses and not lose its influence among them. [Togliatti 1929:21]

We see here the origin of what was to be a major feature of the PCI strategy, the attempt to separate Catholicism from the Church. The Church was attacked as corrupt, but the religious beliefs associated with the Church and held by the people were not at the same time contested. Although, as we shall see later, this strategy is ill adapted to the Communist theoretical analysis of the nature of religion, it has been embraced in Italy as elsewhere as the best approach to a difficult problem.

All of these PCI positions were to be put to the test for the first time with the Communist call to anti-Fascist resistance. The PCI, weak and persecuted under fascism, was in no position to mount a frontal attack on Catholicism at the same time it battled fascism. The Party called on the Catholics to recognize fascism, not communism, as their enemy:

From 1924 on, we have said to the Catholic workers and laborers: Let's unite to win better living conditions, to win liberty and peace . . . we are all slaves of the same oppressor. And still today liberty of conscience is threatened by Fascism! The Communists come offering their hands to the Catholic laborers, without any conditions, with full loyalty, and they are working to convince all antifascists of the importance of uniting with the Catholic laborers to win our material, political and cultural demands, and to defend religious liberty and the liberty of the Catholic organizations threatened by the Fascist government. This unity is one of the principle conditions of success for the victorious struggle of the people against the war and for the liberation of the Italian people. [Togliatti 1938:25]

Here we find what appears to be the awkward position of the Communists taking on the role of guardian of the Church against the anti-Church sentiments of the non-Communist anti-Fascist forces. The PCI is complaining of the poor treatment of the Church by the Fascists!

With the advent of the post-Fascist era, the PCI position regarding the Church remained largely unchanged: "the Communists would not conform to the principles of their own doctrine if, in the words of Lenin, they did not call to this struggle for liberty and for human dignity and welcome as brothers all the workers who *retain* their faith in God, without in any way offending their religious convictions" (PCI 1944:4; emphasis added). Of particular interest in this appeal is the term *conservano*, referring to the workers who still conserve or retain their religious beliefs. The implication, in orthodox Marxist tradition, is that their religious belief is a disability, a vestige of a dying social order that will soon be supplanted.

This recognition of the religious beliefs of the masses as a weakness to be overcome was made more explicit in the Party's explanation of its new statute permitting Catholics to join the PCI as long as they supported the Party program:

the [PCI] Congress has declared that this does not mean that the Party is renouncing its own ideology, which is Marxist-Leninist; on the contrary it remains faithful to the teachings of Lenin according to which Marxism is not a dogma but a guide for action; it is not "something finished and untouchable," but something which develops and progresses as the elaboration of the new experiences of the working class. For this reason the Party accepts in its ranks, with full equality of rights and duties, all those who, though not having yet reached a perfect theoretical consciousness of the historical process in which they are participating, are ready to struggle for the conquest of a progressive democracy, which is today the historical objective which faces the working class and the Italian people. At the same time, the Party has the duty to raise the political and ideological capacity of its militants, and to that corresponds a parallel duty for every member of the Party. [Art. 9 and 41 of the Statutes, PCI 1948:15]

Implicitly established here is a dichotomy between the experts and the novices, a stratification not unlike that found in the Church itself, between those who have access to the Holy Writings and those who have but a partial, imperfect understanding of the Truth.

Tactics of the postwar period

The PCI position on the Church came to a dramatic climax after World War II in the debate of the Constitutional Assembly on article 7 of the proposed Italian constitution, reaffirming the pact signed between the Vatican and Mussolini in 1929. In it the Catholic Church was recognized as the sole official religion of the state and was granted various privileges, such as having the state pay all parish priests and making religious instruction compulsory in the public schools. Clearly, here was a document in sharp conflict wih the normative Marxist view of the proper relationship between politics and religion. Yet, in a controversial move, the PCI decided to cast its ballots for the Mussolini–Vatican pact, thus voting with the Christian Democrats and against the Socialist party, the Republicans, and many of the Liberals.[6]

The PCI backed away from the fight set up by the DC, judging that it had more to lose than to gain from a head-on struggle with the Church. The Party had rapidly acquired hundreds of thousands of new members and millions of sympathizers, yet it was uncertain of their allegiance in a battle with the Church. According to the PCI account, a fight over article 7 would cause a split in the working class between Communists and Catholics. The Christian Democrats used the debate to denounce communism by declaring that the Communist nations persecuted religion. In response, the Communist speakers, rather than condemning the DC attempt to establish a state religion, sought to convince the nation that "there is no contrast between a socialist regime and the religious liberty of the Church, and in particular that of the Catholic Church" (Togliatti 1947:40).

In this sensitive period the PCI often pronounced its opposition to anticlericalism, pointing repeatedly to the article from the Fifth Party Congress of 1945: "anticlericalism has always been condemned by the Communist Party" (*Lotta* March 7, 1946:2). Party spokesmen contended that the PCI was not anticlerical, since the Party judged each clerical individually:

if in a given town a given priest assumes a concrete attitude on concrete political, economic and social problems which the Communists retain contrary to the specific interests of the work-

ers, can the priest, when the existing contrast between this attitude and the interests of the working-class is brought to light,
speak of an antireligious spirit, of violent atheism, etc.? [*Lotta*
June 16, 1945:1]

The implication is that anticlericalism is a groundless antipathy toward all clergymen, in contrast to the Communist
position of judging each priest on his merits. However, this
thesis is questionable. First of all, it is not true, as the
Communists themselves would be the first to point out,
that the old peasant anticlericalism was unfounded. It may
well have come to be generalized in a nonempirical fash-
ion, but rarely did it not allow for individual clergymen to
be looked on favorably. Second, when examined, the PCI
position on the clergy appears little different in substance
from the so-called traditional anticlericalism. The clergy,
as a social body, was seen as an enemy of the people: "The
most important aspect which we must see is that the clergy
is the organizational center of anticommunism and of the
forces of conservatism and of social reaction" (PCI-CRE
1950:52). Thus proclaimed an official Party analysis of the
Church in Emilia. The Church and the clergy who are its
servants are seen in the blackest of terms: "That the Vatican has now become the greatest point of reference and of
convergence of all the most reactionary forces and of all
the most conservative classes of Italian society is a fact
which, I believe, requires no long demonstration" (Crisafulli 1948:339).

In line with the distinction drawn by the PCI between
Catholicism and the Church hierarchy, throughout the
cold war years the Party continually attacked the Vatican
as in league with the forces of reaction. The Vatican was
portrayed as leading the reactionary counterattack, as
stated by Togliatti at the Sixth Party Congress:

Today, after the fascist era and after that which was for the
Vatican the era *forced* to a close by the Committees of National

Liberation . . . we see a new and different bloc of political forces: *today it is the Vatican that has placed itself at the head of the Capitalist State*. There is no longer a fascist bourgeoisie; it is the Vatican directly, through its party and its organizations, that has put itself at the head of the capitalist State: today in Italy we would have a fascist regime under the direction of the Vatican (of the Spanish type) if the working-class did not have the consciousness and the combativeness that it has. [PCI-CRE 1950:10; emphasis added]

The Vatican was seen as the primary political enemy and the DC portrayed as its tool.[7]

The contradictions in the PCI position on the Church in the postwar years are illustrated by the Party argument that the Church was abandoning the "true essence" of Catholicism. The PCI claimed to be scandalized by the politicization of religion: "The religious and doctrinal motives are everywhere giving way to those practical and electoral" (Donini 1953:290). Given a Marxist ideology, the Party leadership could hardly be scandalized; religion is nothing if not political. Yet the Party continued to distinguish between the "real" religion and the Catholicism of the Vatican on this political–nonpolitical, thoroughly un-Marxist criterion.[8]

Only through examination of the Party's internal literature of the period does a consistently Marxist position emerge. An unusual glimpse is provided by the text of a Veneto Party session held to train activists in methods of winning Catholics to the Party. The classified document proclaims that the duty of the Communist activist: "must consist of aiding the popular masses to understand that the problems of peace, of labor, of liberty, etc., can be resolved only outside of the ideological schemes of the Catholic world . . . (PCI-Veneto 1955).

Here it is the ideology of the Catholic Church that is attacked, in contrast with the public attacks that skirt the ideological issue to attack the clergy itself. The fact that the ideology of the Church is reactionary is made clear:

... it is neither strange nor erroneous to consider, in the historical reality, the official Catholic ideology as an ideology either identified with or which becomes identified with the ideology of the dominant classes.

The activism of the masses strikes against, and is dangerous for, conceptions based on the revealed truth. But that, and it is very easy to see it, is of great utility for the capitalist and agrarian bosses. [PCI-Veneto 1955:7]

That this religious ideology must be extirpated is made clear:

Some comrade asks if we ought to work to create the conditions in which the movement of the masses is freed from every tie with religious thought. Without doubt this should be done, however, without falling into the ideological antireligious polemic or positions in anticlericalism. [PCI-Veneto 1955:8]

Perhaps the most interesting public statement of the PCI's openness to religion was made by Luigi Longo, hero of the Resistance, and ultimately Togliatti's successor as head of the Party. Attempting to rebut the charges by the Church that the PCI was "atheist," Longo not only made the familiar statement of the PCI opposition to anticlericalism, but also stated that the "great majority of its [the PCI's] members is of Catholic faith and is practicing" (Longo 1946). Longo proceeded to give religious counsel to the Church, asserting that the "church is and remains in all circumstances only the temple for the adoration of God." He concluded:

Then it is evident that these priests who lower themselves by threatening infernal punishment for political motives not only abuse their divine ministry, but commit also a sacreligious act. Because if it is a sin to take the name of God in vain, it is also a sin to threaten the punishment of God in vain, when there is no justification for it.

Longo caustically noted that although bishops now cried that they could not let 40 million Catholics be ruled by the Communists, they never said anything against them being ruled by the Fascists. And again Longo spoke of the separation of religion from politics:

the priest is qualified, and is only qualified, to give guidance and counsel in cultic matters, not in worldly matters. For political matters, he is, and cannot be considered more than, a citizen, on a par with all citizens . . .

Especially deserving of scorn, according to Longo, were those priests who make a mockery of Catholicism by tying it to politics and using it as an instrument against the Communists. They thereby endangered the spiritual purity of Catholicism:

But what can be said, today, of these priests who dare to refuse baptism to the children of Communists, who refuse the sacraments to the faithful, just because they are members of the PCI? The least which can be said is that they – at least in these moments – cease to be priests, cease to be ministers of a God who wants all men brothers, who calls them all to him. Doing thus, they reduce themselves to the simple instruments of a party . . .

Reproofs of this kind were fairly common in this period, and it was not at all unusual to read Communist charges that the Church was operating in a way "repugnant to the authentic spirit of Christianity" (Alessandrini 1948:203).[9]

Throughout this period, the PCI sought to draw people out of the "Catholic world" and into the "Communist world." The Party decided to compete with the Church for domination of the multifarious aspects of daily life in the villages, towns, and cities. The PCI entered the business of establishing a "church" in the sense of an organization aiming to minister to the needs of its followers in numerous realms of their life: "spiritual," economic, recreational, and intellectual.

The need to provide such an alternative by the PCI was clearly formulated in the Party commission on the Church in Emilia, and approved as a motion by the provincial Party organization:

The Christian Democratic and clerical activity and influence find their organizational and political center in the parish and around the parish, which serves as head of the numerous Catholic organizations . . .

It is therefore at its true *center*, the parish, that we must contest the clerical and Christian Democratic activity, on the political, propagandistic and organizational terrain. For this reason, the two watchwords already put forth by our Party at the Conference of Organization at Florence are confirmed and will be rapidly realized: *a Section of our Party for every* [Church] *belltower*; and the other one: *every Section a community center (casa del popolo), an organizational and coordinating center of all the democratic activities and associations.* [PCI-CRE 1950:107; emphasis in original]

Setting up such a counterparish and removing people from the orbit of Church influence became central activities. For example, concern was voiced over the near monopoly the Church enjoyed in hospital and nursery facilities. A way had to be found to erode the influence of these institutions, and it was felt that the women of the Italian Women's League (UDI) could best do the job: "The women of UDI ought to literally knock at the door of the nursery school, of the nursing home and of the asylum to ask to enter in order to bring little gifts, accompanying these with democratic newspapers and leaflets" (PCI-CRE 1950:60). The battle lines were clearly drawn: "This will permit us to limit and to control the influence that through its charitable activities, the clerics exercise among the poorest elements of the population."

The current PCI position on the Church

With the easing of the cold war, the PCI position toward the Church and religion began to change. The anticlerical rhetoric was toned down greatly, and the Church was seldom publicly identified as the enemy of the worker. This change was made possible in large part by the papacy of John XXIII, with the lifting of the excommunication decree and the possibility of an officially approved Christian–Marxist dialogue. No longer was the Catholicism of the workers referred to as a lamentable superstition from which they must be patiently weaned. No longer were political cartoons depicting corrupt priests to be found in PCI publications. A new era had begun.[10]

This change was marked by a new reinterpretation of Marx. The phrase made famous by Marx, "opium of the masses," was dropped from the PCI lexicon. Indicative are the remarks of Lombardo Radice, perhaps the leading PCI spokesman on relations with the Church, who sharply attacked his Soviet counterpart for maintaining: "Church and religion belong to the capitalist superstructure, they are instruments of the dying classes, a part of the social order which is every day becoming more a part of the past" (Lombardo Radice 1972:18). Yet, though critical of an orthodox restatement of Marx, the PCI claims to be drawing on elements of Marx's thought. Hence Lombardo Radice emphasizes another aspect of Marx's critique of religion: "'It is man who makes religion, and not religion that makes man' (Marx); and that is exactly why, for a marxist, a religion is that which the believers make of it, and for that reason it is not *a priori*, by definition, either conservative or revolutionary" (1964a:87).[11]

The PCI submitted that a Catholic could be a Communist, for a political program need not imply any particular ideology (see Gruppi 1964; and Natta 1972). The appeal to the Catholic is not an appeal to give up his religion, but to find in the PCI the best political program. The implication is that the party of the Church does not abide by the "real" Christian principles. Illustrative is the appeal to the young Catholics made by the PCI youth group (FGCI) during the 1972 election campaign:

CATHOLIC YOUTH, THE GOSPEL IS UNDER FIRE.

THE GOSPEL IS UNDER THE BOMBS OF THE B-52S.

A HUNDRED MEN TOIL FOR THE PROFIT OF ONE.

THE DC IS AN ACCOMPLICE OF THE EXTERMINATION.

THE DC GUARDS THE PROFITS OF THE MONOPOLIES.

DEFEAT IT FROM THE LEFT WITH A COMMUNIST VOTE.

[*Nuova Generazione* April 28, 1972:1]

Similarly, a handsomely printed sheet of paper was handed out by the Bologna PCI Federation to people leaving mass during the 1972 campaign (see Figure 3). Titled "Ai Cattolici," it tells of the "warning" of a prominent ex-partisan who had been the DC candidate for mayor of Bologna in 1956, a priest who later played an active role in the Second Vatican Council. This man, Giuseppe Dossetti, was characterized in the leaflet as an authoritative spokesman of the longing for justice and fraternity among the Catholic masses. Dossetti, the Catholics are told, came to reject the DC as the party of cynical power politics. There follows the PCI conclusion:

Catholic laborers, intellectuals, youths, Giuseppe Dossetti's experience and warning should be heeded by making a political choice that favors peace, brotherhood, justice and liberty, a choice against the DC that, with its conservative political machinations, has betrayed so many expectations and deluded so many hopes.

AGAINST THE DC   VOTE PCI

The current strategy of the PCI, as these examples suggest, is not to argue against religion in general or Catholicism

Ai Cattolici

IL MONITO DI GIUSEPPE DOSSETTI

Giuseppe Dossetti, interprete autorevole, all'interno della D.C., negli anni della resistenza e dell'immediato dopoguerra, dell'ansia di giustizia e di fraternità delle masse popolari cattoliche, e poi figura eminente di sacerdote partecipe e protagonista del Concilio Ecumenico Vaticano II, pellegrino per la « Pacem in terris », nel lasciare l'Italia ha voluto ripensare alle fasi salienti della sua milizia civile e politica:

> « Ricordo con particolare chiarezza l'incontro con Alcide De Gasperi, a casa sua, due giorni dopo il 18 aprile del '48. Gli dissi che da quel momento il partito doveva cambiare rotta, preparare un programma di rinnovamento delle antiquate strutture sociali del Paese.
>
> De Gasperi fu duro: replicò che il partito doveva operare verso il progresso, sì, ma con prudenza. In sostanza indicò una linea di opportunismo politico che io ho sempre rifiutato. Per me fu la più grande delusione della mia breve vita politica e decisi di lasciare tutto... ».
>
> « Quell'incontro è stato la chiave di volta di tutta la politica italiana fino ad oggi e forse ancora per molto tempo.
>
> « Quel giorno la D.C., e per essa De Gasperi, aveva fatto una scelta di conservazione che in seguito ha sempre avallato. Si era inserita definitivamente in un gioco di potere i cui meccanismi funzionano in modo imprevedibile, tanto è vero che De Gasperi fu allontanato poi dalle stesse persone cui aveva dato importanti incarichi nel partito.
>
> « Ma non si può far politica per fare il governo e basta. Il nostro impegno io credevo dovesse essere più arduo: portare una carica spirituale nella vita di tutti i giorni, e quindi anche nella politica ».

Di fronte a queste riflessioni composte e sofferte, il direttore de « il Resto del Carlino » ha reagito con rabbiosa trivialità così scrivendo:

... No, in Italia non c'è proprio più nulla da fare per gente come Dossetti & C., se Dio vuole. La sinistra DC rimane orfana di un " padre " che l'ha messa al mondo (ora confessa) fuori dai santi legami del matrimonio, e non la riconosce neanche come figlia, e che se ne va, se Dio vuole, in mezzo gli arabi. È il posto giusto per lui. E per tutti quelli come lui ».

Lavoratori, intellettuali, giovani cattolici, l'esperienza civile ed il monito di Giuseppe Dossetti vanno accolti e rivissuti in una scelta politica a favore della pace, della fraternità, della giustizia, della libertà e contro questa D.C. che, con la sua meschina politica conservatrice, ha tradito tante attese e deluso tante speranze.

CONTRO LA D.C.   **VOTATE P.C.I.**

Figure 3. A political appeal distributed by the Bologna PCI Federation during the 1972 electoral campaign

in particular but to assert that true Catholic belief is often corrupted by the Church itself.[12] Although in practice the Marxist doctrine is adhered to within the party, and Catholic belief is indeed seen as a sign of weakness, Catholicism is portrayed publicly as a parallel ideology to Communism, an ideology that often serves as the basis for progressive action (Nesti 1965).

Church influence is to be combatted not directly through ideological struggle, but rather through a programmatic and social approach (PCI 1964:69–70). Catholicism is to be distinguished from the Church, and only the latter is to be attacked directly. The theory behind such a tactic is that once social allegiances change, ideological commitments will eventually follow. The individual must first be weaned away from the Catholic world and brought into the Communist social sphere before he can be properly socialized in the Communist world view. Though Gramsci's view of the Church as one of the primary barriers to Communist control of the masses appeared as accurate in 1972 as in 1922, and is undoubtedly shared by the great bulk of the Communist Party leadership, it is a position that is no longer officially acknowledged. Though theoretically faultless, it is strategically dangerous. The PCI would do battle with the Church, but in its own way, on favorable terrain.

Party–Church relations in Albora bear both the signs of the political policies of the Italian Church hierarchy and the national Church policy of the PCI. Yet, as has already been suggested, and as is examined in detail in the following chapters, local-level practice is far from a simple local translation of policy set at national levels. Don Stefano's active public participation in Albora DC activities, for example, is not in line with current Church policy, which suggests a certain public distance be kept between clergy and DC. Similarly, the sentiments, comments, and actions of the Communists of Albora are often at odds with national Party policy of solicitude for the Church. Anticlericalism, denounced in Party literature, is deeply rooted among the Alborese, and not just among the local Communists.

As a 1971 meeting of the FGCI in Albora was about to begin, Alberto Finelli, the *quartiere* Party coordinator, was clearly angry. After opening the meeting with some general remarks, he declared, "This recent business of painting slogans has got to stop. The wall of a church is not the appropriate place to paint slogans. What was it? *Case . . .?*" "*Case Non Chiese*" ("Houses Not Churches"), the FGCI head suggested. "That's deplorable," Finelli continued, "why not write *case non ornamenti* or something like that? That would be much more to the point. Writing slogans like that on the church gives people the wrong impression," concluded Finelli, "they'll get the idea that we don't want a dialogue with the Catholics."

Paolo, a seventeen-year-old, long-haired high school student, looked at Finelli disgustedly. The two were not on good terms anyway, since Paolo was known to associate with one of the ultra-left-wing groups condemned by the Party. Though the other youths present took Finelli's reprimand quietly, Paolo did not: "As far as I'm concerned," he said, "there's no difference between the army and the Church. It's all the same thing." At this, Finelli reddened, replying, "You obviously aren't familiar with the teachings of Gramsci and Togliatti. They taught us the necessity of a dialogue with the Catholics." Paolo just muttered.

Of course the conciliatory position toward the Church does not mean that the clergy are seen as anything other than opponents. During the 1972 election campaign the clergy, indeed, provided the Party with considerable grounds for objection, though, as is made clear in a later chapter, the extent of clerical political campaigning was exaggerated by local PCI leaders. Finelli, speaking to a meeting of Dovero section campaigners a month before the election, warned of the clerical danger:

Comrades, we must recognize the role the Church is playing in this election. More than any time in the last ten years the Church is organizing for the DC and campaigning against the PCI. This is a serious development. Of course the Church is much more sly than before. They don't speak of the necessity of voting DC from the pulpit; they know that would just alienate people. But, just the same, they are active in spreading DC propaganda. This is happening right here in our own *quartiere*. The church is forming a committee to visit people in their homes to get them to vote DC.

A month later, in the report to the Party Federation written by Porri, the slight gain in votes by the DC in the *quartiere* was largely attributed to the work of the priests:

Although the DC augmented its vote by 1.4%, it did not obtain the results they might have, considering that groups of families organized by ACLI [a Catholic association] were voting and considering also the furious activity conducted by the Church, which offered its parish halls for public rallies held by some of the major figures of the DC (Bersani, Elkan and Tesini came to the *quartiere*, in addition to the personal, rabid activity of the priest of Andara).

And so the battle wore on.

6

The Battle for Ritual Supremacy

12 August 1956
FROM THE BISHOP OF PRATO
To the Very Reverend Provost
S. Maria del Soccorso, Prato:

Today, Sunday, August the 12th, two of your parishioners will marry at City Hall, thus going through the civil ceremony only. This is because they have refused a religious marriage. The ecclesiastic authorities have made every possible effort to prevent the commission of this most grievous sin. This gesture of overt and contemptuous repudiation of Church teaching is a cause of profound sorrow for the priests and for the faithful. Marriage, when entered into only *civilly* by two baptized persons, may under no circumstances be considered a marriage, and is, therefore, for all purposes, but the beginning of a scandalous concubinage.

Hence, you, Very Rev. Provost, in conformance with Christian morality and the laws of the Church, shall classify these two persons as *public concubines* and, in accordance with Canons 855 and 2357 of the Canon Law, you shall consider, for all purposes, Mauro Bellandi and Loriana Nunziati as *public sinners*. As a consequence, they shall be denied the Holy Sacraments, their house shall not be blessed, they shall not be accepted as sponsors in Baptism or Confirmation, nor shall they receive Catholic burial . . .

131

This letter is to be read to the faithful. [quoted in Bucci 1969:37]

Bright, festive lights lit up the field. Booths made of metal poles and aluminum sheets circled the 2 acres that for the rest of the year saw no more activity than an occasional impromptu soccer game. The busiest area was the kitchen, where twenty people, mainly older women and men, were furiously grilling *salsiccia*, boiling *tortellini*, cutting the *polenta* and uncorking unlabeled bottles of wine. Radiating from the kitchen stood rows of long tables crowded with eaters of all ages and protected by metal canopies from sun and rain. Across the field, people massed around the cork-pull, with its tiers of prizes for those fortunate enough to find the bottom of their cork colored to match. At 9 P.M., 100 children, some clutching stuffed toys that testified to their parents' earlier good fortune, sat on the grass and on unsteady wooden folding chairs watching a puppet show heavy with Bolognese dialect. The children were allowed to stay up late into the night, for this was the biggest *festa* of the year in this part of Albora, and at midnight the traditional *festa* highlight would come: the goose-pull. With the goose hung by its feet from a scaffolding in the middle of the field, a dozen of the most athletic boys would try to jump high enough to pull off its head, thus winning the goose. On this night, the head proved hard to detach. Giovanni, in a bloodstained teeshirt, swinging and grimacing, his hands engraved on the goose's neck, finally fell to the ground with his prize. Over his head the giant banner proclaimed: *With the PCI Until Victory*.

Posted on the wall of the Proletarian Struggle Cooperative bar was a small black-lined notice entitled *Ringraziamento*, not unlike those found throughout Italy following a funeral. This particular note, however, read:

I would like to express my deepest thanks to the comrades of the Vapori Section for honoring the wishes of my beloved father and providing a contingent bearing red flags at his funeral procession.

Augusto Bonoli

The black, dignified hearse bearing the municipal insignia of Bologna had gone directly from the Bonoli funeral to another funeral, this one in church. The driver needed to stop but a moment to screw the silver cross into its place on the top of the car roof.

It should not be surprising that ritual constitutes one of the important arenas of combat between the Church and the PCI. Power relations in a society are, after all, invariably symbolized through ritual,[1] and ritual serves as a means to reinforce patterns of authority. Although ritual can be an extremely conservative force, it can also provide a potent instrument for struggling against the sociopolitical status quo (Balandier 1970:117). In Albora, as in Italy, the success of the Church in securing the allegiance of the people is intimately tied to its ability to monopolize the realm of ritual. For this reason, the PCI has tried to undercut the Church monopoly on ritual, a task that the Party carries out in part by substituting its own ritual cycle.

The threat to the Church posed by the Communist entry into the field of ritual is recognized by both the Italian Church hierarchy and the clergy in Albora. The priests of Albora complain that the Communists are trying to create an "antiparish" through the use of ritual. Indeed, one priest added, "the very structure of the Party is modeled after the organization of the Church." And at one of the Camolia church meetings held to plan the Decennial procession, don Mario was criticized by a young Church activist for copying the Communist *festa* in an effort to make the

Church procession more popular. Responded don Mario: "I don't see why we shouldn't copy the successful experience of others, no matter who they are. After all, the Communists originally copied us in organizing the *feste*."

Although numerous attempts have been made to explain the Church–Communist struggle for ritual control, most of these focus on the question of how individuals can be both Catholic and Communist, how they can call themselves Communist and participate in the rites of the Church. The Church has been particularly interested in this question, with most observers embracing a theory of "belly" Communism, claiming that the fundamental religious beliefs of the people remain Catholic but that they are attracted to Communism because of economic frustrations. Rank-and-file Communists are presumed to be ignorant of the logical incompatibility between their Catholic beliefs and their Communist allegiance. Hence the Catholic lament:

The people are baptized and confirmed, they "profess" the signs of Catholic practice, they practice in as sizeable a proportion as the others or not less than the others, but they vote Communist. The people just do not want to understand the ideological incompatibility. They merely simplify the relations, claiming: "the priest has to say this, it is his job, but actually things are different." [Bonicelli 1965a:248][2]

In the postwar period, the Church anti-Communist campaign was based on the theory that if the Church could just make clear to the people the ideological conflict between Catholicism and Communism, the people, loyal to the Church, would cease their heretical behavior. The failure of the Church campaign testifies to the inadequacy of this theory.

In analyzing ritual participation in Albora, it is useful to distinguish between *rites of passage* and *rites of commu-*

nity. Rites of passage are taken here in their customary sense to denote rituals accompanying or signifying an individual's change in social status. By rites of community are meant those rituals that are community, rather than individual, centered. Rites of passage, such as weddings and funerals, certainly have important community referents, but the ostensible focus is on a particular individual. The usefulness of this distinction should become clearer as we examine the evidence from Albora, which suggests that the Church has continued to monopolize rites of passage but that the PCI has largely succeeded in supplanting the Church as the sponsor of community rites.

Rites of passage

As is the case throughout Italy,[3] almost all Alborese Communists have their children baptized (see Burgalassi 1970:56, 87; Bonicelli 1965:200–9). Similarly, they send their children to catechism so that they may have First Communion and be confirmed. They are married and buried by a priest.

Not having one's children baptized is regarded as an exceedingly militant act for a Communist in Albora. It results in gossip not only among the non-Communists but among the Communists as well. Indeed, no more than a handful of unbaptized children can now be found in the *quartiere*. Despite this apparent Catholic orthodoxy in fulfilling the ritual prescriptions of baptism, there remains a strong countercurrent of defensiveness, particularly among the Communist activists. Frequently such individuals volunteer the information that they only went through with their child's baptism in order to preserve domestic tranquility, most often in the form of placating the baby's grandparents. Another reason given by the Communists for baptizing their progeny is that unbaptized children are stigmatized by the authorities, especially at school. The defensiveness of the Communists is manifest in another way as well, for rather than approach the local parish priest to arrange for their child's baptism in an Albora church, many Communists have their child baptized while still in the hospital, avoiding the public and local church celebration.

Catechism consists of weekly classes in Church doctrine for elementary school children. First Communion takes place after the first year of instruction, and confirmation at the end of the fourth and final year. Most of the Communists send their children to these Church rites, particularly for the first year. Fewer children attend catechism than are baptized, but most children do attend. As one local priest said, the people have an "exquisitely sacramental orientation." What is important for most Communist parents is that their children have First Communion and confirmation and get it over with. Accordingly, although it is expected that the child should go to church every Sunday until he receives these rites, the parent may well become concerned if the child – particularly if it is a boy – continues to frequent the church after having had the rites.

In a conversation with a group of half a dozen FGCI activists, the youths rather embarrassedly said that they had all been baptized and gone to catechism. They unanimously agreed that their parents had been afraid to be thought different by their neighbors. One girl, whose parents are both Communist activists, maintained that in those days her parents were ignorant. All their relatives and friends told them to send their daughter to catechism, so they went along with the crowd.

One forty-year-old unmarried Communist activist bemoaned the change in his comrades when they had children. He said that when they were young they used to stand up to the priests and were militantly anti-Church. Yet when they had children and the children came of age, they were sent to be confirmed. He said that when they were asked why the change of heart, they would weakly reply that they were afraid that otherwise the children would be discriminated against.

The great majority of Communists in Albora are also married in church. This fact is of particular significance as the wedding ceremony is the first rite of passage in which the participant may be presumed to play a part in the ritual arrangements. Moreover, the Communist has the opportunity to choose between a church wedding and a civil wedding. It is not a choice (as in baptism) between a church rite or no rite at all. Roughly 10 percent of the young Communist men in Albora in fact do choose a civil wedding ceremony, and this is seen by the Alborese as a political statement, a direct repudiation of the Church. These are generally the most militant of the young Communists and their weddings are most often held in the room of City Hall popularly dubbed the *sala rossa* (the "red room").

The tension found in the individual's confrontation with these competing ritual centers is not only demonstrated by those individuals who choose civil weddings. Many a tale is told of a groom adamantly refusing to be married in a church while his bride just as adamantly insisted on it. Nor is the phenomenon new. One woman, whose parents were married in the early years of this century, recalled that they had argued over their church wedding throughout their marriage. Her father, a Socialist, smarted from the embarrassment of having been married in church. The struggle between relatives over a church versus civil wedding ceremony is a common one. One Party activist, when asked if her daughter had been married in a church, embarrassedly said yes, but quickly pointed to the aunt of the

groom as being responsible, saying that the aunt had said
she would not attend the wedding if it were held in city
hall.

It is, of course, difficult to judge to what extent such
explanations are merely ways of creating a scapegoat. As
one Church activist noted:

They themselves, down deep, would like to have the church
wedding, but being Communists they don't want to cut a bad
figure, so they blame the in-law. Those who really are decided
not to have Communion or not to marry in church are very few.
So to save face they say: "But it's the mother-in-law who wanted
it . . ." so they can have it both ways.

Tension in the church weddings of Communists is evident, though, and there are few Communist members who
have a church wedding without some embarrassment. One
indicator of this tension is the fact that numerous people
now do not take Communion at their own wedding ceremonies. The priests of Albora resent this, but say there is
nothing they can do, for they cannot refuse to marry them.
The priest of one parish does, however, make a note in the
church wedding log of which newlyweds refuse Communion.

Although it has been in the interest both of the Church
and the Party not to make a public issue out of people's
divided allegiances, the Communists are occasionally subject to criticism and ridicule from more militant opponents
of the Church who, often in reaction to the Party's conciliatory posture toward the Church, are not PCI members.
Both the barbed nature of this critical position and some
insights into the political importance of ritual are nicely
illustrated by a ballad composed recently by Cesare Malservisi, formerly an elementary school teacher in the city of
Bologna who now lives and teaches in a rural outpost of
the province. Entitled "But Alas Grandmama," the song

tells of the child of a militant Communist. Both the rich original version in Bolognese dialect and the English translation follow:

. . .PERÒ PERÒ LA NONA

La lota dantr' in fabrica
l'an s'met in discusion
anch sl'é un mumant difezil
par la rivoluzion.
Pò adess ch'avan dezis
ed metter so famaja
con la cumpagna ed lota
cl'é una maravaia.

   . . .però però la suocera
   la s'é tant arcmandé
   la vol ch'andagna in cisa
   par eser maridé.
   Si sono idee retrograde
   lo so, al n'é brisa giost
   però la mi Marisa
   l'a gni vol der un sgost.

Me a son sindacalesta
li, la s'e tant arcmandé
la vol c'andagna in cisa
a san sté fortuné.
La lota la va avanti
anch pral so fazen tond
che quand al sarà grand
al sepa miour al mond.

   . . .però però la nona
   la s'é tant arcmandé
   la vol c'andagna in cisa
   parché 'l sepa badzé.
   Mo me a i o i mi prinzepi
   an voi c'um toin in giro
   lasa pur ch'il batazan
   me ai met nom. . .Vladimiro.

Ades che Vladimiro

. . .BUT ALAS GRAMDMAMA

The battle in the factory
continues without diminution
even if it is a difficult time
for the revolution.
And now I've decided
to start my own family
with a comrade in struggle
who is truly a marvel.

   . . .but alas her mother
   begging and harried
   wants us to go to the church
   to get married.
   True her ideas are backward,
   it isn't right I know
   but my Marisa just doesn't
   want to displease her.

I am a unionist and
she a bit retired
since we now have an infant
a baby most admired.
But the battle must go on
and with his little face in mind
I work to make the world a better
place when he grows up.

   . . .but alas his grandmother
   begged and advised
   that we send him to church
   so he could be baptized.
   But I have my principles
   no one can take me for a fool
   go ahead and baptize him
   but I will choose his
   name . . .Vladimir.

Now that Vladimir's

la scola l'a taché
a j o dimondi incarich
coi decret deleghé.
Entrar negli organismi
sanza eser trop seteri
perché la scuola cambi
con spirit uniteri.

. . .però però la nona
la s'é tant arcmandé
la vol che Vladimiro
al seppa cresimé.
Acsé pran feri tort
a la dmanga mateina
a port anch Vladimiro
a lezian ed dutrina.

Gl'impegni di quartiere
im teinen occupè
la Marisa la brantla
la s'é un pucten stufè.
L'idea la condivide
ma boia d'un mond leder
la dis che la ragazol
l'a bisogn anch d'un peder.

. . . però però la mama
l'as pol der una man
l'as beda sampr al cinno
quand in avan bisagn.
Zert li l'a al so abitudin
e cusa vut mai feri
las porta al cinno in cisa
in maz par al ruseri.

(PASSANO GLI ANNI)

A son dantr'al cunseli
d'la lega pensionè
e anch la mi Marisa
la s'é un pucten invcè.
Al ragazol invezi
l'é guintè un bel sturnel

schooling has begun
to my many committee posts
I must run.
Taking part in them
without being a sectarian mission
so that the schools are reformed
through a broad coalition.

. . .but alas grandmama
with a pleading peroration
insists the Vladimir
receive Church confirmation.
And so as not to offend her
each Sunday morning
to his weekly catechism
I must take Vladimir.

with my *quartiere* responsibilities
I've little time to spare
though Marisa's laments
she continues to air.
She agrees with my ideas
but, damn it
she says that a boy
needs paternal attention.

. . . but alas her mama
helps out unpaid
always looking after the boy
when he's in need of aid.
Sure she has her own customs
and what do you expect
she takes the boy to church
so May rosary devotions
he doesn't neglect.

(THE YEARS PASS. . .)

Now I'm on the council
of the pensioners' corps
and even my Marisa isn't
so young anymore.
Our boy though
has become quite a handsome boy

l'a voia ed fer pulid
l'é all'universitè.

   . . . però la zoventò
d'incù an la capess brisa
a ié avanzè ch'al vezi
d'ander sampr in cisa.
E pò an s'acuntanta brisa
ed fer la comunion
lo l'é par al dissans
par la liberazion.

la la la la comunion
la la la la liberazion[4]
me an capes brisa cum l'a fat
a gnir fora un fiol acsé.
So pedar partigian . . .
So medar staffatta partigena . . .
Comunion . . . liberazion . . .
       [by Cesare Malservisi, 1977]

he wants to do well
now that he's at the university.

   . . . but alas I don't understand
young people these days
he's not kicked the bad habit
of going to church, I'm amazed.
Nor is he satisfied with
receiving communion
he says he's for dissent
and liberation.

la la la la Communion
la la la la Liberation
I just don't understand how he
could have turned out that way.
His father a *partigiano* . . .
His mother a *partigiano* courier . .
Communion . . . liberation . . .

As demonstrated by the official city statistics on marriages, the Communists have not been successful in coun-
tering the monopoly by the Church of wedding rites. Of
3,079 weddings in Bologna in 1970, 2,872 were church
ceremonies and only 207 were civil ceremonies (Bologna,
1971:38). When it is recognized that a number of the latter
were unrelated to the Church–Communist struggle, the
overwhelming edge of the Church becomes all the more
apparent.

The two most recent weddings of Albora Party activists
were held in Bologna's city hall, and invitations went out
to all the top Party leaders of the *quartiere*. Indeed, the
invitations to one of the weddings were entrusted to the
highest-ranking Party official of Albora, to be distributed
at a meeting of the local Party leadership. When the mayor
is available, he is prevailed on to conduct the ceremony in
the red room. On such occasions the simple civil ceremony

is embellished with Party ritual. In both recent weddings of local Party activists, speeches were given in the middle of the ceremonies by the two top Party officials of Albora. Each speech, lasting about ten minutes, praised the young couple for their dedication to the struggle and invoked the symbolism of the Party. The Party leaders thus replace the priest in giving the traditional charge to the newlyweds, substituting symbolism of the Party for that of the Church.

Unlike weddings, which are clearly either church or non-church, there is a wide variety of practices in Albora regarding funeral rites. These range from the full church funeral – from confession and Last Rites to religious burial – to the Communist funeral, replete with red flags.[5] The great majority of Communists in Albora has at least some of the church rites, and only a small percentage, no more than 15 percent, of the funerals of Communists are carried out without a priest performing any rite at all. Here again, the tension between Communist and Church is often evident. For example, when a Communist, nonactivist woman died in 1972, her son arranged with the parish priest to have a funeral procession and mass in the church. The procession was led by the priest and an attendant carrying a large cross, followed, in order, by the hearse, the immediate family, relatives, friends, and, lastly, by the leaders of the local PCI section. When the procession arrived at the church, all entered except for the Party leaders, who stood in the street talking quietly among themselves until the funeral mass was over.

The Communist funeral rite involves a procession similar in certain formal respects to the traditional Church procession. No priest is present, nor is any Church symbolism employed. The hearse leads the way, followed by relatives and then friends and comrades of the deceased. The comrades carry red flags, including the flag of the section of which the deceased was a member. Flags of the other Party sections of the *quartiere* are also displayed. At the end of the procession a color guard is formed with the red flags, the hearse passing under them. Remarks are made by a local Party official, extolling the virtues of the decreased and stressing his contributions to the Communist cause.

Rites of community

As indicated earlier, the success of the Church in retaining a near monopoly on rites of passage in the Communist *quartiere* is not duplicated in the case of rites of community. The traditional ritual expressions of local solidarity have largely been usurped and transformed by the Communist Party.

From the point of view of the Church, the most important community rite is Sunday mass. Indeed, Sunday mass attendance is generally seen by Church authorities as the primary indicator of popular allegiance to the Church. One who attends mass weekly is regarded as loyal to the Church; one who attends rarely is of questionable loyalty; and one who never attends Sunday mass is a pariah. Given the importance attached to Sunday mass attendance, the fact that no more than 10 percent of the parishioners of Albora attend mass weekly is the paramount sign of the weakness of the Church in the *quartiere*.

An analysis of the participation of the Communists in the weekly mass is facilitated by the recognition of two cross-cutting variables: sex and Party activism. If we break the latter variable into activists/nonactivists, we can construct a simple table. Using this device to analyze weekly mass attendance, we can make the following generalization:

	Male	Female
Activist	Never attends Sunday mass	Never attends Sunday mass
Nonactivist	Rarely attends: not locally	Few attend regularly, some attend occasionally

As we see here, sex is not a relevant factor for Sunday mass attendance as far as the activists are concerned. For the nonactivist, however, sex is an important factor in determining mass attendance. Women are seen by the Alborese as being "weak" in religious matters. A woman's attendance may be seen as evidence of this sexual weakness. Men are thought to have no such weakness (or rather, to have it to a lesser extent); a man who attends mass is seen as signaling political allegiance to the Church. For this reason, with few exceptions, male, nonactivist Communists do not attend Sunday mass in Albora.

There is some evidence, though, that such people do occasionally attend Sunday mass downtown, where they hope to avoid being seen by anyone they know. The Communist men at the nearby Alborese bars watch on as the people enter and exit from the local churches. This surveillance, ironically, is reinforced by the practice of Communist fathers taking their children to church for catechism and mass and then waiting for them at the nearest bar. Furthermore, the question of who goes to Sunday mass is frequently and widely discussed. Most people who have lived in the *quartiere* for any time can name all those in their courtyard who attend mass.

Communists who do attend mass are extremely defensive. This is evident in the remarks of one of the female

Communist activists on the subject: "The Communists who participate in the church are Party members but they don't participate in any Party activity. They vote Communist, and they might even be members and tell you 'in religious matters I'm a little bad'" (*io sono un pò cattivella*). A dramatic instance of this defensiveness was provided by a young Party activist who was a newcomer to Albora. When, as part of a survey of local Party activists, he was asked about his church attendance, he became agitated and said, "I'm very sorry . . . but I believe in God" (*Mi dispiace molto . . . ma io credo in Dio*). He noted that he went to church on Christmas and Easter. Trying to soothe him, the interviewer pointed out that the PCI statutes held no conflict between being a Catholic and being a Communist. The young activist shrugged this off, apparently feeling that this was a mere technicality that in no way minimized his deviance.

Although participation in church mass for the holidays is greater than that for regular Sunday mass, it too is limited; no more than 20 percent (1800) of the Alborese attend either Christmas or Easter mass at the three churches of the *quartiere*. Considerably fewer fulfill the minimal Church obligation of taking Communion during the year (most often at Easter), according to the estimates of the priests of Albora. The number of Alborese who take Communion or attend holiday mass in the anonymity of another parish is not known. Though possibly considerable, the fact remains that the large majority of Alborese probably do not attend mass on any given holiday, nor do they take Communion with any regularity.

Ritual participation in Sunday mass and Communion in Albora has no strict analogue in the Communist world. The decline of Church monopoly of community ritual and the concomitant rise of Party-centered community ritual is more dramatically seen in another sphere: the annual parish *festa*. These *feste*, occupying an important place in community organization throughout much of the northwest Mediterranean and in Latin America, once placed the churches of Albora at the center of communal expressions of solidarity. Since the war, the PCI has created a system of community *feste* that has helped establish and maintain the place of the Party at the center of community life.

Festa

The annual parish *festa* has received a great amount of anthropological attention and its social importance has been widely recognized. Although their interpretation has been the subject of debate (see Smith 1977), these celebrations have often been depicted as both reflecting and reinforcing the social centrality of the church in the community, as Boissevain argued in the case of Malta:

The festa is thus an occasion on which communal values are reaffirmed and strengthened, as individuals and groups express their loyalty to their patron saint and unite to defend and enhance the reputation of their village. At the same time, the central position which the Church occupies in the social structure is strongly reinforced, for the parish church is the hub around which this festive occasion turns. [1969:59]

As noted earlier, though, ritual is not necessarily a conservative force; it may also serve as an agent of sociopolitical change, and this aspect is quite evident in the Alborese situation. As Friedrich (1966:191) observed, "communal rites and politics, especially political ideology, are interdependent, and change in either may influence or precipitate change in the other." Not only does ritual change in response to political events, but changes in community ritual may themselves influence political processes.

In Albora in prewar days, the communal high points of the year were provided by the *feste* of the church. Virtually everyone participated in these celebrations, and they were the only occasions on which the entire community came together to feast and to play. The *feste* were the subject of great anticipatory excitement and discussion, and the honor of occupying one of the major ceremonial roles in the accompanying procession (such as carrying the Madonna) conferred considerable prestige on the individual. As late as the 1930s the churches in Albora sponsored a full *festa* schedule, as a parishioner recounted:

Don Claudio used to have a festa and a procession for almost all of the saints. There was the big festa of the Madonna of Corpus Domini, then there was the festa of Saint Anna for which there was a little procession; he had a festa for Saint Agnes and Saint Antonio. For all the saints he had a little procession around the church. He really celebrated them. He put lights and decorations all over the outside of the Church.

Many of the processions were quite elaborate. They were led not only by the parish priest but by several visiting priests as well, with higher ecclesiastical authorities present on occasions of major import. Bands were hired to add to the festivity, decorations adorned the church and the homes along the procession route, and the great majority of parishioners joined in the procession, mass, and ensuing festivities.

The largest and most important *festa* in Albora's larger parish was that in honor of the Madonna, held in October every year. Four men, clad in white robes, had the honor of carrying a large statue of the Madonna through the streets of the parish, while numerous visiting priests, dressed in clerical robes, joined the parish priest in leading the procession. Some of these processions lasted over three hours, marching not only through the streets but through the vacant fields as well. The festivities continued at the church following the procession, when food and drink were served, games played, music performed, and novelties sold.

Yet the Church *festa* supremacy did not survive World War II.[6] While the fortunes of the Church in Albora were on the decline, a new *festa*, organized by the Communists, was organized and flourished. Neither the Church nor the PCI minimized the significance of this development, either in Albora or in Italy at large; the struggle for *festa* supremacy was recognized by both sides as an integral part of the battle for popular influence. Indeed, the Cardinal of Bologna became so concerned about the Church's declining role in sponsoring community *feste* that he called for the invigoration of the partially neglected ten-year parish *festa* to draw the people away from the *feste* of the PCI (Toldo 1960:29). That the Communists have been aware of the importance of the competition is evident from numerous sources. For example, the Bolognese Communist weekly *Lotta* (October 2, 1958) featured the following exclamation in a highlighted box:

What incenses the clerics!
  – 276 sectional *feste*
  – 1500 cell *feste*
  – an unprecedented Provincial *festa*
  – 28 million [lire] in contributions

The Communist attempt to destroy the Church monopoly on popular *feste* was national in scope. A report of a Southern Party official recounts that:

The reaction of the ecclesiastical authorities and the Catholic organizations was violent against the popular *feste*, organized last year on the occasion of the Month of the Communist Press. They tried everything to dissuade the masses of the "faithful" from attending, but the lights, the music and the fireworks won out over the threats of excommunication . . . We were expecting this reaction. In Naples, and in general throughout the South, the Catholic Church had an absolute monopoly on the popular *feste*. As a consequence, these have had a purely religious content, a device used by the Church to maintain its ties with the great masses of Catholic laity. [Viviani 1950]

Viviani could not have been more clear in portraying the Party *feste* as a direct attack on the popular influence of the Church, "The popular *feste* have, for the first time, broken the confessional monopoly . . . In many localities of the Province of Naples . . . the success of our *feste* was such that the religious *feste* organized by the local parishes for the same time failed."

In format the *feste* sponsored by the Communists is much like that of the traditional church *feste*. The manifest purposes are, of course, quite different, as are the symbols. Whereas the Church *feste* are proclaimed as tributes to the patron saint or to other saints and as a time of spiritual uplift, the Communist *feste* are organized to glorify the Party, politicize the masses, and raise money for the Party press. Whereas the Church *feste* are marked by crosses, images of the Madonna, and assorted other icons, the Communist *feste* are decorated with red flags and anticapitalist, antiimperialist banners. Just as each parish has its own characteristic annual *festa*, so each section of the Party has its own *festa*. However, today the Communist *festa*, not the Church *festa*, is the biggest community celebration, an event discussed by the local people all year long. Thousands now participate in the sectional *feste* of the PCI in Albora, but no more than 400 participate in the Church *feste*.

Analysis of the content of the Communist *festa* raises a number of points concerning the symbolic import of the community rite.The *feste*, each three to four days long, are held outdoors on land adjacent to that of the local Party section headquarters and the local cooperative bar.

Entering the *festa* grounds, the *festa*-goer is invariably approached by a pair of six- to ten-year-old girls who offer to pin a *L'Unità* card on the person's jacket. This offer is rarely refused, for refusal would connote antagonism toward the Party. In exchange for the card, a small offering is made to the cause. Almost everyone wears this badge of solidarity with the Communist world, which serves throughout the evening to symbolize the political allegiance expressed through participation in the *festa*. Slogans demanding the withdrawal of United States troops from Vietnam, Italy's withdrawal from NATO,[7] and the overthrow of the Greek dictatorship adorn the site. Prominently displayed also are larger illustrations; in one, Vietnamese peasants were dismantling an American flag.

Although the decor of the *festa* is eminently political, the manifest content is overwhelmingly nonpolitical, a continuation of the traditional Church *festa* forms. Food and drink are the center of the *festa*; the largest area contains long dining tables seating 200 to 400 people where the traditional Bolognese delicacies are served along with great quantities of locally produced wine (see Photograph 6). A variety of games of chance is offered, ranging from the cork-pull to the dart competition. For the latter contest the choice of targets in 1972 was between Giorgio Almirante, national head of the neo-Fascist party, and Richard Nixon. Whole families attend the *festa*, eating together and then going to play these games of chance. Each section *festa* in Albora also has one featured game that is associated with the communal *feste* of old and that is especially popular, drawing scores of onlookers at their midnight time slot (see Photograph 7).

The political content of the Communist *festa* centers around a speech made in the middle of the weekend's festivities by a PCI official, usually from the Bologna provincial Party office. The speech is regarded by almost ev-

6. The dining tables are the center of activity at the PCI section *festa*.

eryone as a mere formality, a concession to the official
Party conception of the *festa* as a raiser of political consciousness. Few people in fact listen to the speech; the
great majority continue to eat or play games of chance.

The specifically political content of the Communist
festa, in fact, has been largely delegated to the FGCI, with
the adults concentrating on the more traditional *festa* aspects. The youths, indeed, have taken on the role of de-
fenders of the official political conception of the *festa*, in
reaction to the practices they consider too similar to the
traditional parish *feste*. The youths take it on themselves
to organize political educational activities, such as photo-
graphic exhibits of Vietnam, of Italian substandard hous-

7. The traditional "goose-pull," in which a youth tries to win the goose by pulling off its head, is a highlight of one of Albora's PCI section *feste*, despite its midnight starting time.

ing, of the war in Mozambique, and so on. They show anti-Fascist movies, hold discussions on political topics at the *festa*, and run the only game booth having a political tinge: the dartboard contest. In 1972, in line with their criticism of the nonpolitical content of the Party *festa*, the FGCI youths called on the local Party leaders to close down the food, dance, and gaming facilities during the political speech. The Party leaders opposed this, saying that many people might drift away if compelled to attend the talk. However, by invoking the official Party norms on the subject, the youths forced the Party officials to agree. When *festa* time came, though, this decision was conveniently ignored; the festivities continued without interruption throughout the speech.

Five local *feste* are sponsored annually by the PCI in Albora, one for each section and one for the *quartiere* as a whole. All five are structurally almost identical, though the *feste* of the larger sections have a greater number of activities. The center of each *festa* is the same: a canopied area with long eating and drinking tables. Featured are the traditional Bolognese foods and drinks as prepared by the local Party members. Wine, the *sine qua non* of the communal feast, is procured from a nearby farmer. The sausage is the product of a group effort, with one local Party official rearing the pigs, slaughtering them, and, helped by his comrades, curing and preparing the meat. The *tortellini* and *lasagne verdi*, the most prominent Bolognese food specialities, are made by women in their homes. About a dozen women are enlisted for this chore for each *festa*, each charging her purchase of the ingredients to the Party and spending hours making many pounds of the delicacies.

Strikingly, the kitchen at the *festa* is run jointly by men and women working side by side. Men can be seen cooking *polenta* and *pasta* along with their wives. For Albora and for Italy in general this is an uncommon sight. Normally the Alborese man does none of the kitchen work, particularly avoiding the preparation of food. At the Communist *festa* many share in the kitchen duties with their wives for the only time all year (see Photograph 8).

This behavior can be seen as an expression of Party ideology through the language of ritual, relating to the sexual egalitarian ideology of the Party, the practice of which is something of a sore spot in Party life. Although according to Party prescripts women are equal to men and should take equal political responsibilities, traditional norms regarding women's apolitical nature interfere. Thus, though women take a greater part in the PCI than in any

8. Male and female comrades work in the outdoor kitchen of one of the PCI section *feste* in Albora.

other party in Albora (and Italy generally), Communist ideology has made little headway against the traditional norms. There are few liberated families in Albora in terms of women's role and few Communist families could be distinguished from non-Communist families by this measure. The ritual of men and women working together in the biggest public ceremony of the Party is, against this general chasm between ideology and practice, an expression of adherence to the official Party doctrine.

The egalitarian ideology of the Party is expressed more dramatically by the roles assumed by the Party leaders at the festa. Local leaders become servents, waiting on tables. The hierarchy is ritually reversed, with the politically powerless giving the orders and the political luminaries taking them. The most spectacular case of this reversal, a case frequently pointed out by the *festa* participants themselves, is that of a national senator, originally from Albora, who returns every summer to wait on tables for the *festa* of his old Party section. He plays the role with enthusiasm, hurriedly running around with the steaming plates as if he were afraid of being fired should he momentarily slow his pace.

This ritual is an important one for the local Party, for it symbolizes a crucial Party theme – egalitarianism – and it addresses a frequent criticism, bureaucratization. As one proud young PCI member said, "Can you imagine a Christian Democratic senator waiting on tables?" It might be noted that, like other forms of rites of reversal (Gluckman 1963), this one reinforces rather than threatens the status of the high Party officials. By acting the part of the people's servant on this ritually defined occasion, the top leaders elicit popular approval and validation of their superordinate status.

The political importance of the Communist *festa* in Albora is great, though at first the *festa* appears to be only incidentally concerned with political matters. The Party has supplanted the Church as the sponsor of calendric rites expressing community solidarity. Although the annual processions of the two big parishes are each attended by approximately 200 people, they are no longer the pride of the community, nor are they much discussed outside of the week in which they occur. The role of the Church has been reduced to that of a beleaguered minority stubbornly traveling through enemy territory to demonstrate its continued existence. The adult men who march in the Church procession are few, and all are cognizant of the negative evaluation made of them by the onlooking majority. To participate in the public Church *festa* is to feel isolated from the community; participation in the Communist *festa* expresses solidarity with the bulk of the community. Both Church and Party are aware of the importance of numbers on these occasions. For both, the occasions are displays of strength. Any increase in numbers of people in the Church procession would be taken by all as a sign that the fortunes of the Church in Albora were on the rise. Any diminution in the numbers attending the Party *festa* would likewise be taken as a sign of waning Party power.

The *festa* also serves as a sign to the newcomer to the *quartiere* of power relations in Albora. The size of the Communist *feste* bespeaks Communist ascendancy, whereas the fact that so few participate in the *feste* of the Church indicates to the newcomer that the Church does not represent community power. These may be particularly dramatic observations for the numerous Southern immigrants, many of whom come from villages where the Communists do not have sufficient strength to hold their own *festa*. Thus the immigrant discovers that identification with the Communists, far from ostracizing him from the community, will make him a part of it.

The Communist *festa* is of great local political importance in another respect as well, for it projects a certain image of the PCI, an image in sharp contrast with that assigned to it by its political competitors. The Party, rather than being the conspiratorial foreign-ruled coterie described by its adversaries, is displayed as the open, friendly center of the local community. The *festa*, indeed, is the symbol of community solidarity, the one time all year when the entire community comes together and sits down at the same table to eat. Furthermore, it is a rite involving young and old, men and women, together. The normal social barriers of age, sex, and socioeconomic status are broken down on this ritual occasion. Six-year-old children are enlisted to distribute Party buttons while eighty-six-year-old women prepare the food. Men and women work side by side in the kitchen in a rare expression of sexual equality, and Party leaders express their formal subscription to the egalitarian ethic by taking on the most humble and servile tasks. Alborese who, because of their lack of formal education, disinterest, timidity, or feelings of inferiority, participate in none of the specifically political activities of the Party, can and do, through the *festa*, identify themselves with the PCI and are made to feel a part of it.

Sacred symbols and political combat

In addition to the efforts made by the PCI to substitute its own ritual for that of the Church, the Party has attempted to create its own system of sacred symbols, serving to bind together the Communist community and attract outsiders to the Communist world. As in any other symbolic system, the Communist symbolism is reaffirmed and nourished through ritual. Some of the PCI's major symbols and accompanying rites – such as those embodied in May Day or the use of the red flag – are of foreign origin. Others are of Italian vintage. We turn to the most important of these – *la Resistenza* – to illustrate the use of symbolism in the PCI–Church struggle.

The Resistance movement, conducted in Northern Italy during the last two years of World War II, has been the subject of hundreds of studies and dozens of volumes. Indeed, one of the primary indicators of its political, symbolic importance to the PCI is the number of king-sized, beautifully illustrated books that the Party has had a hand in issuing. It is our purpose here not to investigate the historical question of just what did happen in this period but to show how the PCI has sacralized and thus mythologized this historical event and how the Church has reacted to this process.

The *Resistenza* is in fact part of a larger symbolic nexus for the Party, involving the anti-Fascist movement that began in the 1920s.[8] The Party is portrayed as the primary moral and political force that combatted fascism, the only force courageous and principled enough to do battle with the Fascist regime. Symbols of this equation of the Party with anti-Fascist martyrdom abound. Each of the four Party sections in Albora is named for a Communist martyr from the *quartiere*, assassinated for anti-Fascist activity before the war or killed in combat during the *Resistenza*. Prominently displayed at each section headquarters is a framed picture of the martyr for whom the section is named: the picture hangs alongside other faces in the PCI pantheon: Lenin, Gramsci, and Togliatti (and, in one recalcitrant section, Stalin). There are other local shrines to the martyrs as well. At one, a plaque engraved on a building along via Albora, is written the following: 'Gianfranco Bevani, Communist martyr, killed while combatting the Fascists at the age of 23, on June 8, 1925." Fresh red roses are periodically placed in the attached flower pot.

Various municipal establishments similarly commemorate Communist anti-Fascist martyrs. A large communal sports center, located in Albora, is named after Guido Righi, a Communist hung by the Nazi SS nearby. The symbolism in this case is compounded by the story of his funeral. It is said that his mother, who still lives in Albora, went to get his corpse. The funeral was subsequently held at the Andara church, it is said, with a pair of armed *partigiani* guarding the church door.

The primary symbol of *partigiano* martyrdom in the city is Piazza Maggiore, Bologna's central piazza, where the city hall (and San Petronio, the central church) is located. It was along a wall of the city hall that the Nazis lined up captured *partigiani* and shot them. The commune, since Liberation, has maintained a shrine there, complete with pictures of all fallen *partigiani*, suitable engravings, and baskets of flowers. The symbolic importance of this site to the Communists of Albora was made evident during the election campaign of 1972. All the parties used Piazza Maggiore for their major campaign rallies and the *Movimento Sociale Italiano* Italy's neo-Fascist party, applied for a police permit to do the same. At a PCI meeting in Albora in which this subject was raised, one member after another got up to proclaim, with considerable emotion, that the Fascists could never be allowed to pollute the symbol of our fallen martrys; the Party could never allow it. In fact, the MSI was prevented from using the Piazza.

The *Resistenza* symbolism is expressed and maintained in a number of other ways as well. There are two major celebrations commemorating the *Resistenza*, the anniversary of the battle of Porta Albora in November and the anniversary of Liberation on April 25. For Porta Albora Day, a ceremony was organized at the city gate, well advertised with posters plastered all over the walls of the city. Presided over by the mayor, the ceremony was billed as an opportunity for young students and workers to get to meet some *partigiani*. This theme, of the importance of teaching the young people the lessons of the partisan movement, was taken up in the *quartiere* on Liberation Day, with a special program held at the sports center. Three *partigiani* came to discuss the *Resistenza* and to comment on a brief film depicting the partisans' struggle. The call to the meeting proclaimed: "Quartiere Albora, on the anniversary of April 25, is sponsoring a meeting especially intended for the youths and elementary and junior high school students, to teach them of the high political, social and moral values of the *Resistenza*." The moderator stressed to the sixty people present the importance of teaching the children of the *quartiere* what fascism really was, because every time they tried to enter the schools, the door had been

shut in their face. (The schools are nationally administered, that is, by DC authorities.) The only Albora partisan
on the panel was the secretary of the Vapori PCI section.

In 1972 Liberation Day was used for more direct PCI
purposes, as it came in the middle of the election campaign. In Albora the youths of FGCI carried a leaflet to
each home, calling on the people to vote PCI. The leaflet
began:

We are celebrating 27 years of peace and the recovery of liberty.
While in all those who lived through the sadness, the privations,
the suffering of the war and those who in that dirty war lost
those most dear to them or who were injured themselves,
thoughts turn to the anxiety and the hopes of 25 APRIL 1945,
bitterness also lives on in the thought that, thanks to the com-
placency of the DC, the fascists . . . are being permitted to speak
on radio and T.V. This fact profoundly offends all democratic
laborers, but, above all, it offends the Constitution, born from
the popular spirit of the RESISTENZA.

The continuing attempts to link the Party with the *Resistenza*, to portray the PCI as the champion of antifascism,
and to paint the DC as soft on fascism are not limited to
electioneering. A PCI wall poster from November of 1971,
for example, entitled "No More Fascist Criminality" began
as follows: "If the fascists and their accomplices delude
themselves into thinking they can profit from the weakness
and the incapacity of the DC and the center-left government, they are hereby warned that the COMMUNIST
PARTY will not stand idly by."

But the *Resistenza* symbolism is even richer and more
complex than has so far been indicated, for it serves the
Party not only as a mythical charter of its moral superiority
but also as a symbol for national unity. Indeed, the *Resistenza* is pointed to by Party spokesmen at all levels as proof
that a government of national unity is possible, that Catholics and Communists can work side by side for the benefit

of the nation. This imagery rests on the participation of various Catholic forces in the *Resistenza*, among them priests and lay leaders who later entered the DC. Throughout the 1970s, as the PCI struggled to be accepted as a partner in a governmental coalition with the DC, the Party made liberal use of the *Resistenza* symbolism both as a precedent and as a sacred sanction.

Whereas the *Resistenza* is a sacred symbol for the PCI, its symbolic value for the Church is more complex. There are two primary strands in the Church attitude toward *Resistenza* mythology: attempts to demonstrate the participation of members of the Catholic world in the *Resistenza* and attempts to desecrate the whole mythological constellation. Of these, the former is the less important, though, as shown by the fact that the one DC section in Albora is named after a fallen *partigiano*, it has not been discarded.

The people of the Catholic world of Albora have ceded the symbolism and ritual of the *Resistenza* to the Communists; they do not participate in its rituals nor recount its stories. However, they are not indifferent to the myth, for they see it as building Communist strength at their expense. In our conversations, the priests and Church activists of Albora often brought up the subject of the *Resistenza*. Typical were the comments of Pelti, the young church activist, who, referring to the "myth" of the *partigiani*, said the truth was that 80 percent of the *partigiani* were cowards. Unfortunately, the school teachers cannot let their students know about this, he continued, because the Communists have so much power.

Don Giorgio held forth at some length on the subject, giving his account of the *Resistenza*.

Many priests were killed in Bologna when the Germans were driven out, killed by the *partigiani*. They killed the priest of San Vitale and a number of others. When the Americans arrived, everyone called himself a *partigiano*. Now you even find people born after 1945 claiming they were *partigiani*. Of course there were some people who had high ideals and risked their lives during those years, but at the time the Americans arrived there was just a bloodbath, people killed for personal or economic reasons, not on account of their politics. In fact, in this *quartiere* a number of people were taken from their homes and executed. They were just regular people like everyone else; they hadn't done anything anyone else hadn't done. But they were killed. You hear a lot of talk about how horrible the German soldiers were here. Well, the truth of the matter is that the vast majority were just regular boys. They were sent here; they didn't choose to come. There was one town near here that was just about wiped out thanks to partisan activity; about 1,300 people were killed. The *partigiani* would shoot German soldiers in the back, knowing that the Germans would retaliate by executing ten local residents. Meanwhile, after shooting the German solider, they would just go back in the hills, so they didn't have to suffer the consequences of their action.

Battling through ritual

Communist efforts to establish an alternative to the traditional Church ritual system have, as we have seen, met with only partial success. The PCI has failed to substitute its own rites of passage for those of the Church (Burgalassi 1970:57), but it has succeeded in wresting control of the *festa* system. Thus the majority of the Alborese participate in two ritual systems, turning to the Church for the private rites of passage and turning to the Party for the public rites of community: first and foremost the annual *feste*, but also May Day, Liberation Day, and celebrations in honor of their martyrs.

The Communist rites of passage remain a sign of the unusually dedicated Party member. Almost all children are sent to catechism and, through the childhood rites of the

Church, are indoctrinated in the importance of these rites for their own children. Meanwhile, on the local level the Party is constrained in its attempts to establish an alternative ritual system by the national Party policy of not publicly opposing Church ritual. There can be no open attempts to build up the Communist ritual through castigation of Church ritual. Despite this public posture, the Communists are aware of the Marxist view of Church ritual. Local Party leaders send their children to catechism in order to have First Communion, yet refuse to attend the celebration of the child's rite. The family is sure to baptize the child, but tries to make the baptism as secret a ceremony as possible, just the opposite of the community ceremony exalted by the local priests.

Church retention of a monopoly on rites of passage is of no small significance in the struggle between the Church and the PCI. Indeed, the power of the Church over the Communists stems in good part from this monopoly. Through childhood rites the Church is able to influence the Alborese at a formative stage in their lives. Were it not for these rites most children would have little contact with the priests, with the Catholic faithful, or with the ideology and organization of the Church. Similarly, the Church monopoly on mortuary rites gives the Church considerable influence over adults. Dealing with the anxieties engendered by the prospect of death, aiding one in dealing with a dying parent or spouse, providing a ritualized expression of social solidarity on the death of a loved one, the priest plays an important role in people's lives.

Only rarely does any Communist in Albora directly attack the theology of the Church. Rather, often heard are attacks on the "hypocrisy" of the Church and the subservience of the Church hierarchy and clergy to the "bosses" (*padroni*). Many people make known their opinion that, far from being inseparable, high morals and churchgoing often conflict. Thus the refrain is often cited and lamented by the priests that morality can best be taught to the child at home. One story, possibly apocryphal, told by a top Alborese Communist official about his grandmother, is revealing here:

She used to go to church every week. Then her son, my father's brother, was sent to the African war (1936). The priest in Camolia at the time was a real Fascist. My grandmother was at mass and the priest preached the glory of having a son die for the motherland. My grandmother walked out in the middle of the mass and never returned to church again as long as she lived.

The woman's quarrel was not with Catholicism but with its "perversion" at the hands of a right-wing priest.

When asked about the Communist members in Albora, the Party *quartiere* coordinator maintained that the large majority are "Catholic" and that, though nonpracticing, they believe in God. Their objection, he said, is only to the political usage being made of the Church. Unfortunately, the investigation of people's religious beliefs is exceedingly difficult, for there are various levels of often contradictory beliefs and elaborate defense mechanisms. Also, though there is a certain amount of correlation between Party affiliation and antipathy to the Church, the chain of causation is much more complex. There are non-Party members in Albora who are as atheist as the most militant Communist. Indeed, there are some who refuse to join the PCI because of its conciliatory position toward the Church. There are also active Communists who subscribe to the Catholic cosmology.

The contradictions in belief systems are readily apparent to the outside observer. Commonplace in Alborese homes is the joint hanging of two holy pictures, one alongside the other: Jesus (or Mary or Pope John XXIII) and Togliatti, the PCI leader. Many of the Communists wear silver crosses on chains around their necks, though a number of the more militant Communists wear a silver hammer and sickle in its place. Speaking with older women who are Party members, one often learns that Jesus was a Socialist. The Communist Party, in effect, is portrayed as the historical bearer of the message of Jesus, a message that has been perverted in the Roman Catholic Church.

As was illustrated by the defensive reaction of the young Communist activist who occasionally went to mass, attachment of any kind to the Church is regarded as a weakness among Communist men. In a sense, there is a return to a classical Marxist position, in contrast to the backing off from that position by the Party national hierarchy.

When asked why he sends his children to catechism classes at the church, the usual answer given by the Communist is "tradition" or "superstition." These explanations are also given by the churchgoers to account for the behavior of the Communists. The two terms, "tradition" and "superstition," are often used interchangeably, as evidenced by the explanation provided by a faithful churchgoer for the presence of the children of Albora's Communists at catechism: "It's a matter of tradition not belief." Asked to elaborate on what he meant by tradition he thought a moment and responded, "It's really a matter of fear. They are afraid of the spiritual consequences of not sending their kid to catechism and not having the various rites of the Church. It's basically just superstition."

Perhaps more interesting than the fact that the priests and churchgoers brand the behavior of the Communists as superstitious is the observation that the Communists themselves account for their Church behavior in the same terms. Defensive about admitting any belief in Church dogma, the Communist often uses the cover of superstition to explain his participation in Church rites and to indicate to the outside world that this participation is not fully serious.

One day before Easter in 1972 don Francesco got a message from the workers in a little local factory asking him to give the Easter blessing at their factory. The workers, all Communists, had refused the annual Church blessing the year before, but in the past few months they had experienced a series of accidents. They decided to take no chances this time. The priest responded to this call and blessed the factory but later complained that this was superstition not religion.

"Religion" and "superstition" can be profitably seen as contrasting folk categories. Both are used to refer to ideological systems, having social referents, that embody a concept of superhuman power. In fact, the social referents, or rites, of the two systems may often be overlapping, and the ideological foundations largely the same. What is different is the evaluation made of the system. "Superstition" is used as a label when the evaluator wants to claim that the behavior is not to be taken seriously. In the Alborese politico-religious context, allegiance to religion – the Roman Catholic Church – is seen as a political statement implying allegiance to the DC. By referring to his behavior as superstitious, the Communist is able to participate in Church ritual and the Catholic belief system without being labeled anti-Communist.

The Church is equally concerned to separate the superstitious from the religious, for through such a distinction a discrimination can be made between those who are politically loyal to the Church and those who merely perform some Church rites – a distinction, in other words, between those considered to be part of the Catholic world and those considered to be outside it. In claiming that someone's decision to baptize his child is superstitious rather than religious, the Church people are saying that the rite does not signify a statement of political loyalty to the Church. The Church reserves for itself the right to specify what is truly religious, that is, behavior that meets with the official approval of the Church. The Church bases this claim on its monopoly of the divinely revealed Truth, but it may profitably be analyzed in political terms, that is, the power to set certain standards and to retain control of belief and ritual systems. When Durkheim, for example, complained that in Egypt and India "popular superstitions are . . . confused with the purest dogmas" (1915:5), he too established himself as a political authority, judging the claims of various religious systems to political ascendancy. In this light, what is most interesting in the Italian case is not that those who monopolize religious authority are concerned to separate superstition from religion, but that those in the opposing political camp are equally content to employ the same distinction.

In Albora, as elsewhere in Italy, apparently contradictory social pressures abound. Communists regard priests as forces of evil, yet they insist that their children go to the priest for lessons in Church doctrine. They see the Church as the co-conspirator of the bosses, yet a full rejection of the Church is regarded as deviant. But simply to brand people's beliefs and behavior as the product of confusion or ignorance, as has often been done, is erroneous. The absence of any coherent, codified ritual ideology should not be taken to mean popular ignorance of the normative antagonism between the Church and the PCI. The position of the Italian bishops in this regard is naive: "many adhere to atheist Communism not knowing all of the doctrine and often only in the illusory hope of economic advantage" (in Boschini 1965:178). The majority of Catholics certainly are not aware of all of Church doctrine. In any case, the Alborese does not affiliate with the PCI thinking that either the Party or the Church believes a division of loyalty to be theoretically consistent. The conflict of institutional norms and hegemonic goals of the Church and the PCI does not mean that people expressing divided loyalties are ignorant. Rather, the individual makes his own decisions on allocation of allegiance on the basis of his own personal interests as he sees them.

This does not resolve the intriguing question of why the Church rites of passage have remained relatively unaffected while the rites of community in Albora have largely been usurped by the Communist Party. The data permit no more than a hypothesis: Rites of community are more susceptible to changing political influence than are rites of passage. Just why rites of passage are so conservative would require a treatise in itself to examine.

The questions raised here are far from merely academic. The continued influence of the Church in Albora hinges in good part on its continued monopoly of rites of passage. Without this contact, without the years of catechism, without the necessity of having ritual relations with the parish priest, the majority of parishioners might well drift entirely away from the influence of the Church. As long as this attachment to the Church rites of passage continues, the Church will remain a major competitor of the Communist Party for the allegiance of the people of Albora.

7

The Immigrants

Pietro Busi first came to Albora in 1962, when he was assigned to the army barracks in the *quartiere*. There being no work in his Sicilian *paese*, he remained in Albora when he was discharged from the army the following year, finding a job as an assistant barber downtown. Though his job paid little, he cut every corner he could to save money for his two goals: bringing his family to Bologna and getting married. To accomplish these he had to raise enough money to acquire his own barber shop and a suitable apartment for a family. Two years later, his fortunes on the rise, Pietro returned to his village to seek the hand of the girl he had chosen. Though she had only spoken with Pietro two or three times before, she accepted his proposal. Her widowed mother, however, had been less smitten with Pietro, so a wedding by abduction was arranged, with Pietro's uncle acting as the lookout. Faced with the fait accompli, the bride's mother came to accept Pietro and before long had moved into the newlyweds' apartment in Albora.

Pietro also succeeded in bringing his own family, first one of his brothers, then another, and finally his parents and the two youngest boys. Both the elder brothers work as bartenders, helping support their invalid father, while the two youngest brothers attended elementary school. All six of them live in an apartment just outside Albora, where every Monday, Pietro's day off, Pietro, his wife, mother-in-law, and three-year-old child go to visit them. Pietro laments the fact that he sees his sister so seldom, for she lives with her Sicilian husband in Milan, but he realizes he is more fortunate than his wife, who sees few kin, for almost all of them have migrated to Argentina and the United States.

Although Pietro's wife never worked in Sicily, soon after her arrival in Albora she began taking in clothes to mend, thus augmenting a family budget strained by the purchase of a new car. Their son is out of the house much of the day, attending a municipal nursery school six days a week, where he gets a hot lunch, at a cost of twelve dollars per month. Pietro's mother-in-law, though, rarely leaves the apartment, except for her Sunday trip to the church for mass. Her daughter, who in Sicily regularly accompanied her to church, now goes only on the major holidays. Pietro almost never goes to church in Albora, though sometimes on Christmas or Easter he goes to one of the big churches downtown. Soon after moving to Albora, Pietro took out his PCI membership and, later, his wife joined the Party as well.

The success of the Party in Bologna, as in many of the larger cities of northern Italy, is attributable not only to its ability to win the allegiance of long-time city residents but also to its capacity to win over the new immigrants who have been swelling the urban populations. In the case of Bologna, with its strongly Communist hinterland,[1] the challenge for the PCI has not come from the large numbers of immigrants from the province (Ardigò 1959, 1963), but rather from the growing number of immigrants from Southern Italy, *i meridionali*. As many of these people come from areas in which the Church is at the center of community life and the Communists are a persecuted minority, large-scale Southern immigration could undermine Communist hegemony and strengthen the Church. Yet, in fact, no such erosion of Party strength has occurred in Bologna. Just why this has been the case, why the Church has not profited from this influx, is the question to which we now turn.

Prejudice and politics

Prejudice against Southerners is widespread in the North and appears to be a worsening problem (Anfossi 1962:180). At the root of this prejudice are the pronounced socioeconomic differences between North and South: the North is industrial, the South is rural; the North enjoys a relatively high standard of living, but the Southern standard of living is one of the lowest in Europe (Lopreato 1967:51). Because of this economic disparity, Southerners by the tens of thousands have, in the postwar years, poured into the cities of the North. Whereas just 11 percent of Bologna's immigrants were from the South in 1951, 23 percent of the 1970 immigrants came from the *Mezzogiorno* (Bologna 1966: graph 3; Bologna 1971:53).[2] The rate of Southern immigration to Albora, as one of Bologna's poorest *quartieri*, is even higher, with 28 percent of Albora's immigrants in 1970 coming from the South and approximately 12 percent of the *quartiere* population Southern born.

Anti-Southerner feeling has been an important basis of Catholic–Communist solidarity in Albora, providing an identity that cuts across the Church–Party split. The native Communist in Albora has two identities – Bolognese and Communist – which lead to different and conflicting social action. Which identity determines behavior depends both on the situation in which interaction takes place and on personal factors, most notably how militant a Party mem-

Table 23. *Immigrant population by zone of origin, 1970 immigrants*

	Albora		Bologna	
Origin	No.	%	No.	%
Province of Bologna				
Mountains	8	3.9	580	4.6
Hills	12	5.8	1,779	14.2
Plains	27	13.1	1,437	11.5
Total province	47	22.8	3,796	30.3
Other provinces of Emilia	46	22.4	2,279	18.2
Total Emilia	93	45.2	6,075	48.1
Other regions				
Northern Italy	26	12.6	1,783	14.3
Central Italy	27	13.1	1,188	9.5
Southern Italy	42	20.4	1,845	14.8
Insular Italy	16	7.8	912	7.3
Total other regions	111	53.9	5,728	45.9
Italy	204	99.1	11,803	94.4
Foreign	2	1.0	705	5.6
Total	206	100.1	12,508	100.0

Note: The official figures tend to be deflated, for they refer only to cases of people who renounce their previous home as their permanent domicile. Thus, for example, a Southern immigrant who moves to Bologna and who works there for years may not be listed in the census if he indicates his Southern hometown as his "permanent" home.

Source: Comune di Bologna 1971:58.

ber the person is. In some sense, though, the Catholic–Communist division can be conceived of as a family feud, with the whole family (of Northerners) recognizing its common identity in opposition to nonfamily members, the Southern immigrants. This can even be seen in the behavior of children, whose parents rarely are concerned about the Church versus PCI allegiance of their small child's playmates, but often do warn them against playing with the "dirty" or "ill-mannered" Southern children.

The very term *immigrato* carries a distinctly pejorative connotation in Albora. The people living in Buca, the decrepit settlement whose 100-year-old stucco buildings are crumbling, are stigmatized by being *immigrati* and poor, the two conditions being associated in the minds of the Alborese. Buca, it is often said, is full of illiterate immigrants too lazy to work and so lacking in willpower that they spawn hordes of children. Referred to as *vagabondi*, it is said that the inhabitants would rather go on welfare than do a day's work.

Although the Alborese are extremely chauvinistic about Bologna, any trace of comparable sentiments by Southerners is met with anger. One woman's comments are typical. In speaking of her dislike for an elderly Southern woman, she explained: "I can't stand how she's always praising Sicily. If it's so great there, why did she leave in the first place?" In the opinion of many Bolognese, the South is the refuse heap of Italy, in terms of people, economy, mores, and politics. The Southerner in Albora is thought to be too lazy to work and his children too lazy to study. Thus the fact that one lives in poverty and the other is failed in school is seen by most Alborese as the fault of the Southerners themselves.

One evening in February, at one of the bars in Albora, a drunken card player jumped up from the table, took a pistol out of his pocket, and shot his card partner. Both the murderer and his victim were Southerners living in Buca, but another man, the Bolognese bartender, was seriously wounded when he tried to disarm the assailant. For days this event was the main topic of conversation in Albora, and the comments were familiar ones – the Southerners are no good; all they bring is trouble. The topic of the Southern influx to Albora was brought to the fore:

Buca is a bad zone, full of Southerners, bad people. They don't want to work. The Southerners are mostly rotten; there may be a few decent Southerners, but mostly they're no good. They don't have any courage. If they get in an argument, right away they use guns. One of them shot another here just Sunday night, right here at the bar. The man was drunk out of his mind, just like a Southerner. Thankfully, the City isn't going to let any more of them move into Buca.

The sixty-year-old man who made this statement, it should be noted, is a Communist member and past activist. The murderer was a fellow comrade, a member of his Party section.

Three days after the killing, the topic was still being heatedly discussed, with the following discussion between a woman and a man in a bar indicative of the tone and content:

Woman: Everybody's talking about Sunday night's murder at the bar. The murderer is a Southerner. He has four children here, four children down South, and another one on the way. Those Southerners! Now three families are ruined. The only one I care about is the bartender. He's a good man. The man who was killed was a good-for-nothing himself. No one is going to mourn for him. He was always drunk. He was a Southerner himself. You ought to talk to this man here, he was there just a few minutes before the shooting.

Man: I've lived here for forty years and there have never been any murders here that I know of, except for some Southerners like these. You never see any Bolognese do anything like that. If a Bolognese gets in an argument, he'll talk it over, or at worst he'll punch someone. He'd never think of using a gun against anyone. The South has an entirely different set of customs; it's altogether different from here. If someone has his pride injured he'll just go get a gun and shoot you. We have a lot of them here, a lot of them. They're ugly people [*brutta gente*].

Although the Bolognese deny that their *razzismo* is comparable to white racism in the United States, some of their remarks have an uncanny similarity: "Uva used to be a very nice area until a few years ago. There were a lot of good people living there. But then when some of the Southerners started moving in, all the good people moved out. Now it's not so nice anymore."

In the eyes of the Southerner

The Southern immigrants in Albora clearly perceive this strong anti-Southerner prejudice, and few Southerners differentiate between Communists and Catholics in identifying the sources of this prejudice. For the immigrant, the most important social dividing line in Albora is that between Northerner and Southerner, as is reflected in the remarks of one particularly discontended Southern immigrant in Albora:

The Bolognese are always claiming, among themselves, that we Southerners aren't up to them in intelligence or in industriousness or in anything else. But it isn't true; it isn't true at all. Up here they have big mouths, but when it comes to a test the Southerner always does better than they do. They keep to themselves. Even at work they always keep to themselves with other Bolognesi; they form their own clique and, no doubt, bad mouth those from the South; they're always criticizing. We Southerners try to get together with them, but just as soon as they see that there's a group of them, they leave you and go off to their side. And they say, "If you don't like it here, why don't you go back where you came from?" And I always tell them that if there were work back in my village I would never have come to Bologna; Bologna rubs me the wrong way.

In day-to-day interaction, whether in bars, the courtyards, or elsewhere, Southerners tend to socialize with other Southerners. Every day in the PSC bar, for example, the Southerners present sit together at one or more tables, though if they are Communists they may be greeted by their Northern comrades as they enter. The housing patterns reinforce this social segregation, for the Southern immigrants are heavily concentrated in the poorest housing zones of the *quartiere*. On Sundays the Southerners often visit their relatives or *paesani* living in Bologna. At these weekly gatherings they can speak in their own dialect and talk nostalgically of their *paese*.

Further alienating the Southerners from the PCI, beyond these social, cultural, and economic differences, are the political attitudes of the Northern Communists, stemming in part from orthodox Marxist dogma. In the South the PCI is organizationally weak and, according to the belief of many Alborese Communists, the Church is at the center of village social life. Thus the Southerners are viewed suspiciously, presumed to be Church and DC partisans, if not Fascists, and to have been indoctrinated in anticommunism. The Marxist conception of the role of the *Lumpenproletariat* tends to reinforce this antagonism; the Southern immigrants are viewed as opportunistic, ready to join whatever party – Communist, Christian Democratic, or Fascist – offers them the greatest immediate material benefits.

Indeed, there is a fair amount of political cynicism among the Southern immigrants, as is reflected in the remarks of one thirty-five-year-old man:

Here, the majority is all Communist, while down South it isn't. On this account, too, they look at us askance, because they say that we are Democrats (DC), and that because of us the Party doesn't win, because the majority are Southerners.

In the village where I was born, one time there was a Communist Secretary. He had organized a section; he had done everything. But they said that he was doing bad things, that he was doing certain things that he shouldn't do, and then they arrested him; they arrested him and he was never seen again.

I say that any party is fine as long as it gives everyone work so that we can all eat. Not that we must make a big jump ahead, but at least so that we can eat a piece of bread. For me the Communists are all right, the Socialists are all right; all the parties are all right, just as long as they stay calm and as long as they don't give us a lot of baloney, as long as they give us jobs.

These remarks illustrate a number of points already discussed. First, many migrants realize that the Communists are suspicious of them because of the perceived anticommunism of the South. Second, coming from a village setting where in many cases the Communists were a minor and persecuted force, the Southerner may be wary about being associated with the Party. Third, many Southerners recognize no important differences between the parties in dealing with their most pressing problem: economic well-being for themselves and their families.

The Church and the DC

Despite the popular image of the Southerners' life as being organized around the local church, few Southerners in Albora attend church with any regularity.[3] Southern men are virtually absent from Sunday mass, and no more than a fifth of the immigrant women attend Sunday mass on a regular basis; only the older women attend mass in a decidedly higher proportion than their Northern counterparts. Southern women over sixty years of age probably outnumber all the rest of the Southern immigrants attending Sunday mass in the *quartiere*.

Although systematic data on church attendance of the immigrants in their natal *paesi* are lacking, many of the migrants maintained that they used to frequent church more often before their move north. Many of the immigrants attribute their nonattendance to the different role of the Church in Albora, compared to its role in their *paese*, a comparison made in the following remarks by a Southern man:

Religion is felt more in the South. In the South, in every place I've been, you hear the church bell ring first thing in the morning and then the priest goes into the church. That gives you notice that the church is already open. They also have the ceremonies for all the holidays, while here the Camolia Church is falling apart. In my hometown there's a beautiful church, a church that would knock your eyes out. Down South the church is almost like a family, because when it's Sunday everyone goes to church in the morning, and then they have those *feste* and they all go. Here everyone has money, and they go dancing or to the movies or to the ocean. Who goes to church? Nobody. If you go to church here, the people look at you crooked, because that means you're a Christian Democrat and not a Communist.

You see all the people at the Communist *festa*; you see how many people there are, eating and drinking? Well, if it were a Christian Democratic *festa*, no one would go. Everybody would just pass by; no one would stop.

The women's alienation from the Church is also considerable, particularly considering the tradition of women attending Sunday mass in the South. Like the men, the women refer to the different role of the Church in Albora in explaining their changed behavior. As one woman said:

Things are totally different here. The Church here just isn't at the heart of the community the way it is in Sicily. In the communities in Sicily the Church has many *feste*, and these are at the center of community life. Here in Camolia the Church isn't very important. They just have the one procession through the streets in October. We used to have a lot more back home.

Indeed, this woman, who attended Sunday mass unfailingly in her home town, became a PCI member with her husband within two years of moving to Albora. She voices no hostility toward the Church; there is little evidence of any change in her religious beliefs; yet her behavior has changed dramatically.

The alienation of the Southerners from the DC is obviously related to their alienation from the Church. The route of recruitment to the DC that has been earlier described – that is, recruitment of churchgoers – fails to bring the Southerners into the DC net. Although a number of Southern women do attend church, as noted earlier, women generally follow their husbands into the Christian Democratic party. This is accentuated among the Southerners by the stronger norms proscribing women's political participation. Perhaps half a dozen of the forty local DC members are Southerners, a significant percentage in terms of the small section but an insignificant proportion of Albora's immigrant population. None of the officials of the Albora DC section is a Southerner.

The alienation of the Southerners from the DC is attributable not only to their alienation from the Church but also to the class composition of the DC and particularly the DC leadership. Whereas a large proportion of the Albora DC membership is of middle- and upper-class status, and the top leadership of the section is of upper-class status, the Southern immigrants are overwhelmingly manual laborers. The anti-Southerner prejudices common to both Communists and Christian Democrats are compounded in the case of the DC by this socioeconomic chasm.

The Southerners and the PCI

The winning of Southern support has been one of the most important and most frequently discussed problems of the PCI (Tarrow 1967a). Historically, the PCI has proclaimed the duty of the more highly developed Party cadre in the North to lead the way for the Party in the *Mezzogiorno*. Referring back to Gramsci, the Party proclaims: "Only with the support and the guidance of the working class of the North can the peasants of the South liberate themselves from the conditions of exploitation and of subordination and shatter the bloc of reactionary power" (PCI 1972:131). To meet these goals, Northern comrades must treat their Southern brethren as equals: "The substance of the question is to defeat any tendency to break the bond which unites the workers' forces of the North with the great popular masses of the South who are struggling for the restructuring of Italian society" (Occhetto 1972:3).

It is in this context that PCI–Southerner relations in Albora must be seen. Both the national Party norms and the increasing numbers of Southern immigrants to Albora make the inclusion of Southerners an urgent task of the local Party organization. At the same time, the anti-Southerner prejudice of the Alborese militates against such an inclusion. The integralist impetus of the Communist world is compromised by the solidary behavior of Communist and Catholic Bolognese against the Southern immigrants.

Yet the Party has thus far avoided any serious Southern threat to its supremacy in Albora. The immigrants, once established in the *quartiere*, begin to support the PCI and, as has been noted, keep a goodly distance from the Church and the DC. Examination of the 1972 election results for the twelve electoral seats of Albora lends support to this observation. As can be seen in Table 24, a high concentration of Southern immigrants generally corresponds with a high PCI vote and a low DC vote. The zones of highest concentration of Southerners are generally the zones of lowest socioeconomic status. Correcting for the PCI bias of these lower- and working-class voters, it appears that the Southerners vote much like their neighbors. There is certainly no indication that the Southerners vote disproportionately for the DC, with one instructive exception. The exception is provided by the voting district (entry 1 in the

Table 24. *Southerm immigrants and voting in Albora, 1972 assembly elections (listed in decreasing order of Southerners in district)*[a]

Voting seat	Southerners as % of all voters	% PCI vote	% DC vote
1	20.2	53.0	18.3
2	18.5	71.5	10.0
3	17.7	70.6	11.2
4	16.3	70.2	13.3
5	12.6	74.7	11.0
6	12.5	71.1	13.1
7	12.3	59.4	19.2
8	9.4	56.4	23.0
9	9.2	60.1	15.8
10	6.4	69.0	10.3
11	5.1	54.9	18.7
12	2.9	64.1	18.0
Quartiere	11.8	64.1	15.7
Voting seats 1–6		69.9	12.7
7–12		58.3	18.7

[a] Based on a 20% random sampling of voting lists.[4-]

table) that in 1972 contained a new public housing project, inhabited largely by Southern immigrants. These people had entered the *quartiere* just a few months before the election and, moreover, lived in the only part of the *quartiere* lacking a PCI-controlled cooperative bar. In short, they had not yet been integrated into the Communist-dominated social structure of Albora.

Although the vote among Albora's immigrants is favorable from the PCI viewpoint, Southerners are underrepresented on the Party's membership lists. Taking the Vapori section as an example, we find that only 6.9 percent of the section membership consists of Southern immigrants, though the zone of its jurisdiction has a 12.1 percent

Southern adult population.[5] PCI membership of the Southerners is low relative to that of the Northerners in Albora, but it is many times that prevalent in their home towns. Although there are only 1.9 PCI members for every 100 residents in the South, as much as fifteen times that rate pertains in Albora. The rate of Party membership by the Southerners in the *quartiere* is thus intermediate between the rate in the South and the general rate of membership in Albora.

The rate of participation in Party affairs by the Southerners in Albora is extremely low. None of the forty Party officials in the *quartiere* is a Southerner, and only one Southerner is active in local Party affairs. Few Southerners attend Party meetings, where they appear to feel ill at ease among the Northerners and hesitant to speak publicly. Indeed, both Southerners observed to speak at Party meetings began their remarks by apologizing for their dialects.

If Southern men are largely absent from Albora's political activities, the immigrant women are entirely divorced from any public political work, including the various PCI-related voluntary organizations. For example, when asked if any of the UDI activists were immigrants, the Albora Women's League head responded with a sigh: "Ah! If we ever got an immigrant activist that would be some conquest!" She elaborated:

It's hard as hell to get to them. There are some men whom you can reach a little. But the women . . . it's always the same story. If you talk to them a little they'll say, "Beh! my husband thinks about those things. I'm a woman, I stay home." They are just submissive, they still haven't understood anything. And to make them understand, who knows how long that will take?

The lack of participation of the Southern immigrant women in the PCI, most evident from their absence from Party meetings, is also reflected in the local PCI membership rolls. Only 23 percent of the Southerners belonging to the Vapori section are women (compared to 43 percent of all Albora Party members), and 60 percent of these come from the province of Rome, the most northerly point in the Southern region (*La Società* 1977:58–9). This reflects the pattern prevalent in the South: In 1972 only 14.1 percent of the Southern PCI membership was female, compared to 30.1 percent in the Red Belt and over 40 percent in Bologna (Barbagli and Corbetta 1978:23). Although the Southern women join the PCI in Albora in greater proportion than is the practice in the South, no stunning breakthrough has yet been made. The Southern immigrant woman is unaccustomed to participating in community politics, and this background, her family-focused social life, and her feelings of social exclusion combine to prevent her from becoming involved.

Conclusions

The Southern immigrants in Albora are stigmatized, and the stigma that divides them from the native Bolognese population mitigates the social distinction between Catholics and Communists in the *quartiere*.

Why, then, given the hostility of the Communists, do the Southerners support the Party and reject the Church and the DC? The reason is that the immigrants do what they can to adapt themselves to the local social milieu, to minimize the ill effects of their stigma. The Church is largely abandoned because it is seen as peripheral to local social life and public allegiance to the Church is viewed as socially hazardous. Thus allegiance to the Church may be a more locally bound phenomenon than often thought, dependent on the social role of the church in the community rather than on a universalist ideology.[6]

In addition to the social forces operating in the *quartiere*, most immigrants are influenced by their experience at work in other parts of Bologna. Although no fieldwork was conducted in workplaces outside Albora, the work experience clearly puts the immigrants shoulder to shoulder with an overwhelmingly Communist native workforce. The political importance of this work experience is emphasized in a study of immigrant behavior in Turin: "For these people, largely young men distant from the social environment of their hometown, the workplace, with its daily experiences, represents a powerful modelling force for new behavior" (Zaccone Derossi 1962:235). Although, in the case of the immigration to Albora, we are dealing with women as much as men, the same considerations apply.

Though neither the Church nor the PCI has dedicated itself to winning over the Southern immigrants in Albora to the extent of campaigning actively against anti-Southern prejudice, the PCI has been the relative victor of the competition for the support of the newcomers. The fear that the Southerners would constitute a bastion of Church and DC support has proved to be unfounded. Indeed, the Southerners are now recognized by the local priests as the population furthest removed from Albora church life. Although the Southerners are not active in public political affairs, they have fallen in line with Alborese voting behavior. By identifying with the Communists, the new immigrant can make some claim to the sympathies of the general population of the *quartiere* and can establish his membership in the local collectivity. Though this claim to in-group status is tarnished by the stigma of being a Southerner, it is a serious claim; to slight a comrade on account of anti-Southerner prejudice is a normative offense in the PCI. Membership in the Party provides a means of establishing a bond of equality and ongoing social relationships with all other Party members in the *quartiere*. Such a claim to equal status and general social acceptance cannot be made as well through the Church, both because the Church does not have the same official egalitarian ideology as the PCI and because only a small minority of the local population identifies itself with the Church.

8

Storefront Church

Like most of Uva's buildings, the four-story structure was old and decaying, the home of several poor immigrant families who had not yet made their way into public housing. That this building was unlike all others in the *quartiere*, though, became obvious as soon as the metal roller protecting the ground floor storefront was raised, revealing a translucent glass wall adorned by a small red cross. Though the appearance of this Church outpost set tongues wagging in September of 1971, few people ventured in to slake their curiosity. If they had, a small sign identifying the premises as *Comunità di San Giuseppe* would have greeted them in the hallway. Inside, the wall of a two-room apartment had been torn down to erect the sanctuary of the new church, whose austerity contrasted starkly with the richly decorated interior of the two old established churches in the *quartiere* (see Photograph 9). In the place of pews stood simple benches bereft of kneeling boards; in the place of the large, raised altar, stood a modest table, covered with a white cloth, some flowers, and a candle. And don Francesco, the young priest, wore not the traditional robe and white collar of his colleagues of Albora, but a black turtle-necked sweater or open-collared shirt. In a room on the other side of the dark hall was the church library, with its illustrated biblical tales and assorted Communist publications.

9. The austere interior of the storefront church chapel.

It was not fortuitous that the new church was established in the poorest part of Albora – Uva and neighboring Buca– the area having the highest proportion of Southern immigrants. These socially marginal Alborese were to be the main targets of the storefront Church's appeal. The church reflected a new strategy in the Catholic competition with the Communists, based on the premise that only a change in ideology and political policy of the Church could stem the Communist erosion of the Catholic world. Only by embracing the cause of the poor and by rejecting all ties with the DC could the Church hope to regain the allegiance of the masses.[1]

In examining the way this strategy was applied in Albora

and the reaction of the PCI and the local people to the new church, two issues will be considered. The first concerns the importance of ideology in determining people's allegiance to Church or PCI. It has often been claimed that Italians have been repelled by the political conservatism of the Church, flocking in reaction to the Communist Party, seen as the champion of the poor against the rich. Almond (1954) and others have proposed, following this logic, that the most effective means for combatting the PCI would be a politically more progressive Church. Ironically, the official PCI analysis of the Church shares the same premise, that the rejection of the Church by the masses is a product of the Church's conservative political ideology.

The advent of the storefront church is interesting in this regard because it provides the people with an alternative political ideology within the Catholic world. The success of the new church should provide a measure of the importance of ideological factors in Church allegiance. To put it simply: Is allegiance to the PCI based on the ideological tenets of anticapitalism? Can the Church defeat the PCI by co-opting its ideological appeal or are ideological factors less important in the local-level struggle than other, social factors?

Second, the storefront church provides a test case for the official PCI policy of conciliation with the Church. As discussed in Chapter 5, publicly the PCI only opposes the use of the Church for politically conservative purposes. "Progressive" church movements are applauded, and PCI cooperation with progressive churches is formally endorsed. We have expressed the view that this policy is essentially contradictory and un-Marxist. The test of whether it is contradictory is in its application on the local level. Given official Party doctrine we should expect to find the PCI in Albora solicitous toward the new church.

Observations to the contrary provide support for our argument and call for a reexamination of the relationship between official Party norms and local Party practice.

Church of the poor

The establishment of the new church in Albora was largely the work of its founding pastor, don Francesco. The twenty-nine-year-old priest, the child of a poor Bolognese family and a seminary student during the years of the Second Vatican Council, was attracted by the movement whose central symbol was the "church of the poor." As he explained in his proposal to the bishop, he wanted to work toward the creation of a new kind of church:

It is part of the conception of the Church that had been somewhat buried, somewhat clandestine, but which with Vatican II has been rediscovered, that is, the Church is principally defined as a church of the poor and that is interested principally in the poor, not to use them or to exploit them politically or economically, but rather to serve them in the spirit of Jesus.

In consultation with the priest of Camolia, the bishop's office assigned don Francesco the northwestern corner of Albora for the establishment of his parish. The people of Albora were puzzled by the appearance of the storefront church. Many assumed that don Francesco had been exiled for some misdeed, being placed in the most miserable of ecclesiastical circumstances. This surmise was in fact not entirely inaccurate. Don Francesco's unorthodox theology had gotten him in trouble in his previous parish in the nearby *quartiere* of San Pietro. The lay leadership of the San Pietro parish consisted primarily of the same middle-class individuals who formed the backbone of the local DC organization. Though the leadership was middle class, the bulk of the parishioners were working class, and don

Francesco propounded his theology of Church poverty, his opposition to the DC as a party of the bourgeoisie, and his opposition to Church support of the DC. The lay leaders of the parish soon petitioned the bishop to have him replaced.

The physical novelties of the new church in Albora reflect the symbolism of the "church of the poor." Don Francesco, indeed, seized on his parishioners' questions about these innovations to proselytize for the Church:

At first, the people said: "Do you call this a Church? It doesn't look anything like a church." And I let them speak on a bit, and I told them: "What is it that makes a church? After all, Jesus was not ashamed to be born in a hovel, a cave of pastors. He, the son of God, was not ashamed to be surrounded by dampness and dirt."

In addition to these theological justifications, don Francesco took advantage of these discussions to bring his social message to the people:

During my Easter visits to people's homes, there was almost always an argument over when we would build a new church. I told them that for many reasons I did not want to build a new church, but the primary reason I gave is that they are living without decent housing now, they live in houses that are not for men but for animals. So, I said, the problem of a new church shall come up later, only after their housing problems are resolved through the efforts of all of us.

In order to bring this message to all those in the parish, don Francesco began issuing parish bulletins. Appropriately enough, they were mimeographed, in contrast to the slick printed publications of the two old churches of Albora. A new version of the political ideology of the Church was presented:

It is true. Fear, complicity with the political powers that be, with the privileges of the Concordat, the wealth and the hypocrisy–

like the commerce in the Sacraments–are present in the Church of Christ. But these are the heredity of sin which the Spirit will steadily purify. There is a new face of the Church which the Spirit is creating. We must work for this: a church stripped of means of power, poor and one with the poor as was its teacher.

He thus expounded a vision of the Church that contrasted sharply with that presented by the other churches of Albora, a Church that repudiated the powers-that-be, that recognized its past errors in taking the part of the rich at the expense of the poor.

As might be expected, these views did not endear don Francesco to the other priests of the *quartiere*. The relations between the new priest and the parish priest of Camolia were formal and diplomatic, the disapproval each had for the other's mode of operation never being publicly expressed. Don Francesco never went to don Mario, the previous pastor of the people of Uva, for advice or information on parishioners. This hostility, however, was not generally perceived by the Uva parishioners. Not atypical, indeed, were the comments by one individual that the Uva church originated when don Mario called on his good friend don Francesco to help him out with his oversized parish.

While rebelling against the conservatism of the Church, don Francesco was also sharply critical of the PCI. He recognized that the Communist domination of his new parish made his efforts to draw people to the Church extremely difficult.

The people are afraid to go to mass because they will be thought supporters of the DC. The PCI has tried to set itself up in direct competition to the Church, establishing its own parish organization on much the same lines as the organization of the Church. In taking over the control of leisuretime activity, for example, the PCI has gained control of the cooperative bar, the only social center in Uva. It is only human for the people to want to pass their time at the bar, so the result is they want to be on good terms with the Communists. In short, Uva is a Communist fiefdom: They truly have a thousand percent control here. For example, I am almost certain of being watched in the moves that I make; everyone knows them. I have the impression that they fear me, that they fear I will whittle away the supremacy they enjoy over the people.

The means used by the Communists to discredit the Church focus on the identification of the Church with the DC, with the rich and powerful. For don Francesco, attracting people to the new Church meant combatting this image propagated by the Communists:

I think it's difficult for the people here to participate in the mass, given that there are still many prejudices in the zone. In fact, I have heard it said that those who participate in the mass are Christian Democrats, that I'm a Christian Democrat. But it's just not true. I think that people, and especially the men and the boys, feel very conditioned by this thinking, and I have the impression that the Party does nothing in this to serve the truth.

Don Francesco sought to explain to the people that the Church is not and should not be identified with the DC. The task was to portray his church as on the side of the poor and anticapitalist forces, struggling together with the working class and the poor to create a new and more just society. In short, the goal was to present an image of the Church that was substantially similar in ideological appeal to the Communist Party appeal to the downtrodden.

Like the other priests of Albora, don Francesco found himself in a defensive position in the Communist *quartiere*. However, whereas the defensiveness of the Andara and Camolia priests was expressed in reaction–that is, by direct counterattack–don Francesco's defensiveness was characterized by protestation. For the successful execution of the new Church strategy, he had to protest his innocence of anticommunism and his and the Church's independence from the DC. The extent of this defensiveness was hinted at in his second church bulletin, announcing his Easter home visits: "To those who will not receive me as a priest, I ask you to accept me as a man who intends to respect other people's consciences and therefore to get to know everyone without any kind of prejudice, desiring only to recognize the good, the true and the just wherever they may be." The tone was both defensive and conciliatory toward those in the Communist world. Never did he specifically refer to the PCI, but his declaration was clear: This church will not castigate those in the Communist world; rather, it welcomes them. This was part of the larger strategy: to bring people into the social orbit of the new church by establishing supportive social relations with them. If people became friendly with don Francesco and his aides, it was felt, they might be drawn into the church through this friendship. In this vein, don Francesco's top aide remarked: "We face a wall of division in the community between the Communists and the Catholics. This barrier will only be dissolved slowly as people get to know us."

Participation

Insight into some of the strengths and weaknesses of the storefront church can be gained by examining its lay leadership. No one in the parish could be described as a lay leader or Church activist in the way in which we have used the term for the other churches of Albora. Yet the Uva church probably had the most cohesive and active group of lay leaders of any of Albora's churches. The leaders, though, young devotees of don Francesco and his "church of the poor," came from San Pietro, don Francesco's previous parish.

The seven youths who formed the nucleus of the activist

group range in age from sixteen to twenty-five. Deeply affected by the new currents in Italian Catholicism, they had responded enthusiastically to don Francesco's vision of the Church. Resenting their own church for its conservatism and its dismissal of don Francesco, the youths followed the young priest to his new parish, though they continued to live with their parents in San Pietro. The Uva church became for them not only the center of numerous church-oriented activities but the focus of much of their leisure time. Two couples of boyfriend–girlfriend were among the seven, and the group united together regularly for recreation. For example, after Sunday mass each week, the group gathered with don Francesco at one of their homes for an extended lunch, alternating homes from week to week. The youths regularly offered their services to the new church, and the two most active youths worked at the church every day.

These youths are the children of the San Pietro church leaders and their parents range in socioeconomic status from skilled workers to white-collar workers and merchants. All the youths are students, most at the university, and most hold part-time jobs to help pay for their education. Typical is the case of Carlo, don Francesco's most active assistant.

Carlo is twenty-two years old and lives with his parents in San Pietro. His parents are DC activists and his father is a DC *quartiere* counselor. Carlo refers to them as right-wing. Under parental influence, Carlo was active in DC youth activities until five years ago. Then, coming under the influence of Vatican II and some of the left-wing movements in the Church, he abandoned the DC and began looking for other forms of Church activity. He wandered from group to group, independent Catholic social action organizations, but found none of them satisfactory. At that time don Francesco came to San Pietro and, as Carlo

acknowledges, "he changed my whole life." Together with
the other San Pietro youths, Carlo became committed to
the conception of the "church of the poor," and he devoted
all his free time to aiding don Francesco in its construction.
All the political parties, as he sees it, are corrupt, and the
DC is the most corrupt of all, founded on religious hypocrisy and the rule of the rich.

The ties binding these youths to don Francesco are deep.
Not only do they spend hours together each week at the
church and in each other's homes, but they plan their
vacations together. In the summer of 1972, three of the
youths went with don Francesco for their vacation, camp-
ing in Sardinia. They also went on a pilgrimage to the
former parish of don Milani, one of the most prominent
figures of the revolt within the Italian Church. In addition,
don Francesco and some of the youths discussed sharing
an apartment in Uva.

Since participation at the leadership level is limited to
"outsiders" previously committed to the new church, we
must look at mass attendance in order to determine the
extent of popular participation in the Uva church. These
figures reveal that, as of its first year of operation, the
church of the poor had not succeeded in changing the
balance of power in the *quartiere*. The same low level of
popular participation in Sunday mass is found in the new
church as is found elsewhere in Albora. Indeed, the rate
of attendance is lower than the *quartiere*-wide rate, as indicated by the data in Table 25, collected at five regular
Sunday masses (the storefront church holds but one mass
each Sunday) from January through March of 1972. With
a total parish population of approximately 1000, attendance
at the new church in its first year of operation was proportionately less than that of the poorly attended churches
of Andara and Camolia. If we subtract the San Pietro
outsiders from the congregation, we find average attend-

Table 25. *Sunday mass attendance at storefront church*

Date	Total present	Men	Women	Children	San Pietro youths
January 16	44	2	12	22	8
January 23	48	2	15	22	9
February 13	42	2	19	14	7
February 27	43	4	20	14	5
February 12	31	2	12	11	6
Mean	42	2	16	17	7

ance at Sunday mass of only thirty-five parishioners, or 3.5 percent of the parish population, a total almost entirely composed of women and children. Only two men in the parish attended mass with any regularity, and the men who even occasionally appeared at mass were few.

Examination of attendance at the special holiday masses at the storefront church reveals a similar pattern. Midnight mass in 1971 was attended by seventy-five people, of whom fifteen were youths from outside the parish. By Easter Sunday mass, which may be a better indication of the first year, because by then everyone in the area was familiar with the new church, ninety-two people attended, seven of them San Pietro youths. Of the eighty-five local parishioners in attendance, only seven were adult men, the rest being women and children. Male nonattendance was even more dramatically illustrated by the First Communion service, held on a Sunday early in June. A total of sixty people attended, including twelve children who were celebrating their First Communion. Only six men attended, the two regulars plus just four fathers. Thus over the course of the first year, the storefront church made practically no headway in attracting men and did not seem to have increased the rate of attendance of women or children.

If the ideological and social appeals of the new church had little initial effect on the adults of Uva, don Francesco did succeed in bringing to the church a number of children whose contact with the Catholic world would undoubtedly have been much more limited otherwise. Working with the children, in fact, took up more of the church's time than any other activity. In part, this was a tacit admission of inability to change the ways of the adults in the zone.

The principal children-oriented program of the storefront church was the *doposcuola*, literally an after-school. The church provided remedial lessons each afternoon to over a dozen elementary and junior high school students. Most of these youths were Southern immigrants whose inferior school background and problems with dialect were the source of much public school difficulty. Although the *doposcuola* began spontaneously when a child asked don Francesco for aid with her schoolwork and then told her schoolmates of the service, it was in keeping with the church-of-the-poor concept as enunciated by the renowned don Milani (Milani 1957, 1970; Barbiana 1970).

Through the *doposcuola*, which was taught jointly by don Francesco and the San Pietro youths, children were brought into the church whose parents never attended. Although don Francesco was careful to state that all were welcome at the *doposcuola* and that religious topics would not be discussed, a group of youths was formed through the *doposcuola* for whom the Uva church served as social center. For the first time in their lives, the Church had become their central point of extra-family orientation. Frequenting the church every day, the children not only received lessons, but spent time cleaning the chapel and running errands as well as attending mass every Sunday.

They also regularly went as a group to a nearby park where don Francesco and the San Pietro youths led them in play.

While attracting a number of youngsters to the church, don Francesco's "progressive" ideology antagonized some individuals who otherwise might have supported the church. The Uva parishioners with public DC ties would have nothing to do with the left-wing priest. In fact, they continued their weekly attendance of the Camolia church despite having been notified that they were now in the Uva parish. To give but the most prominent example, Giuseppe Rocco is a rich farmer and landlord whose land and home fall within the boundaries of the new parish. For many years one of the pillars of the Camolia church, he has often been rewarded for his contributions of time and money by being given the honor of carrying the statue of the Madonna on his shoulders in the annual parish procession. He is a public supporter of the DC and regularly attends local DC campaign meetings. Rocco continued to attend mass at Camolia, where he socialized with the other lay leaders of the Camolia church, DC supporters like himself. He never set foot inside the Uva parish and never spoke with don Francesco. Don Francesco himself recognized this hostility:

These families have very close personal relations tying them to Camolia, relations which have existed for years. But I have the impression that essentially the reasons are more of a political than a religious nature, attributable to the political position openly taken by don Mario, as we have seen in the last election. The big and the little *padroni* here find in the priest a local authority with whom they can ally to form a common authority; so they keep going there.

Don Francesco's ideological position not only separated him from these well-known, wealthy DC and Church leaders, but also created friction with the working-class DC supporters of the parish, who otherwise might be expected to have strong bonds with the new church. These people, many of whom sought to conceal their anti-Communist sentiments in the Communist *quartiere*, expected to find in the new priest a political confidante with whom they could share triumph and defeat, and perhaps through whom they could derive some material benefit from their pro-Church politics. Thus it was not only the Communists of Uva who assumed that don Francesco was a DC supporter in disguise, but also the adherents of the DC:

In fact they consider me a Christian Democrat politically just the same. In two families that I went to see after the election – because for just those reasons I avoided visiting anyone before the election – two families immediately began telling me that *we* won the election, etc. And then I had to explain a little; I don't know if they understood. I said: Look, I'm not here to represent any party; I'm here to represent the Lord and his Word, to create the unity of the children of God around his altar."

That don Francesco felt it advisable not to visit any families during the campaign period is indicative of his defensiveness vis-à-vis the Communist world. Yet despite his sermons, his church bulletin writings and his personal conversations, the idea of a church independent of the DC proved difficult for his parishioners to accept.

Don Francesco's political posture proved a disability in attracting parishioners in another way as well, for by divorcing himself from the DC, the young priest renounced the political patronage system through which the Church had served and influenced numerous parishioners through the years. The system of *raccomandazione*, of the priest acting as a broker for his parishioners in dealing with the rich and the politically powerful, is largely dependent on the priest's ties with the DC. By declaring his independence from the DC, don Francesco removed one of the bases for popular allegiance to the Church. The young priest bore the burden of this marginal political position:

The priest ought to help a man get a job, but without compromising his [the priest's] personal liberty. The problem is that the employers who are willing to do a favor for the priest are apt to soon ask for an exchange on a political or social level. They'll ask that the priests avoid any positions which will hurt them.

Recently a man came to ask for a letter of introduction to get a job working for the city. He wanted a job as a streetsweeper, and everyone knows that to get City employment you have to have the support of a politician, that the positions are always assigned on the basis of the internal political forces. Thus the PCI, having the strong majority, dispenses a majority of the positions, recommending its members for them. Likewise the DC, etc. Well, I told this man that I couldn't, and I explained the reason. I told him that I could speak with a DC or a PCI politician, but then afterwards what would they ask me in exchange? They would do me a favor, I'm sure, but I have to hold on to my personal liberty, to the liberty of the community. I cannot allow it to be conditioned, so to speak, by the bosses, by those who have the power to hire and fire.

Thus, by not acting as a DC-backed broker, don Francesco offered the people of Uva no alternative to the PCI brokerage system, further tying them to the Communist world. He has cut off one of the important bases of local Church support.

The Communist response

The leaders of the Giuliari PCI section looked on with concern as the new church was established in their backyard. Until then there had been just one uncontested social center in Uva, the building, owned by the Party, which houses the cooperative bar, ARCI, and the Giuliari section itself. There is one other small bar in the area that doubles as a milk store, but the cooperative bar allied with the Party section held an undisputed monopoly on male adult social life in Uva. Though it has a large immigrant population, Uva has been one of the most staunchly Communist areas in Albora, giving over 70 percent of its vote to the PCI. The heads of the cooperative and of ARCI and almost all the storekeepers are PCI members. All public events are sponsored by the Communists, and all complaints about city government are channeled through the local PCI leaders. It was this Communist stronghold that don Francesco entered with his vision of the church of the poor.

According to official PCI policy, the local Party leaders should have extended a warm welcome to this progressive Church movement in their midst. That in fact this did not happen, that the PCI leaders looked on don Francesco from the beginning with decided hostility, is something that came as no surprise to anyone in Uva, including don Francesco. Despite the national PCI position, no one expected there to be anything but conflict between the new church and the PCI.

Although the hostility of the PCI leaders quickly became evident, there were no soap box speeches denouncing the new church or the new priest. The local PCI leaders knew not only that this would have been counterproductive but that it would have led to swift denunciation from the PCI Federation. The antagonism simmered under the surface.

This attitude of the PCI toward the Uva church was expressed, first of all, in the posture assumed by the Giuliari section leaders vis-à-vis don Francesco and the Church. Though don Francesco made a point of trying to greet all his parishioners, the PCI leaders crossed the street to avoid him and often ignored him when they did pass one another. This served not only as notification to don Francesco of the Giuliari section's attitude, but also as an example for the parishioners. None of the PCI leaders ever entered the new church and their example was scrupulously followed by the men of Uva. As we have seen, only two local men regularly frequented Sunday mass, and one of these had been certified by the state to be mentally ill and was regarded by all as deviant. Though the Giuliari PCI leaders sent their children to catechism, none of them attended his children's rites of passage in the church. In 1972 the daughter of the secretary of the Giuliari section was confirmed and the son of another section committee member received First Communion. Though neither father attended the rites, both mothers did.

Even those men who entered the Uva church in a non-religious capacity were subjected to peer pressure. Such was the case of two local unemployed carpenters who were hired by don Francesco to renovate the church building. Though they never went to mass, they were derided by their peers in the Uva cooperative bar for frequenting the church.

Pressure was also applied to those male teen-aged youths who attended the church's *doposcuola*. A few such teenagers came only once. One youth, who was having difficulty with French, came to the church *doposcuola* with obvious trepidation, exhibiting considerable discomfort in the priest's presence. The youth, whose parents are PCI members, was concerned not only about what the others would say of his being in the church but about the new priest's reaction to his Communist Party activities and his absence from Sunday mass.

More dramatic was the case of Pasquale, a fifteen-year-old impoverished Southern immigrant. Stigmatized by poverty and a father in prison, Pasquale was economically responsible for his nine siblings. He was befriended by the youths of the FGCI and much of his leisure time was spent in their company. Having had little formal education, he decided to go to the Uva church to learn English and thus not be the "ignoramus" of the group. He came to the *doposcuola* one afternoon and began his first lesson. This he thoroughly enjoyed, both for the personal attention he was getting and because it offered the prospect of some intellectual accomplishment. He made an appointment for the next day to continue his lessons. As Pasquale walked out of the Uva church, the secretary of the PCI section was waiting outside the front door. They somewhat awkwardly greeted each other. That night, at the FGCI headquarters associated with the section, the Communist secretary called Pasquale into a separate room and spoke with him about his church attendance. Pasquale did not keep his *doposcuola* appointment for the next day, nor did he ever again attend the church *doposcuola*.

Don Francesco's difficulties in establishing a new church in this Communist zone became increasingly evident during the 1972 national election campaign. Despite his own condemnation of the DC and the Church support of the DC, don Francesco was the object of an attempt to discredit his church by linking him to the Christian Democrats. The attempt was not the result of a' calculated fabrication by the PCI leaders. Rather, it may best be understood as an ingrained response to the Church during election time. The majority of the Communist leaders see the Church as the foremost anti-Communist force in their *quartiere*, and they are accustomed at election campaign time to find the local churches operating as the centers of the anti-Communist drive.

Thus rumors to the effect that don Francesco was campaigning for the DC began spreading throughout Uva and throughout the Party organization in Albora. One local PCI leader told people that don Francesco was instructing the aged and the feeble-minded how to vote for the DC. Similar stories circulated, spread by other PCI leaders of

Uva. When the election results were finally in, the local PCI leaders felt their suspicions were vindicated by the Uva PCI vote, which had dropped from 75 percent in 1968 to 70 percent in 1972. There was one man seen as responsible for the PCI decline, don Francesco, and the Uva pastor was denounced at a local PCI leadership meeting for his DC propagandizing.

Conclusions

Despite official Party policy, the Catholic world is treated both as monolithic and anti-Communist by the Party members of Albora. This observation leads to the larger question concerning the actual bases of conflict between the Church and the PCI. The fact that the local PCI organization was antagonistic to the new "progressive" Church movement suggests that degree of ideological compatibility is not directly related to the institutional compatibility of the Party and the Church.

The Church on the local level is not merely a threat to the PCI insofar as it directly campaigns against the Communists and supports the DC. The Church is also a threat by providing an alternative social center, alternative allegiances, and an alternative ideology. Political allegiances are based on social groupings, and any institution that threatens the Communists' social influence in the *quartiere* ultimately threatens its political ascendancy.

Indeed, in some respects the progressive church movement may be more of a threat to the Communist world in Albora than are the traditional, politically conservative churches. The symbolism and arguments used in the past by the Party in Albora to draw people away from the churches, away from the Catholic world, are of little use in combatting the left-wing church. The storefront church could not be accused of flaunting Church opulence in the midst of human need, nor, over the long run, could it be accused of politicking for the rich and the DC.

The co-opting by the church of the symbolism of defender of the oppressed and spokesman of the worker against the bosses may pose more of a threat to the continued appeal of the PCI in the working-class *quartiere* than does the interclassist position of the two old churches. In light of this ideological similarity, indeed, the PCI should find it much more difficult to deal with any attempts at political organizing by the new church. For example, should don Francesco decide to initiate a social action project and ipso facto challenge local PCI political authority, it might be difficult for the Party to provide an adequate response. Any such attempts by the priests of Camolia or Andara could easily be discredited by demonstrating their DC-serving character.

It is, of course, just this co-optation of the political ideological appeal by the "progressive" Church movement that makes it so potentially valuable to the Catholic world in the struggle against the Communist Party. The emergence of a left-wing faction in the Italian Church in response to the rising popularity of a secular left-wing movement is hardly new. Such a strategy was used to bring disaffected elements back into the Catholic orbit in the case of the Catholic peasant leagues of the late nineteenth century and in the case of the early Christian Democrats such as Murri at the turn of the twentieth century. The dissenting Church groups challenge the prevailing conservative political ideology of the Church, but they do not challenge the authority of the hierarchy nor the importance of the unity of the Catholic world. The strength of the Catholic world lies less in the inculcation of a particular ideology than in the creation, on the local level, of a broad web of social allegiances.

This is not to say that all local PCI forces throughout

the country act toward moderate and progressive elements in the Church in a suspicious, antagonistic way. In keeping with the theoretical position we have outlined, we would expect Party–Church relations to be strongly conditioned by the local-level social context. Albora presents us with a case in which the PCI pervades local social life and in which the Church has, to a considerable extent, been socially isolated. It is in this circumstance that the Party is most likely to rebuff any effort on the part of Church forces to launch an untraditional appeal, an appeal aimed at bringing under Church influence segments of the population that had been estranged from the Church.

If we consider a very different social context, one in which it is the Party that is isolated and the Church that is at the center of community life, the Party might well find another response more rewarding. Fortunately, we are able to turn to Stern's study of just such a social setting, found in the Church stronghold of Veneto. Here, as Stern describes it, the greatest problem for the PCI has been establishing its legitimacy at the local level. In struggling to establish its legitimacy, the Party found it disastrous to attack the Church. In fact, its locally perceived illegitimacy is bound to the label, pinned on it by conservative Church forces, of being antireligious and anticlerical. In attempting to overcome this stigmatic symbolism, local Party leaders have in recent years sought to establish ties with moderate and progressive priests and other Catholic leaders. A local Party leader, for example, seized on the opportunity provided by a young priest who was willing to enter into a series of public discussions with him on the common ground shared by Marxism and Catholicism. Here it was the Church, with strong DC urging, that cut short an attempt at Party–Church cooperation (1975:253).

One last question that might be posed here is whether the discrepancy between official Party precepts and local

Party practice is a symptom of poor articulation between national and local Party organization or whether the conflict is in fact built into the system. The answer to this question should be clear from our earlier discussion (Chapter 6). The contradictions stem from PCI reaction to a particular historical circumstance – a conservative Church tied to the ruling national party but enjoying the allegiance of the bulk of the nation's population. It seems unlikely, given both the explicit nature of Marxist and Gramscian doctrine on this point and the actual array of forces on the local level throughout the country, that the PCI national leadership believes an ultimate conciliation of the Communist world and the Catholic world to be likely or desirable. The ability of the Party to sustain this conciliatory position is dependent on the scarcity of left-wing Church groups, that is, Church groups that challenge the PCI to live up to its conciliatory national policy. In this light, churches such as don Francesco's provide the leaders of the PCI in Albora with a dilemma; they must choose between subscribing to formal Party policy and dealing successfully with a threat to their social influence.

If allegiances were primarily based on ideology, we would expect left-wing Church movements to undermine a good deal of Communist support. Yet this view fails to recognize the importance of local social factors. As we have seen, don Francesco succeeded least in attracting people through his specifically ideological appeals (e.g., sermons and church bulletins) and succeeded most where the appeal was almost entirely social (e.g., the *doposcuola*). There is little evidence to support the view that the people of the Communist zone favor the concept of the "church of the poor" over the traditional medieval conception of the rich church. This is indicated not only by lack of mass attendance but also by the behavior of the parishioners on other ritual occasions. For example, the parishioners voiced much opposition to the idea of housing a church in such shabby quarters. Given the simplicity of the chapel, combined with the guitar accompaniment at mass, people were overheard referring to the new church as a dance hall. A church, they claimed, should be something beautiful, something in splendid contrast to their own drab dwellings. Thus of the three women of the parish married during the church's first year of operation, two requested permission to have their weddings held elsewhere, one forthrightly explaining that she did not want to be married in the "dinky" church. Don Francesco's ideology of the nonauthoritarian church, of the church that is one with its congregants, was apparently not immediately appreciated by the bulk of his parishioners.

Related to the ineffectiveness of its ideology is the conflict inherent in the apolitical stance assumed by the storefront church. Don Francesco's defensiveness in the Communist *quartiere*, as we have seen, consisted in good measure of asserting just this apolitical status of his church. But a "progressive" ideology in the absence of any political action may leave the parishioners skeptical of the church's commitment to its progressive ideals. Taking action on these problems, though, translating the ideology into practice, would mean not only risking offense to the DC and the Church hierarchy but antagonizing the PCI as well.

A related problem is faced by don Francesco in his sermons. He wants to convey his solidarity with his parishioners in protesting against their oppression, yet he is loathe to mention specifics for fear of being charged with taking a politically partisan stance. The result is that his sermons are full of generalities and biblical references whose significance often goes over the heads of his unschooled congregants. Thus his sermons often denounce capitalism and point to the Christian virtues of socialism yet never mention socialism or communism by name, nor does he mention the DC in referring to the corruption of the capitalist system.

Don Francesco was restrained from demonstrating his political independence too by the popular presumption of his DC support and anti-Communist sentiments. Even a fraternal gesture proffered toward the Communists might be misinterpreted. And so it was, for example, that Francesco resisted the pleas of his *doposcuola* children to attend the big *festa* of Uva, the Communist *festa* of the Giuliari section. He explained his refusal as follows:

> What confines me the most is the opinion that they have of me, for I have become inexorably convinced that the Party perceives me to be its enemy. So I have to be careful not to act in a way which they can interpret as provocation. I didn't attend the *Festa dell'Unità* for just that reason, because I thought that my presence would be seen as provocatory . . . as a spy watching over them.

Finally, the question must be raised as to whether the church of the poor actually appeals principally to the poor at all. As we have seen, the core of the lay leadership of the new church was composed not of new converts from "religious indifferentism" nor from the Communist world, but rather of individuals coming from the traditional wing of the Church. This reliance on outsiders is both symptomatic of and contributory to the social isolation of the storefront church. Though the youths were valuable in providing certain services to the people of Uva – most notably in teaching the *doposcuola* – they obviously were less suited for creating the nucleus of a solidary grouping on which allegiance to the new church could be built. Not a single university student lives in the Uva parish; a half dozen such students descending on the zone constituted something of an invasion. The irony is that the control of the church of the poor fell into the hands of the middle class, just the phenomenon whose rejection led to the abandonment of the traditional Church ideology and the embracing of the "progressive" Church.

Though the future of the Uva church and other churches like it in Italy is difficult to predict, one thing is clear: Simply presenting a progressive ideology does not automatically increase the popular appeal of the Church in a Communist, working-class zone. Despite all the rhetoric of conciliation, both don Francesco and the local PCI leaders recognize that they are in mutually antagonistic positions. It is don Francesco's task, as part of his mission of building up the Catholic world in Uva, to whittle away at PCI power in the parish. The PCI leaders are well aware that any increase in popularity for the new church can only lead to a diminution in their own authority; consequently, they will continue to discourage people from developing an allegiance to the new church. The Party may well have to find new ways of doing this, for the customary anti-Church symbolism – the identification of the Church with wealth and the DC – will probably become less effectual as the parishioners become more familiar with don Francesco's conception of the church. It is don Francesco's task to make this conception known to his parishioners and to counter charges of conservatism by portraying himself and his church as part of an insurgent movement of the poor. His primary problem is the lack of a local social base of support, yet it is doubtful that the youths being brought into the new church by the *doposcuola* will remain in the parish long enough to form such an adult base of support. After the church's first year of operation the adults of Uva remained estranged from the Catholic world.

9

Catholic *Gruppetto* and Communist Power

The storefront church was not the only new Catholic group in Albora. It was preceded by another group that was similar in theology, political ideology, and sense of mission and that, like the storefront church, took special aim at the socially marginal Southern immigrant population of the *quartiere*. Both groups directed their attention to the presumed weak link in the Communist control of the *quartiere*, attempting to build a local organization independent of the Communist world. Although the ideology of these two groups was politically heretical from the point of view of the conservative Church hierarchy, they claimed their legitimacy in the Second Vatican Council. Both rebelled against the alliance of the Church with the DC and against anticommunism as the primary organizing principle for Church social and political action. Both saw the salvation of the Catholic world through the identification of the Church with the plight of the poor and against the *padroni*.

The Catholic *gruppetto*[1] that entered Albora in 1969, two years before the advent of the storefront church, had no official ecclesiastical status. Hundreds of such *gruppi spontanei* had arisen throughout Italy with no formal organization nor even a name, but sharing the purpose of serving the poor in the name of the Church. The great majority of these were short-lived, encountering a variety of problems: difficulty of sustaining the interest of the group members, the hostility of the Church and of the political parties, and the diffidence of the very people they were seeking to aid.

Examination of the Catholic *gruppetto* in Albora raises the question of whether a left-wing Catholic group can successfully challenge PCI political authority. This complements Chapter 8, in which we inquired into the possibility of a left-wing Catholic Church successfully challenging the Communist world on formally nonpolitical grounds. In examining the political challenge posed by the *gruppetto*, we are also provided with an example of how the PCI in Albora organizationally copes with a direct political threat to its hegemony. We begin by describing the composition, program, and early history of the *gruppetto* and then proceed to an analysis of the battle between the new group and the PCI.

Organization of the gruppetto

The origins of the Albora *gruppetto*, like those of the storefront church, lay entirely outside of the *quartiere*. Like the storefront church, its appearance in Albora was largely fortuitous. Neither had any previously existing social roots in the *quartiere*.

The half dozen youths who initiated the Albora *gruppetto* had all been active in their parish churches and came from families firmly entrenched in the Catholic world. However, with the stirrings of the progressive movements in the Italian Church they sought an outlet for Catholic social action outside of the parish structure. As a result, in the mid-1960s these youths, from different parts of Bologna, joined the group Sing Out, the Italian branch of the organization based in the United States. Though not limited to Catholics, the singing group was primarily promoted through the Church and attracted mostly young Church activists. Sing Out was regarded as something of a social mission, preaching peace and brotherhood.

After participating in Sing Out for two years, the youths began to complain that the organization was getting nowhere, that it was all talk and no action. What needed to be done, they said, was to stop talking about the social problems of the day and start doing something to solve them. Following the example of the much discussed Catholic *gruppi spontanei*, they decided to quit Sing Out and devise their own social action project. While the group was struggling to formulate a plan of action, one of the youths spoke with a friend who was temporarily living in Buca, Albora's poorest zone. As a result of the friend's description of the poverty of Buca, the decision was made to undertake their project in that zone. The purpose of the *gruppetto*, as they conceived it, was simply "to try to do something for others." Formally, the group was to be aconfessional, open to all regardless of Church ties. This claim to aconfessional status was bolstered by the later addition of two "non-Catholics" to the group, both drawn in through previously existing social ties with founding members. One of these "non-Catholics" had served in the army with a core group member; the other was a schoolmate of another. Both were nominally Catholic, but not churchgoers. They belonged to no political party.

In all, ten youths became active in the *gruppetto*. None of them had ever lived in Albora, much less in Buca. Furthermore, their family backgrounds contrasted with those of the residents of Buca. None of them was a Southern immigrant and the great majority came from middle-class families. In addition, their education contrasted

Table 26. *Characteristics of gruppetto membership*

Name	Age	Occupation	Education	Father's occupation
Luigi	24	Typist	8th grade	Bricklayer
Bianca	19	Teacher	High school	*Carabiniere*
Paola	21	Student	University	Banker
Angelo	25	Medical student	University	Engineer
Francesca	21	Medical Student	University	Professional
Rina	23	Student	University	Professor
Enrica	21	Student	University	Banker
Giancarlo	22	Student	University	—[a]
Antonio	23	Student	University	Truck driver
Guido	24	Carpenter	High school	Farmer[b]

Note: Data as of spring, 1972.
[a] No data available.
[b] Owns large farm employing numerous farm laborers.

starkly with that of the people of Buca (see Table 26).
Whereas Buca had no university-educated residents, seven
of the ten youths were university students.

One important exception to this pattern was Luigi, the
informal leader of the *gruppetto*. Coming from a socioeconomic background similar to that of many Buca residents,
Luigi grew up in small, decrepit apartments, in economically precarious circumstances. His father was an irregu-
larly employed bricklayer; his mother took in washing and
ironing. Because of their poverty, his parents sent Luigi to
live with his aunt and uncle in Veneto for the first six years
of his life. He returned to live with them in a converted
garage, the nearest outhouse being 200 meters away. The
home had holes in the ceiling, and all the children slept in
the same bed. Luigi's mother was very religious, turning
to the Church for relief from her worldly problems, and
Luigi became active in the Church from an early age, a

member of Catholic Action in his parish for ten years. After dropping out of junior high school in order to go to work to help his family, he found employment as a typist. He still lives with his parents, who moved into a public housing project apartment a few years ago.

Thus, though the youths sought to insert themselves into the lives of the people of Buca, only Luigi had any claim to having shared in their circumstances. For the majority of the group, university students living in their parents' comfortable homes, such sharing would be largely vicarious.

The object of the *gruppetto* can best be described in the words of its members. After their first few months of activity in Buca, the group wrote a document of self-analysis:

We are a group of youths of diverse if not opposing social, cultural, political and religious backgrounds. As a group we are aconfessional and independent of all political parties. As a common base we have the following:

– sincerity . . .
– nonpartisanship: our action is not taken either to gain votes for any party or to indoctrinate the people with pseudo-revolutionary theories, etc. Not having to carry water to anyone's mill, we are consequently free.

In a later self-critique, Luigi described the group's mission:

We are seeking to form a popular movement, a diffusion of ideas, in order to attempt to resolve in a new way certain very grave problems: housing, schools, etc., to resolve them with the direct participation of the people. The most serious problem is that an individual or a number of people, outside of the parties or the unions, do not have any power and are not able to exercise any power. It is this situation that we want to change.

The youths had an ambitious goal: the defeat of the parties in Albora and with it the end of PCI monopoly of public power in Buca.

Buca contains seventy apartments, each renting for ten to twenty dollars per month; these apartments are inhabited by approximately 300 people, in large part migrants from the South and from other economically depressed areas of the country.[2] In order to gain entrance to Buca, the youths planned to begin by befriending the children of the zone – playing with them and caring for them – until ultimately they would be accepted by their parents as well. The youths recognized that the adults of Buca would be suspicious of outsiders and of the ulterior motives of those who claimed to want to help them; it was consequently decided that a long-term commitment was needed if the project was to have any chance of success.

Although theoretically aconfessional, the *gruppetto* originally used the Camolia church as its center of operations. The children of Buca were befriended and, in groups of five to fifteen, taken to the church to play games, put on puppet shows, and stage dramatic productions. In cooperation with the priests, the *gruppetto* youths also began a weekly Bible reading session at the church, in which the Buca children did not generally take part. Although their activities were made known to the parishioners of Camolia, only one young Church activist of Camolia became involved in them.

The alliance of the *gruppetto* with the Camolia church, however, was short-lived. As long as the youths were engrossed in their preliminary goal of winning over the children, there was little basis for conflict between the conservative and the progressive Catholic factions. However, once the youths began to move beyond their initial access activity and started discussing their political goals with the adults of Buca, conflict with the Camolia church arose. As the youths' anti-DC politics became evident, a number of influential Camolia parishioners prevailed on the priest to dissociate himself from the youths and to dissociate the youths from the parish church. As a result, the youths relinquished all contact with the church. Children were no longer taken there, the weekly Bible reading class was disbanded, and the one local church member who had participated in the youths' activities permanently withdrew from them. The public reason given by the priests for this split was that it was better for all concerned. It was better for the youths themselves, they claimed, because otherwise people would look on their efforts with suspicion, as an insidious plot to drag people into the church. As for the church, they said, it was better that it have nothing to do with the youths, or the church would be charged with organizing against the city government.

Political organizing

After several months of contact with the children of Buca and after a number of contacts had been made with Buca adults, the *gruppetto* youths decided to begin political organizing. Their first move was sending a letter to the *quartiere* council party heads complaining about the lack of social services in Buca. The letter included a detailed analysis of the socioeconomic situation of the residents of Buca, along with a critique of the failure of the schools and other public agencies to deal adequately with these problems. The result of this mistreatment and prejudice, said the letter, was that the zone was "being isolated, forming a real ghetto." Their letter was ignored.

The youths then decided that political action could not be taken without some formal organization of Buca residents to give them legitimacy. The result was a call to a public meeting, a leaflet distributed to all the apartments of Buca:

On Sunday, May 31, 1970, at 7 P.M., a series of meetings of the inhabitants of this zone will begin. The meeting place is in the courtyard opposite the restaurant. At this first meeting the problem of housing will be discussed. Participating in these meetings will be the residents of the zone and a group of youths whom many of us know. There will be meetings, friendly discussions, but having the intention of achieving something concrete and resolving all our biggest problems (housing, schools, work, etc.). We hope that from these meetings we will succeed in reaching a common position in order to be able to act and make our voice heard to the *quartiere*, to the city, and to the Region.

The leaflet was signed: "A group of residents of Albora street, a group of youths." Thus began the efforts of the youths to build a front organization. The leaflet had been written by the youths, though they did show it to two or three local adults with whom they had become friendly.

It is hardly surprising, given the strength of the PCI in Albora, that the Party lost no time in trying to find out what this new group was doing in the *quartiere*. Party leaders had been forewarned by the letter sent to the head of the PCI delegation to the *quartiere* council and, with the appearance of this leaflet referring to an independent political organization in the *quartiere*, the local PCI leaders became seriously concerned. There was no grass roots political organizing in Albora outside of the PCI, and the Party had no intention of seeing a competitive structure arise.

And so it was that at the first public meeting of the "group of Buca residents" a local PCI leader was one of the half dozen Alborese to attend, attempting to squelch the new group before it could get started. Luigi, in his diary, wrote caustically of the PCI leader's participation that evening:

Last night at the meeting a man I had never seen before intervened. From his long discourse-propaganda he clearly let it be understood that he belonged to the PCI, which is trying to absorb in its ranks all those who move outside of it. It wants to systematically monopolize and exploit all those who try to do anything outside of it. He proposed having meetings at the ARCI headquarters, saying that it is a group without any political ties (it's for the PCI).

In the days that followed, the word was passed throughout the *quartiere* that a group of DC youths was organizing in the *quartiere*, that they were trying to exploit the lamentable situation of the people of Buca. An attempt thus began to discredit the youths. A few days later, the highest party official in the *quartiere*, a PCI candidate for city council, decided to give a campaign speech (for the 1970 city council campaign) in the main courtyard of Buca to counteract the anti-city-government talk inspired by the Catholic youths. The speech was a denunciation of the "youths of the DC" who, acting as self-appointed missionaries, had come to foment trouble in Buca.

Although the early association of the youths with the Camolia church lent public credence to the charge that they were a DC front group, the antilandlord rhetoric and action of the youths began giving people some cause to doubt this assessment. The youth's attitude toward the DC was well expressed in a letter to the DC written by Luigi a month before the first public meeting in Buca. He wrote in response to a campaign letter sent to him by the DC:

I, who believe I am a Christian, am unable to understand how a party which calls itself Christian Democracy has the nerve to present itself with this name to the people and to act like all the other parties (if not worse) . . . We are in a state which calls itself democratic and no one represents the people! The people who ought to govern the country have become just a mass of 30 million individuals that is called upon every 5 years to vote, to elect its representatives. These charges become still more uncomfortable when they are aimed at a party that has added to its program the word Christian. With what conscience can a Christian who ought to love all men as brothers permit an absurd and inhuman economic system that is based on profit and not on the good of men?

The youths opposed all the political parties on the grounds that all are merely interested in preserving their own power and in exploiting the people. The DC was the most heavily criticized for its claim to be Christian, a blasphemous hypocrisy in the youths' view. Although the Church pictured the PCI as the enemy and the DC as the savior, for the youths there was little difference between the two, as Luigi wrote:

In the DC I think that the only Christians remaining are the two dots between the D and the C. The Italians and Italy, or better yet, man, is very strange: two large parties exist which monopolize everyone in their own spheres of influence, two parties – conservative – each in its own sphere: the PCI and the DC, and both of them (and most especially the DC I think) exist just because the other one does.

These sentiments did not endear the youths to either the Party or to the local Camolia church.

As the youths' activity continued, the conflict between them and the PCI increased. They decided to hold a public meeting in Buca, inviting the municipal official in charge of housing to speak on the possibility of the city providing public housing for Buca. This meeting also attracted a PCI leader, the mayor's representative for Albora (*l'aggiunto del sindaco*). After the housing official spoke, the *aggiunto* gave a defense of the *quartiere* council, claiming that it was doing everything within its power to get public housing for the Buca residents.

After the youths' Wednesday night adult discussion group had been meeting for a few weeks, they began to identify themselves in leaflets and letters by the signature: "A group of Buca residents." Gone from most such docu-

ments was the additional identification of the outside
youths. Such was the case, for example, when the youths
decided to call on the city housing and sanitation authority
to inspect the dwellings of Buca. The youths went from
door to door, collecting thirty-two signatures of local residents for the letter they had written. None of their own
names appeared on it.

This total of thirty-two adults enlisted to sign the letter
indicates the high point of the youths' popular support in
Buca. The Wednesday night meetings, the primary organizational activity of the *gruppetto*, rarely drew as many as
a dozen adults, and often drew no more than three or four
local residents, all men. The great majority of Buca residents never directly participated in the political activities
of the *gruppetto*, apparently viewing the outsiders with
suspicion and with cynicism over their claims to be able to
improve the lot of the Buca residents. Only one Buca man
could be called an activist. Alfonso, a thirty-two-year-old
immigrant from the rural hinterland of Rome, had long
been vocal in criticizing living conditions in Buca and,
meeting the youths through their interaction with his children, he became the local center of the group's activities.
Whenever correspondence was sent by the *gruppetto* to an
official, his name and address were used for return correspondence. In addition, Alfonso's apartment was the one
reliable gathering center for the youths in Buca. Alfonso
alone could be counted on to attend all the group's meetings, usually bringing a couple of neighbors with him.

PCI response

The early surveillance of the *gruppetto* by the PCI in Albora soon gave rise to a variety of techniques designed to
crush the incipient challenge to local Party hegemony.
Although the youths were few in number, the local Party

officials had long been concerned with the new Southern immigrants and uncertain of their loyalties. Whereas an attempt by a group of outside youths to organize the Bolognesi proletarians would have been dismissed as absurd, the Party was not so confident about the reaction of the people of Buca to the *gruppetto*.

Since the youths had taken their case to the *quartiere* council, in which other parties were represented, the PCI was obliged to fight back through the council. Thus in response to the letter sent to the council by the youths and their subsequent visits to the council party heads, a council meeting was called. The *gruppetto* youths attended this meeting as spectators, but few Buca residents came. A PCI council member spoke on behalf of the Party, maintaining that the problems of Buca were well known to all present and that there was no need for outsiders to come to tell us about them. He rejected the youths' approach to the problem, saying that the matter could not simply be dealt with piecemeal for it was part of the larger problem of Southern immigration, a result of national (DC) policy that had created this influx of the poor. The council would have nothing to do with the outsiders and took no action on the complaints of the *gruppetto*. Furthermore, permission requested by the *gruppetto* to be allowed the use of a municipal building in which to hold their meetings was denied on the grounds that the group could offer no security guarantee, not being sponsored by any political party or public agency.

The PCI informal campaign against the youths continued, with the secretary of the Vapori section, which has jurisdiction over Buca, spending many hours speaking with the men of Buca in the courtyards and at the cooperative bar. The secretary called on Alfonso and told him to do whatever he wanted but to let the city government alone. The fault, he maintained, was not theirs. Meanwhile, the

word was spread throughout Buca by PCI partisans that
the youths were being backed by people seeking to undermine the city government, by anti-Communist bosses seeking a way to smear the Communist municipal *giunta*.

While the Party was trying to discredit the youths
through such gossip campaigns, they recognized that their
own position would erode if they could not demonstrate
the superior ability of the Party to provide decent housing
for the people of Buca. They recognized that the appeal
and the danger of the youths were based on valid complaints and a cynicism on the part of the people of Buca
that the Party was willing to do anything for them. The
issue was especially sensitive as it involved an attack on the
Communist city government for not providing people with
decent housing at the same time as the PCI nationally was
hailing the Bologna city government as the shining beacon
for all of Italy. Some plan had to be devised to show that
the Communists would not allow a few Catholic youths to
wear the mantle of social reformers at the Party's expense.

The limited municipal budget for public housing had
already been allocated, while available national public
housing programs were primarily geared toward the wealthier workers rather than toward the unemployed and the
poor. If there was to be an immediate promise of relief for
the people of Buca, it could not come directly from these
sources. The answer to this problem, devised by Albora's
top Party leaders, was to have the housing cooperative of
Camolia, the PSC, sponsor a low-rent housing project
geared specifically toward eliminating the housing problems of Buca. The PSC, though legally a housing cooperative, had not actually been involved in cooperative
housing since the original dreams of its founders over a
half century before. At long last, it would fulfill its charter
and organize low-cost housing for the people of the *quartiere*.

This plan of the PSC was, in fact, first announced publicly at a meeting of the PCI. The meeting was well publicized in Buca as a demonstration of how the Party would solve the people's housing problems. At the meeting, attended by over fifty men and women of Buca, a PCI leader told the people that only the cooperatives could provide them with housing at low cost. Any other approach to the problem would be a waste of time. The PSC was requesting national public housing funds to finance the construction of 750 apartments in Camolia; the plans called for the demolition of the Buca apartments and the relocation of the Buca residents who join the PSC into the new housing project. The *gruppetto* youths attended this open PCI meeting and became angry at what they saw as an attempt to undermine their work. They became particularly upset by the militant rhetoric of Porri, the Party head in Albora. Porri told the Buca inhabitants that "we" must struggle together for better housing and take whatever measures are necessary to attain that goal. One of the *gruppetto* youths at this point interrupted to say that he was making a note of Porri's promises, which he hoped "were not just demogoguery." Porri became enraged by this insult by an outside youth in his own Party section, and there ensued a heated shouting match, with the meeting ending in chaos. Thereafter, the Party stopped claiming that the youths were attached to the DC and spread the word that they were Fascists.

Following the public announcement of the PSC plan to get public housing for the people of Buca, the youths approached the president of the PSC and requested that he come to speak to the Buca inhabitants (the youth-sponsored group) about the cooperative's specific plans. At first the PSC president agreed, but then, after conferring with other local Party leaders, he informed the youths that no separate meeting would be held, that the PSC itself would hold a public meeting to explain the plans to everyone.

In frustration the youths attempted to go over the heads of the local Party officials by sending a stinging letter to the mayor of Bologna, hoping that the harshness of their charges would provoke the city government into responding publicly to their complaints. The letter was signed by their local contact man, Alfonso, and written as if penned by the people of Buca, though it was drafted by the youths:

We write to you, mayor, because you are the head of the city and you have the right and the duty to know in what condition its citizens live.

Who are we? We are those who are of no use, those who are not useful because they have no power, because it doesn't matter to anyone what we have to say. We are not of any use, but we count. We are like numbers. Everyone seeks us out before the elections, they delude us with promises that afterward things will change. We are the disinherited. Too many are illiterate . . . Everybody wants to speak in the name of the poor, but no one allows them to speak. All fear those who are in the right.

They offend us. We have lived here for a long time; many times people have come to give us charity. These people are the rich. The parishes spend millions to construct sports centers, billiard rooms, then as their apostolic duty they organize the rich to distribute charity. It's time that they stopped considering us as tranquilizers for their consciences. We should not accept the charity which comes from the rich. The parishes get in the race just like the sections of the parties. They have taken on the task of obtaining votes. The parties every once in a while put up big posters along our streets, send leaflets to our homes, and come to sell us their newspaper, though knowing that many of us do not know how to read. It's a commercial operation; they are not interested in having the people know and therefore able to decide. They are only interested in numbers: the more sheep there are, the more you can command.

We have followed the democratic path, that of democracy made for those who rule, which unfortunately also you, mayor, have accepted.

A year ago we wrote a letter to all the delegation heads of the *quartiere* council of Albora, in which we detailed the conditions in which we live. The *quartiere* is supposed to serve as an expression for the local people. Instead it is just a little parliament, in which only those elected by the parties may speak. The people are not allowed to speak, IT IS ANTIDEMOCRATIC! We have tried to collaborate, to unite ourselves, to find out. The parties, the *quartiere*, the various institutions, all have shown that they are annoyed at just one thing: we wanted to think with our own heads! We ought to act together, united. There exists the money to construct the houses, only the will is lacking! Let us go get it together; you who represent a city of 500,000 inhabitants, you have much more force than we do, we who are weak and few.

We want to know!
  – what concrete things can you do, together with us, to solve this problem?
  – at what point are the arrangements regarding the PSC/ Buca plan?
  – with what criteria will the work contracts be assigned? Are they already assigned?
  – what criteria will be used in assigning the apartments?
We ask:
  – to continually be kept up to date on how they are using our money.[3]
  – to be part of, and not just to watch, the commissions in which the assigning of apartments is decided.
We await your response, which you can send to this address: Savelli Alfonso – via Albora 448, Bologna.

No response was ever forthcoming from the mayor. No credence would officially be given to the claim that this was a bona fide group of Buca residents.

Soon after this letter was sent, the youths temporarily suspended their political activities. The immediate cause was a PCI meeting held at the Vapori section, to which the Buca people were invited. They were told by the Party leaders that the youths were hindering the efforts of the PSC to get public housing built in the *quartiere*. The youths had, in fact, lost momentum and were being rapidly isolated by the Party, which had been able to submit a concrete plan of action where the youths could only try vainly to attract the attention of the powerful sources of public funding.

Political downfall

In the spring of 1971 a crisis point was reached in Buca, a crisis that left in its wake the shambles of the *gruppetto's* political organization. The youths had rapidly become anathema to the great majority of Buca residents to whose initial suspicions of the outsiders' motives was added the fear of the social ostracism that came from association with them. The two or three men who had allied themselves with the *gruppetto* were the subject of strong verbal attacks by the Communists in the courtyards and at the *circolo*. The local Party leaders refused to greet the men when they entered the bar, and warned those who did talk with them that those individuals were not socially acceptable.[4] The social costs of allying with the Catholic youths were great and the possible advantages remote. Weakened by this isolation, the *gruppetto* was left in too weak a position to resist outside threats to its integrity, and it was through such association with outside political forces that the *gruppetto* was ultimately discredited.

In 1970, with the appointment of a local *aggiunto* drawn from the PSIUP, the left wing of the Socialist movement, PSIUP began organizing a party section in the *quartiere*.

This drive was headed by the *aggiunto* himself, who came from a neighboring *quartiere*. Having no power base in Albora and lacking any clearly defined ideological differences with the PCI, the PSIUP leader was looking for an issue around which to organize the local section. From his experiences as *aggiunto* he had become familiar with the youths working in Buca, and he knew that they had put the PCI in a defensive position. Thus the PSIUP leader decided to meet with the Buca group to see how his party might get involved. Several PSIUP members, all but one of whom lived outside Albora, attended the meetings of the citizen's committee for the next two months. The youths were initially happy about this development, since they had been losing their struggle with the PCI and the city government. They saw in the PSIUP *aggiunto* a potential power broker whose connections could be employed to sustain the group's political activities.

The youths acted together with the PSIUP nucleus of three to four people, distributing a leaflet from door to door in which the Buca citizens' committee pronounced its "fatigue and impatience in waiting for that which never arrives." This coalition with the PSIUP did not last long, however. The youths, though excited by having someone with political connections on their side for the first time, were suspicious of the motives of the PSIUP leader. The youths had insisted that the committee be independent of any party, and though the PSIUP people had agreed to this, it became clear that their own purpose was to use the Buca issue as a means of gaining local support for their party. In addition, the activities of the local PSIUP leaders were getting them into trouble. The PSIUP was in the city government coalition with the PCI and was vulnerable to any criticism of the municipal government. Furthermore, the PSIUP relied heavily on PCI patronage, and when the Alborese PCI leaders informed the PCI Federation officials of the PSIUP activities in Albora, pressure was brought to bear; the PSIUP *aggiunto* resigned.

At the same time, another political organization sought to benefit from the *gruppetto*. This group, *Lotta Continua* (LC) (Continual Struggle), was also based outside Albora, having no participants from the *quartiere*. A national, ultra-left-wing organization almost entirely composed of young people, *Lotta Continua* arose in the aftermath of the 1968 student rebellions. Strongest in the schools and universities, it proposed a plan of direct political action on the part of the poor to wrest power from the reformist (PCI) and the capitalist (DC) parties. In the spring of 1971 a national drive was begun for the seizure of new housing by the poor. The slogan *Lotta Continua* shared with other such ultraleft groups was: *la casa si prende, l'affitto non si paga!* ("seize the housing, don't pay the rent!"). Such seizures had already received copious publicity in Milan and in other cities; the youths of Bologna's LC were eager to add Bologna to the list of *Lotta Continua* triumphs.

The LC members were first attracted to Buca by leaflets distributed in downtown Bologna by the *gruppetto*, describing the poverty of the zone and the uninhabitable state of the housing. The LC youths, however, had no local contacts in Albora, much less in Buca, and they decided to utilize the "citizens' committee" of Buca as a means of entering the zone. They began attending the Wednesday night meetings and, during this period, worked with the Catholic youths in putting up a poster throughout the city denouncing the municipal government for not doing anything about the Buca housing situation. This was signed "Buca citizens' committee."

Having thus made some contacts with the people of Buca, the LC youths began organizing on their own, under their own name. They plastered the walls with their posters and painted on slogans. Each week they sold their national newspaper in Buca and distributed a variety of leaflets, building up to their attempt to organize an occupation of a new public housing project in Bologna. The housing project, they claimed, was excluding the poor of the city; they tried to approach the Buca residents directly to enlist their participation in the housing seizure. Failing to elicit any positive response, the LC youths returned to the Buca's citizens' committee, proposing a vote on the motion calling for a housing seizure. With five or six local residents present, the motion was voted down. But again the youths returned to the citizens' committee, again proposing the motion. This time just two Buca adults were there, one voting for the motion and one against. This the LC took to be a mandate for action.

The ability of the LC youths to move in so quickly and, in effect, take over the citizens' committee reflects the weakness of the *gruppetto*. Having been crushed by the PCI after two years of political activity, the youths no longer had confidence in their own proposals, for they had begun to recognize where the power lay and how and by whom it would be influenced. As a result, though most of the youths bitterly opposed the LC strategy, they could not argue alternative courses with any conviction. Furthermore, two of the youths, frustrated by their unsuccessful political organizing attempts, backed the housing seizure proposal of *Lotta Continua*. This internal division further weakened the group, leaving it open to a partial takeover by outside forces. The weakness, too, stemmed from the organization's ideology, that of openness and spontaneity. Luigi mulled over these problems, writing in the midst of the LC episode:

Faced by these tightly organized and dogmatic groups or parties we have made no counterproposals; rather, we have been divided, and strangely we who know the people and the affairs of

Buca well have not proposed anything, but instead have accepted proposals of people who have been here 15–20 days (and only on Wednesdays). Not only, therefore, have we not, together with the others, made our own decisions, but we have progressively become Psiupanized or Lotta Continuized. The committee of Buca really no longer exists, save for the participation of Alfonso, Giuliano, and Mauro. To continue with activities or actions which presuppose a large base of support not only is false, but is only creating other "bosses" who administer on behalf of the people.

The housing project seizure did take place, in another part of Bologna, and the LC youths were finally able to find three Buca families to participate in it. The occupation was a severe embarrassment to the city administration, and the Communists, in Albora and elsewhere, attacked the occupation in harsh terms. After occupying the building for several days, the LC youths and the poor families evacuated in the face of a threatened police assault.

This brief period of association with *Lotta Continua* was used by the PCI in Albora to brand the *gruppetto* youths as irresponsible adventurists. The Catholic youths were discredited by association. In these months, also, the FGCI was activated by the Party to counteract the influence of the *gruppetto*. The latter had undertaken a door-to-door survey in Buca, noting medical complaints and sanitary conditions. The FGCI reacted by undertaking virtually the same survey, and the word was spread throughout Buca not to cooperate with the outsiders, but to aid the efforts being made by the young Communists. The Party sought to demonstrate to the people of Buca that the young people working in Buca were neither representative nor responsible. The FGCI published its survey results in pamphlet form, distributing a copy to each apartment in Buca.

The attitude of the PCI toward the Catholic youths is reflected in the comments of the Vapori section secretary:

All the problems were caused by people from outside the *quartiere*. They began by speaking badly of the PCI and the city. They took advantage of the unhappiness of the citizens of Buca, above all because they are Southerners, and also because they truly live in such terrible housing, so they are fixated on the problem of housing. They made a lot of propaganda against the city, denigrating the city and the PCI and they tried to exploit the people. They went from house to house, making a lot of promises, and saying why haven't the Communists done anything? and why doesn't the city give you this and give you that? and they got a grip on the people. Then when last year we succeeded with the young people (FGCI) in going from house to house and telling the people who those others were and who we were . . . they divorced themselves from those other people. They were eight or ten youths who didn't live here, not one of them, and they wanted to call themselves a committee of tenants of Albora, this was at the bottom of their leaflets. They were *gruppetti*. There were a whole bunch of them. There was a group from the church, a group of young Catholics who were working with PSIUP. The *gruppetti* were all joined together, working together, working against the PCI and the city.

The theme of "outside agitators" was thus emphasized in the Communist anti-*gruppetto* drive.

In speaking of this unfortunate episode, local Party leaders not only stressed the fact that the troublemakers were from outside the *quartiere* but stressed that those who came under their influence were also outsiders, Southern immigrants. This theme was also taken up by Porri in analyzing the Buca conflict: "In the *quartiere* some groups of *Lumpenproletariat* exist. These *Lumpenproletariat* are divided, with one part being local, Bolognese, and one part being immigrants. Now as for the local *Lumpenproletariat*, we have strong bonds with these little people of Bologna. With the others the bonds are more tenuous." In the face of this outside threat to the Party, branded as backed by right-wing forces, the Party response was clear – have nothing to do with the troublemakers: "We made the decision to build a wall between ourselves and them and our attitude proved to be correct. We slammed the door in their face; they came with external elements to put pressure on us, even coming to our homes to harrass our families." And the final element to discredit them: Not only were they outsiders and not only were they sponsored by the right, but they were from bourgeois and Catholic backgrounds:

I remember one coming to our meeting and he said: "I don't agree with what comrade Porri said." And then I said: "Excuse me, whose comrade are you? You're no comrade of mine. You get out of this room because if you don't I'll take a chair and break it over your back." And then he said: "Oh, that's all right for you since you already have a house." And I told him: "Yes, I have an apartment, and I'm going to keep it for myself. If you want to give one away, give away yours, give them yours and there's also a maid to go with it."

Although the PCI successfully met the threat posed to the Party in Albora by the *gruppetto*, the youths continued their regular visits to Buca, returning there every weekend throughout the following year. The citizens' committee had been abandoned and no political activity was undertaken. The youths reverted to what they had concentrated on in their first weeks in Buca, playing with the children and providing certain social services to their parents.

Somewhat surprisingly, perhaps, the youths did not become allied in their activities with don Francesco and the new Uva church. Don Francesco had arrived in Albora only after the big political confrontation involving the *gruppetto*. Although the Buca youths went to Uva as soon as they heard of the new storefront church, don Francesco did not offer to join in their activities, although Buca was part of his new parish. No alliance was formed, although the youths shared don Francesco's theology, political attitudes, and conception of the Church's social mission.

Don Francesco's decision not to ally with the *gruppetto* was due largely to his fear of the consequences of a direct confrontation with the PCI. The task of starting a new church in this bastion of Communist strength would be difficult enough without entering an open political battle with the Communists as soon as he arrived. Using terms similar to those employed by the priests of Camolia, don Francesco maintained that it was better for the youths that they not be formally linked to the church:

On my part I haven't taken any step toward becoming involved with them, toward doing anything with them. In part this is because I know them so little and in these things you can succeed or you can fail. I'm happy that they are there in Buca, but they don't limit the nature of my activity just as I don't limit theirs. They intend to carry on a Christian activity which is also political, political in the good sense. Luigi comes every once in a while to see me, but only once in a while. This seems to be best for them because in this way they escape the accusation of being my dependents.

From don Francesco's point of view, in fact, there was little to be gained and much to be lost through association with the *gruppetto*. Joining the youths in 1971 would have been jumping onto a sinking ship.

Conclusions

The failure of the Catholic *gruppetto* provides both a lesson in the power of the PCI in Albora and an indication of the weakness of new Catholic movements in combatting the Communist social-political hegemony. The Catholic world is sharply divided, whereas the Communist world is not, and neither major current in the Catholic world has been able to challenge the PCI supremacy successfully. Only outside Catholic forces have taken any sort of new initiatives to win over the people of Albora, whereas the old, established churches have clung to a defensive and conservative posture. But the outside Catholic forces are severely handicapped by their outsider status in the *quartiere*. Although their ideology is in many ways in substantial harmony with that of the Communists, they are social pariahs and, consequently, face extreme difficulty in winning local people over to their side. The Communists recognize this weakness and exploit it as much as possible. Thus the *gruppetto* youths were stigmatized through identification with ingroup–outgroup symbolism.

That this symbolism was employed by the Communists is made especially interesting by the fact that most Buca residents are themselves regarded as outgroup members, Southern immigrants. The Communists dwelled on an ideal of local community solidarity, together with an ideal image of proletarian unity, to turn the people against the *gruppetto*, despite the fact that neither of these ideals was much reflected in daily social practice. The symbols were powerful not because they represented the prevalent pattern of social solidarity but because the immigrants saw greater potential gain from accepting that symbolism than from exposing it as hypocritical. These advantages were of both a social and a political nature. Although they were outgroup members in the Albora context, the Southern immigrants could assert their claim to ingroup status through common opposition to a third group. By standing against the *gruppetto* youths, the Buca residents had the opportunity to establish their loyalty to the Alborese Communist world, expressing their social solidarity with it. Added to this was the recognition by many of the people of Buca that the political power of the community lay firmly in the hands of the Communists. The Communists and not the *gruppetto* youths were recognized as potential power brokers, the only effective means of access to political authority.

As indicated earlier, despite their youth and lack of political experience, the youths of the *gruppetto* were perceived as a threat by the Communist leadership of Albora. Although in the end this threat was handled rather easily by the Communists, at the time it was the subject of numerous worried meetings and discussions by Party activists. The way in which the PCI countered this threat provides a demonstration of the strategic importance of the PCI-allied organizations. The Party itself was in no legal position to sponsor public housing, yet it sought to circumvent the fixing of responsibility on the Communist municipal and provincial authorities. By having the PSC provide a housing proposal, the PCI both absolved the municipal government from responsibility and at the same time put the housing movement under Party control. They were able, in short, to maintain the message that the people's best chance for material progress lies within the Communist world. At the same time, the Party was able to shift the responsibility for the lack of public housing funds onto the national DC government. This effort was supplemented by the use of another PCI-allied organization, the FGCI, whose members were used to go door to door in Buca, demonstrating that the conflict was not one between encrusted old power brokers and young reformers. The image of the struggle to be conveyed to the people was rather that of a battle between outside trouble-making Catholic *borghesi* and the local working-class community, the Communist world.

Of course in the long run the ability of the Party to attract the support of both newcomers and long-time residents of the city is linked to its fulfillment of its promises, its effectiveness in meeting the valid demands made on it by its citizenry. Although in the short run the *gruppetto* challenge could be fended off through organization and pledges, without satisfactory action the people would eventually lose their faith in the PCI. In fact, the Party, through the efforts of the municipal government, was eventually able to provide modern housing for the people of Buca. Though new housing did not come as quickly as some wanted it, the dilapidated dwellings of Buca were torn down and public housing was erected in its place. In 1976 the mayor came to Buca to cut the ceremonial ribbon, marking the opening of the modern housing facility and providing another indication to the people of Albora that the Party looks after their interests.

It is not surprising that both of the marginal Catholic groups organizing in Albora – marginal from the point of view of the traditional Church structure and ideology – chose to concentrate on the socially marginal immigrant population. Launching a direct threat to the Communist world through the solidly Communist Bolognese working-class population was felt to be a far more difficult task. It was supposed that the poor immigrants, lacking strong ties with either Church or Party, could be more easily incorporated into an alternative structure. The Communists, however, showed that they hold considerable influence over the immigrants and the poor, influence stemming both from monopoly of the social centers of the *quartiere* and from control of political brokerage. Cut off from the political party of the Church, the marginal Catholic groups find themselves in a politically impotent position. Representing an idealistic middle-class revolt against the conservatism of the embattled Church, the personnel of these Catholic groups are social, economic, and geographic outsiders to the *quartiere*. Any direct assault on Communist power in Albora by such marginal Catholic groups is likely to be isolated and defeated.

10

The Social Bases
of Political Allegiance

Most studies of Communist allegiance in countries not governed by Communist parties have focused on ideological factors, a focus that has also characterized many analyses of the Church–Communist struggle. In these studies it is theorized that people become Communist because they feel oppressed or dissatisfied with the governing political forces. Or in cases where an area has been largely Communist, political socialization, subculture, and tradition are invoked. When seen in these terms, the problem of Church–Communist struggle is approached as the subject for ideological analysis and the study of values. By contrast, in these pages we have tried to point out the importance of social factors in understanding people's allegiance to the PCI and the Church and in analyzing the ongoing battle between them. No claim is made that ideological factors are unimportant; certainly the identification of the PCI with the interests of the working class has been a crucial element in this context. Rather, an attempt has been made to counterbalance the excessively mentalistic bent of much of the literature.[1]

Proselytizing, in this perspective, is a social process in which ideological and programmatic appeals are not necessarily primary. We should reconsider the common distinction made in the analysis of political organizations between activities that serve to win recruits and activities that serve to keep the allegiance of those who are already adherents. An illustration of the dichotomy is provided by Lange's study of PCI sections in the center, suburbs, and periphery of Milan:

> Similar differences in the character of the mobilizational work of the section groups appear when we look at the themes of the public assemblies they sponsored. In the peripheral sections, the large majority of such assemblies were concerned with what I have previously termed "celebratory" themes; that is, they were intended to commemorate a major PCI or Communist movement anniversary. Only rarely were they called as a party response to a national or international event. Furthermore, section leaders indicated that these latter assemblies tended to discuss the general themes of the PCI's history and strategy rather than specific aspects of the party's program. From these observations it would appear that the peripheral sections tend to carry out mobilizational initiatives appealing primarily to those already sympathetic to the PCI; assemblies concerned with celebratory or very general national issues would seem to have little likelihood of expanding the party's social support. [1975:287–8]

What attracts new supporters, from this viewpoint, is the party program; proselytizing is seen as a largely intellectual activity of argumentation.

In contrast, the study of Albora shows that no simple dichotomy between "celebratory" and proselytizing activities is possible. What attracts people to the PCI or to the Church is as much the celebratory element as the ideological, as much the aura of social solidarity as the programmatic pleas. For the growth of PCI influence, better one *festa* than a dozen public meetings presenting the Party's pension, housing, and public safety proposals.

Communists, social scientists, and social pathology

Before considering the ways in which people react to the competing claims for their allegiance made by the Church and the PCI, it is worth asking just what it means to be a Communist in Albora. Alternatively, it is instructive to clarify what being a Communist does *not* mean. Party membership in Albora bears no resemblance to the model of Communist Party membership that flourished in the cold war period and that remains the most common image found among the American public: communism as social pathology.[2] In this model, Communist Party membership, rather than being seen as an aspect of social life to be investigated in the round, is portrayed as a pernicious form of institutionalized pathology. Given these premises, investigation focuses on the psychological problems of members or potential members rather than on the actual life of the Party in the community. As should be clear from the rest of the book, this approach is both analytically sterile and grossly inaccurate.

Perhaps the archetypal study of this tradition is Gabriel Almond's (1954) *The Appeals of Communism*. Almond's study is, like many of the same genre, plagued from the outset by a defective methodology attributable to its anti-Communist assumptions. Almond supervised a study of Communist Party organization in which none of the researchers ever attended a meeting of any of the parties studied, nor did they speak with any party members. Rather, disillusioned and vocal ex-members of the party were interviewed as well as a number of psychiatrists who had ex-Communists as patients. That Almond and his collaborators did not see this warped sample as discrediting any generalization regarding the Communist parties under study may be attributed to their apparent belief that those who quit the Party were more normal than those mentally unbalanced enough to remain in it. That such a study could be so widely heralded for such a long time is a token of the influence of political ideology on the practice of social science. In this context, Almond's statement on the value neutrality of his methodology is a monument to self-deception: "It is one of the obligations of the scientific calling that while ethical impulses may affect the selection of a problem and the purposes for which the findings are used, they may not enter into the scientific process – that is, affect the methods of research or the findings themselves" (1954:370). Almond undertook an anti-Communist study, and his premises led inescapably to his anti-Communist conclusions.[3]

What we have tried to highlight, and what is neglected in Almond's study and others like it, is the establishment by the Communist Party of a comprehensive and satisfying social system providing a basis for strong emotional ties while addressing economic and social problems. The remarks attributed by Almond to a former Italian Communist are particularly erroneous: "Party discipline does not admit of friendship. So human a sentiment would bind together individuals who must be Communists above all, rather than normal men. Friendship would also interfere with the careful reciprocal surveillance among the comrades" (1954:120). Almond went on to note the high incidence of Italian respondents who "described personal relations in the Italian party as detached and functional or as characterized by fear, suspicion and distrust" (1954:123). This is, of course, just what Almond expected to find. However, this portrait of a tight-knit, conspiratorial organization is fallacious. This has been demonstrated for Albora, and may be generalized on the basis of scattered observations at Party sections throughout the Red Belt and on the basis of the other empirical studies that have been conducted to date on local-level Party activity. Nor can the difference in time of the two studies account for the discrepancy. Though the Party was ideologically more rigid in the early 1950s, it was in certain respects an even greater center of popular activity, and the sense of solidarity and comradeship was probably more intense among the members in that period.

The portrayal of the Party as a haven for fanatics colors Almond's description of the Party member as being continually involved in Party activity. The Communist Party is seen as fundamentally different from any other party or voluntary organization, as, "It would be difficult indeed to find another political organization which could lay claim to most of the spare time of more than half of its rank and file" (1954:150). Again, this is a totally inaccurate view of the Party in Albora, and it is just as inaccurate nationally. From 1945 on, one of the major laments of Party leaders has been the lack of ongoing political participation by the bulk of the membership. Over half of the rank and file not only does not spend the majority of its spare time on Party activities, but spends hardly any time on them at all. In this light the quotation of an Italian former Party member is misleading: "They try to keep the party members constantly occupied from morning to night, and to really tire them with a load of tasks and assignments . . . The result is that the individual becomes accustomed to thinking of the party from the moment he awakens to the moment he goes to sleep" (1954:148). There are no more than a handful of Party members in Albora for whom such a description is even remotely appropriate, and these are the local Party leaders. Although in the immediate postwar period there was a greater degree of popular participation in the political initiatives of the Party, at no time were the majority of local Party members spending even 10 percent of their leisure time in PCI activities.

The level of membership participation in Albora, moreover, reflects the national pattern, as a review of studies
done elsewhere demonstrates (Barbagli and Corbetta
1978:36–9). Lange (1975:298), for example, examining a
large number of sections in the Milan area, concluded
that:

only about 10 percent of the members of most sections made
any contribution to section initiatives during a nonelection year.
There were, of course, occasions (the festivals, for instance)
when participation rose markedly and the average attendance at
section assemblies was usually between 15 and 20 percent, but
otherwise the burden of running the section fell on the few
(*pochi ma buoni*) who were willing to devote two or three evenings a week to party affairs.

The participation rate was lowest, in Lange's study, among
the urban sections, with 83.1 percent of their membership
labeled "never active" (1975:300). Gori's study of fifty-seven
PCI sections in Florence arrives at similar figures; he estimates that 80 percent of the membership can be classified
as "simple adherents," whose only annual activity is the
taking out of membership. "The personal involvement in
party activity is zero" (Gori 1975:251). Gori notes how revealing these figures are, "given how widespread the belief
is of the PCI as a party cadre and of mass mobilization"
(1975:250). Earlier, Galli (1966:165–6) had reached similar
conclusions in examining the national Party picture, esti-
mating that just 10 percent of the PCI membership attend
Party meetings and, according to official Party figures, 25
percent attend the section congresses. At the height of its
organizational mobilization, in the mid-1950s, about 8 percent of the Party members could be considered "active
militants." Ten years later, no more than 5 percent of the
membership could be so classified (1966:152).

The assumption behind the portrait of fanatic devotion

to the Party, as is shown in Daniels's (1962) *The Nature of Communism*, is that Party members are social misfits, people who are desperately seeking a cause in which to immerse themselves:

The Communist movement provides a special haven for the alienated. It is a cause to identify with, a group to belong to, and can offer an embittered and rootless individual an opportunity to remake his personality around the movement [1962:340].

The party member characteristically exhibits complete devotion to the movement. He has faith in the infallibility of the party, its leaders, and its line [1962:343–4].

Again, though this model bears little resemblance to Italian sociopolitical life, it coincides neatly with the popular American anti-Communist stereotype. Along similar lines, Cantril (1958), in his influential book *The Politics of Despair*, distinguishes between the "militant Communist" and the "protest voter." In this way those exhibiting Communist sympathies are portrayed as fanatics or as not really pro-Communist at all. Such a framework renders the Alborese situation unintelligible. Few are the PCI members in Albora who meet the criteria of either category.

The Catholic Communist

Of the ways in which the local-level conflict between the Church and the PCI has been conceptualized, two are by far the most common. In one, the Catholic Communist model, the mass of Communist Party members and voters is portrayed as fundamentally Catholic. In the other, the two-worlds model, two mutually exclusive social spheres are distinguished, the one Catholic and the other communist. At both the popular and the scholarly level, each of these models has many adherents in Italy. The Catholic Communist construct, in particular, has become a part of the nation's folk wisdom, enshrined in the tremendously popular tales of don Camillo.[4] In these stories and in the films made from them, the parish priest turns in exasperation to Jesus for guidance in coping with his Communist parish. He is told, in turn, to be gentle with the local Communists, for they do not understand what they are doing. Following this counsel, don Camillo outwits the local Communist officials, who come to him for advice.[5]

Ironically, though it is the PCI that contends that one can be a good Catholic and a loyal Communist and the Church that denies this possibility, the Catholic Communist thesis has most often been espoused by people close to the Church. Although the Party issues programmatic statements on the compatibility of communism and Catholicism and points to illustrious people who call themselves both Communist and Catholic, the Communist intellectuals have not been interested in documenting the divided allegiances of Party members. In contrast, although Church strategy calls for the condemnation of the Catholic Communist identity, in practice the Church bolsters its own image by claiming a high number of such half-breeds.

In the Catholic Communist model, the Communists are divided into two categories: the mass and the elite. Only a handful of the hardcore Party leadership, in this view, has abandoned the Church. For the great mass of Communist members and voters, allegiance to the PCI entails no rejection of the Church, no abandonment of a Catholic identity.[6]

Perhaps the most cogent ethnographic support for this thesis is provided by Faenza (1959), in a study of a rural community not far from Bologna, outside Rimini in Romagna. San Lorenzo a Monte, the *paese* studied by Faenza, is particularly interesting in that its vote is similar to that of Albora, with the PCI receiving an absolute majority and the DC receiving just 20 percent of the ballots cast.

As described by Faenza, the Communists' allegiance to the Church is striking. On Sunday two-thirds of the parishioners regularly attend mass, and men and women are equally represented. Only three or four of the Communist core group members do not attend Sunday mass, and even these few go to church on Christmas and Easter. Furthermore, on all the major holidays, 60 percent of the parishioners take Communion, with only the same three or four Communist activists never participating. Every one of the inhabitants was baptized, confirmed, and had First Communion; all are married and buried by the Church. The Communists see no conflict between their Party membership and their ties to the Church:

"Everybody goes to church," declares one comrade with energy. "Ah! Communism has nothing to do with the Church; we've already understood that well enough. The priest warns about it, but it's just a confusion, all *zizzania*. Seventy percent of the parishioners go to church and who do you think they are? They're the Communists. It's always us."

According to Faenza, the anti-Church sentiments of the Communists, insofar as they exist at all, simply reflect antagonism toward the wealth and power of the Church, elements that have been under attack among the masses for centuries:

The priest is an integral part of everyone's social environment and spiritual life. A Communism without priests is inconceivable. One opposes the representative of the Church, but striking higher up, because the distinction between the Church of the rich and the Church of the poor is a characteristic of peasant evangelism, as are the distinctions . . . between the Gospel and the Church, between the clergy and the Gospel, and between the teaching of Jesus and that of the clergy. [1959:180]

The people's attachment to communism is portrayed as

limited, not comparable in depth to their ties to the Church:

> Communism remains, for these sharecroppers, an exclusively sindicalist fact, the claim of a profoundly felt material exigency: private ownership of the land. And the dilemma which the parish priest belabors in order to impose the choice on the faithful – either Communist or Catholic, either with Satan or with God – does not necessarily elicit any profound echo in the hearts of the parishioners, nor provoke any agitation in their spirit. It falls like an empty abstraction, it slides like water from marble. Why choose? The farmers are unable to feel this need because they have never abandoned Catholicism . . .[1959:80–81]

The facts of Albora should make clear that the San Lorenzo a Monte pattern cannot be generalized to describe Catholic–Communist relations throughout Italy. The theory of "belly Communism," implicit in Faenza's analysis, fails to account for the strength of the Communist Party. This is particularly notable in the case of Albora, where a considerable rise in the standard of living has had no effect on Communist strength. In fact, many of the Alborese are former sharecroppers and children of sharecroppers who have risen economically in the world.

The majority of men in Communist San Lorenzo attends weekly mass, yet not one in twenty of the Alborese men does so. Whereas in San Lorenzo only three or four men fail to take Communion every year, in Albora the large majority fails to meet this minimal Church prescription. Perhaps even more telling is the fact that although in San Lorenzo there is no widely held folk distinction between Catholic and Communist, such a distinction is commonly made in Albora. According to Faenza, a question such as "Are you a Catholic?" would be nonsensical to a San Lorenzo resident. In contrast, in Albora such a question is not only sensible but provides a basis of social pigeonholing.

Though a simplistic Catholic Communist model is inadequate to account for the situation in Albora, the model does point out a number of important characteristics of divided allegiances. By leading in the opposite direction from the Communist-as-fanatic portrait, the model calls for an examination of the ways individuals respond to conflicting calls for their allegiance. At the same time, we are forced to distinguish between institutional norms (of Church and Party) and the norms and behavior of those who in some way identify with these institutions. The Catholic Communist argument has heuristic value, but insofar as it makes substantive claims, it must be used with caution. Different patterns of allegiance are found in different social environments. The question of greatest interest is what factors account for this differentiation? If we are ever to answer this, many more studies of the ways in which people deal with the competing institutions are needed.

The two worlds

The concept of the two worlds – the one Catholic and the other Communist – has already been introduced. Analytically, this model contrasts with the Catholic Communist scheme, as it depicts a social universe that is divided into two spheres. Support for the two-world concept has come both from national institutional analyses and from local-level studies. The institutional evidence is provided by the integralist designs of the Church and the PCI, the ways in which these institutions attempt to encapsulate people socially through a series of organizations and networks. On the local level, populations have been identified that are closely tied to the Church and populations have been identified that are closely bound to the "Socialist tradition."

This social division is linked to the network of allied

organizations associated with each institution. The integralist designs of these organizations have been noted for the European Communist parties by Duverger (1964:117) and others. The organizational efforts of the Italian Church have been seen in similar terms, as in La-Palombara's comments: "there are Catholic organizations corresponding to every facet of the Italian's existence. In providing this kind of infrastructure for millions of Italians the Catholic Church seeks to isolate them from other groups and organizations in society whose values and possible influence the Church considers damaging" (1965:294–5). In the two-world concept it is implicitly recognized that ideology may be a product of such social groupings, that the individual who is segregated in the organizational sphere of the one world is not likely to change his allegiance as a result of ideological conversion.

The structural similarity between the Church and the PCI, in this model, stems from their common integralism, with both Church and Party trying to place themselves at the center of their adherents' social, political, ritual, and ideological life. This structural comparability between the Communist world and the Catholic world has been observed in other national contexts as well. For example, a study of Italian immigrants in France concluded:

Communism, as it is presented in the region, like Christianity as it was and is perceived by these immigrants, appeals to the identical psychological motives: daily self-sacrifice, generosity translated into action, fraternity and solidarity. In the one as in the other, one works, one votes today, counting above all on the future . . . The cell, like the local church, guards you and remembers you. [Bonnet et al., 1962:70]

The founding fathers of communism also noted the parallels between the Church and the Communist movement. Engels devoted considerable attention to the study of early

Christianity and the incipient Communist movements.[7]
His classic study of the peasant wars in Germany (1926)
similarly draws a parallel between a heretical Church
movement and a proletarian Communist movement.
Gramsci's notion of the structural similarities between the
Communist Party and the Church is implicit in his depic-
tion of the functional equivalency of the Church and the
Party. Although couched largely in ideological terms,
Gramsci's position foreshadowed the postwar PCI tactic of
constructing antiparishes.

The Church's integralist norm is clear, though it has not
gone unchallenged. The faithful are called on not only to
perfom the various rites of the Church and to believe in
the Church's eschatological precepts but also to follow
unquestioningly the counsel of the Church hierarchy
against all those identified as the enemy. The integralism
of the Communist Party is more complex, and it is officially
repudiated by the PCI, but the allegiance sought is as
comprehensive as that called for by the Church. The ideal
Party member not only follows the political line of the PCI,
but also spends his extrafamilial leisure time in the secure
network of organizations close to the Party.

In communities in which the Party organizational infrastructure is strong, the world view of Party members is an
outgrowth of their social bonds. Children of Party members become members themselves, and the centrality of
the Communist social sphere attracts outsiders as well,
both immigrants and local people from non-Communist
families. Yet even in Albora, where the Church is weak,
it is unusual for the child of a family firmly in the sphere
of the Catholic world to take on a Communist allegiance,
although it is not uncommon to find such young people
who are dissatisfied with the conservative ideology espoused by the Church.

In Albora hundreds of men regularly gather together

under the direct or indirect auspices of the PCI, whereas their association with the Church is occasional at best. The brokerage duties traditionally performed by the learned and politically well-connected priests of Albora are now more often performed by PCI-tied personnel holding Party or governmental positions. Public rituals expressing community solidarity are now centered around the Party rather than around the Church. The wealth of organizational life of the Church, referred to earlier by La-Palombara, simply does not exist in Albora. Indeed, the Church in Albora never entirely made the transition from political ruling body to political competitor, the transition that prompted the national formation of these Church-sponsored mass organizations.

Given this setting, the concept of two worlds provides a helpful framework for analyzing the organizational conflict between the Church and the Party. It is helpful too in its predictive value, pointing out areas where we might expect conflict to arise, where there is competition over specific spheres of behavior. It also provides a means of evaluating the success or failure of these two institutions by focusing on the ways in which they have succeeded in penetrating into the various aspects of social life.

The defect of the two-worlds scheme becomes evident when we try to use it to describe the behavior of individuals. As has often been mentioned in these pages, the fact that the two institutions make certain claims on individuals does not mean that the institutional norms are popularly compiled with. The fact that the Church forbids those who regard themselves as Catholic to vote for the PCI does not tell us what people actually do. Likewise, the fact that official norms state that every Party member should be a militant tells us little of how politically active Party members are.

The most difficult problem in using the two-worlds concept is in dealing with just those topics that are assumed in the Catholic Communist model. Preeminent among these is the question of participation of people regarding themselves as Communist in the ritual life of the Church. How does one account for the fact that the great majority of Communist Party members goes to the Church for rites of passage or that many wear crosses around their necks? The two-worlds model is of little use here.

Subculture and hegemony

The concept of two subcultures – one Catholic and the other Communist – is obviously similar to the two-worlds model. Among the first to employ this subculture terminology in the Church–PCI context were Pizzorno (1966) and Galli (1966), both of whom cite American sociological sources as their inspiration. Galli advanced the idea of two subcultures existing alongside a predominant national culture, a lay bourgeois culture produced by the capitalist industrial revolution. What distinguishes a "subculture" from a "culture," in this scheme, is that the former characterizes a minority group: "The two subcultures were, on the one hand, the remains of a once dominant culture (the Catholic) and, on the other, the product of a new cultural attitude bound to new cultural developments, namely, Marxist-inspired socialism" (1966:249–50). Galli portrays the subcultures primarily in ideological terms, though he recognizes the importance of social factors:

The defining characteristic of a subculture is that it has its own set of values, different and often contrasting with that of the dominant culture. It is a set of values that reflects its own patrimony of language, of songs, of rites, of *feste* – all characteristics that we find in both the Catholic and the Socialist movements. Political attitudes are one of the aspects of this patrimony, handed down from generation to generation. [1966:250]

Pizzorno also identifies subcultures with minority groups, particularly groups whose members feel disadvantaged in comparison with other groups in society. But Pizzorno emphasizes social rather than ideological elements as defining characteristics. People in a subculture do not reject the values of the larger society, rather, they seek security by limiting their social sphere to others in their position (1966:273–5). In these terms, much of local political life in Italy, transpiring in local sections of the mass membership parties, is seen as a process of social segregation:

The mass parties tend to be composed of two strata, distinct in both norms and activities. At the lower level, that *grosso modo* of the sections (though there are certain types of sections which follow a different model) – the associational and cooperative life is organized, permitting the old and the new members, the latter in general being the children of the former, to continue living [*durare*] in a system of values and faith which is solid but without particular stimulus toward true political action.

The subculture thus implies cultural homogeneity, permitting people to avoid the unpleasantness of contacts with people who are socially and culturally different, even if they have the same political ideas. [1972:36]

The concept of subculture, insofar as it is used to elucidate the social presence of the Church and the PCI, may prove to be more misleading than enlightening. The subculture concept itself has been under anthropological attack for a number of years (see Valentine 1967), so that it now is used more frequently by sociologists and political scientists than by anthropologists. The Italian political literature has done nothing to clarify the conceptual distinction between culture and subculture, with a subculture being variously conceived of as equivalent to a culture but pertaining to a smaller group of people, or as some sort of subdivision of a larger culture. "Subculture" is sometimes used to refer to an organizational nexus (as it appears to be in Lange 1975) and at other times (as in Galli's case) to a system of values.[8]

If, as is most often the case, a subculture is thought to refer to a system of values and modes of perception, the danger of speaking of unitary subcultures of Catholics and of Communists should be apparent. The beliefs and behavior of Communists in Bologna are different from those of Communists in Calabria, and the same could be said of Catholics. Even in the same locality, as is recognized by Pizzorno, different social strata associated with each of the two institutions exhibit different beliefs and behavior. It would not appear, then, that the concept of subculture provides a useful tool for analyzing loyalties to Church and Party.

"Hegemony," one of the most common terms in the Italian political lexicon, is a more fertile concept in understanding Church–Communist struggle, for it can be conceived in terms of process rather than as a static trait list. Employed widely by Marxists and non-Marxists alike, the term has been assigned a wide variety of meanings.[9] Sometimes referring simply to a nationally ruling party (Wiatr 1970), it has a broader definition in Gramscian terms, referring to a class that is politically dominant and that is able to monopolize the cultural symbols and the socialization process of a society (Gruppi 1972:88–9).[10]

The Gramscian usage of "hegemony," although recognizing social factors, accentuates the ideological nature of the political process. The substitution of the hegemony of the Church by the hegemony of the Party was, for Gramsci, largely a matter of substituting one world view for another. But the concept of hegemony may be made more useful, in the present context, if given a more social emphasis, for ideological appeals cannot be extricated from their social content. Conversion or socialization to the hegemonic sphere of the Church or the Party is as much a matter of social factors as of ideological allure. Though our Western intellectualistic heritage biases us toward a belief in the primacy of ideological factors over social forces, there is no justification for seeing social behavior as derivative from ideological principles.

Hegemony, then, should be seen as a process, and as such is a matter of degree, the extent to which people are embedded in the social networks, organizational structure, and symbolic system of a political force that seeks their allegiance. Both Church and PCI have hegemonic aspirations and both have established hegemonic spheres. Yet these spheres cannot be simply measured by voting behavior or political opinions. In some areas, for example, a high Communist vote is found without the organizational infrastructure necessary for the establishment of Party hegemony. In such cases the hold of the Party over the people is tenuous. The hegemonic designs of the Church and the PCI are necessarily in mutual conflict, both in the social and the symbolic sphere. In terms of people's response to these competing hegemonic bids for their allegiance, conflict may be more acute in the social sphere than it is in the symbolic. Human ability to syncretize diverse symbolic systems is legendary, and people are under no constraint to adopt only nonconflicting symbols.[11] Yet people have less freedom in the social arena, where mixing and matching can be untenable. The Italian evidence bears this out, for although a variety of syncretized and apparently disjointed mixtures of symbolism have been documented, the mixture of social networks associated with the competing political forces is more limited. The individual who participates in the web of Church organizational life does not particiate in its Communist counterpart. In much of Italy, similarly, the person wrapped in the organizational life and social networks associated with the Party is divorced (excepting involvement linked to rites of passage) from the social networks and organizational system of the Church.

Making things more complicated

The Catholic Communist and the two-worlds models of Church–Communist conflict in Italy share the virtue of simplicity, a virtue that, in this case, is indicative of their inadequacy. The former scheme roughly describes people's behavior in certain places; the second reflects the organizational logic of institutional strategies. What is needed is a perspective that can deal both with behavioral data at the local level and with organizational strategies and structures. Toward this end, it is useful to distinguish among five different spheres of analysis: (1) national institutional policy, (2) organizational structure, (3) local organizational policy and activity, (4) people's norms, and (5) people's behavior.

National institutional policies and norms are basic to an understanding of the Catholic–Communist conflict on the local level; they affect all four other spheres of analysis. The characterization of national institutional norms is complicated by the fact that in many cases there is no normative consensus (though in both the case of the Church and the PCI this is minimized in public declarations). Disagreement over norms at the national level is reflected at the local level when competing local factions take advantage of the normative diversity to justify their own position and to discredit others. Such was the case, for example, of the Uva storefront church, where Pope John XXIII was continually cited to lend legitimacy to the unorthodox undertaking. Another kind of heterogeneity of norms at the national level also exists, a disjunction between overt norms (those publicly adhered to) and covert norms (those privately held). Institutional action is in some cases better understood through reference to covert norms than to those that are publicly endorsed. The PCI attitude toward the Church provides a complex case of a unitary overt norm contrasted with a diversity of covert norms regarding the mutual compatibility of Catholicism and Communism.

The nature of organizational structure reflects national party strategy at the same time as it constrains it. The effectiveness of institutional norms and strategies can in part be measured through an analysis of the organizational structure. This is particularly important in the case of the Church–Communist struggle, because of the integralist aspirations of the two institutions. The wider the net of organizational presence and the greater the number of people participating in the organization, the stronger is the Party or the Church.

Local policy and activity link the national strategy and organizational structure to the local community. They reflect national policy, but as constrained by local social factors and political strength. Local party leaders can fruitfully be seen as brokers coping with the national institutional demands in a setting in which they cannot afford to take all official guidelines too seriously. Although both the Church and the Party hierarchical structures are unusually tight-knit and efficient, with intricate systems of control from above of activities below, the fact that local-level activity varies so widely from one locality to another testifies to the number of factors that intervene between national policy and local action.

Studies of people's norms, often tapped through formal questionnaires, are among the most common of sociological topics. As the case of Albora should make clear, though, norms are an exceedingly slippery subject. Not only do different people have different norms, but the same person has conflicting norms. Moreover, what people verbalize as their norms may have little to do either with what they consider their norms or with the actual attitudes and values that guide their action. The divergence between people's beliefs and their public statement of beliefs is well illustrated in the case of Italy by the consistently and significantly smaller number of people who have told survey researchers that they were Communist supporters than actually identified with and voted for the PCI. A related problem also exists, with Communists and Catholics providing the official position of Party or Church as their own, though in fact they may hold dissenting opinions.

Finally, there is the question of individual behavior as seen by an outside observer. Strangely enough, this is one of the least studied areas in the Catholic–Communist literature. Scores of studies have been published analyzing national policies, organizational structures, local-level policymakers, and people's norms, but few have appeared that address the question of what the mass of people actually do. This reflects both a methodological bias and larger cultural factors (such as a fascination with elites), resulting in a serious gap in our knowledge of Italian society. If a social perspective is substituted for an intellectualistic perspective, if people's beliefs are seen as largely socially determined, the lack of local-level studies of behavior is particularly lamentable.

How, then, can the behavior of the Alborese best be described and, ultimately, explained? The national strategies of Church and PCI have been examined, the organizational structure depicted, the nature of local-level leadership and policy-making probed, and local beliefs and behavior investigated. The two-worlds concept has been found to be misleading, given the lack of mutual exclusivity between Church and Party allegiances among the people, but this need not entail slipping back into the Catholic Communist model.

The Albora case shows that the coexistence of ties to Church and party cannot be simply attributed to popular ignorance, as Faenza and others have done. As discussed in our conclusions to Chapter 6, it is a self-delusion for the Church to claim that the great bulk of those who support the PCI do so in ignorance of the "real" Communist doctrine, misled by PCI rhetoric. Although, like the mass of Catholics themselves, the Communist member and voter does not know all his institution's official doctrines, he is not being duped. Not only does the Communist Party present a concrete plan for economic betterment of the worker, but it also provides a web of social organizations and social reinforcement. There is no adult in Albora unaware of the Church's fierce opposition to the Communist Party. The Alborese does not affiliate with the Party thinking that either the Party or the Church believes a division of loyalty to be theoretically consistent. The inconsistency at the institutional level, though, should not be taken to entail ignorance on the part of people expressing such divided loyalties. The strategy of the individual is entirely different from that of the institutions; the individual can seek to obtain the proverbial "best of both worlds." He may increase his local prestige and gain entrance to a desirable peer group through association with the Party; at the same time he may ask to be buried by a priest in order "not to take any chances." He may subscribe to the Party program of economic reforms and still believe in the divinity of Jesus. Both Party and Church struggle to win the individual over to an undivided allegiance, but there is little reason to assume that all or even most individuals should find such undivided loyalty to be their most attractive option.

Given that the exact nature of popular allegiance to the Church and the Communist party varies from locality to locality and from person to person, there remains the question of whether any pattern of divided allegiance can be discerned and explained. The mapping of Italy along this dimension is not yet possible, given the scanty observational data, but some general observations can be made. In the space of a small corner of Italy, from Veneto to rural Romagna to Bologna, markedly contrasting systems are found. In Veneto the Church provides the central symbolism of community solidarity, with allegiance to the PCI being seen as heretical and antisocial. In the Romagna described by Faenza, the symbolism of Church and Party provides the symbolism of community solidarity, and allegiance to the one without the other marks a person as socially marginal to the community. In Albora, the Party provides the predominant community symbolism, but social isolation from the Church, if absolute, marks a person as socially anomalous.

The two poles described here are not mirror images of each other. If only because of the pervasive Church monopoly of rites of passage, in even the most heavily Communist area the Church continues to be part of the mainstream social landscape of the community; some contact and identification with the Church is considered to be a normal part of social life. Yet in the communities where the Church is at its strongest, publicly expressed PCI allegiance is rare and socially stigmatic. The public attitudes of the priests toward the Communists in Veneto also contrast with the publicly expressed attitudes of the Communist leaders toward the churchgoers in Bologna. Although the former range from hostility to patronism (Stern 1975:243), the latter are more tolerant. The tolerance of churchgoing behavior by the Party, reflected in statements of local Party officials, has its limits, though. Regular church attendance is frowned on by the Communists and is seen as a sign of antagonism to the Communist collectivity.

The two major questions that arise from this portrait are

(1) What accounts for the difference in balance of forces between Church and PCI in different localities? and (2) What accounts for the continued widespread subscription to Church rites of passage? The former is a historical question to which a substantial literature is addressed. Stern (1972), for example, in contrasting the strength of the Church in Veneto with its weakness in Emilia, refers to the identification of the local clergy with the interests of the prevalent small landholders in the former case and the clergy's close ties with the large landholders in the latter case. The role of the clergy in the economic system, the nature of foreign political rule and the position of the clergy as rulers or as mediators between the rulers and the interests of the local people, the land holdings of the Church, the nature of the liberation from fascism, and a variety of other factors are involved here.

The constancy of Church influence even in the areas in which the Communist Party is strongest, especially through Church control of rites of passage, raises the classic question in the study of religion: Why are rites of passage virtually a cultural universal? In this context the more specific question can be posed: Is there any reason these rites must be monopolized by the Church and cannot be expropriated by the PCI? Is there any reason why the PCI has been able to wrest control of rites of community but unable to win control of the rites of passage?

Given a social conception of the nature of religion, there appears to be no reason why the Church could not be substituted by the Party as the fount of all ritual. If ritual, as Durkheim portrayed it, is essentially the expression of societal sovereignty over the individual, the transcendental character of ritual does not consist of a prior belief in the supernatural; rather, the supernatural quality is a product of the social experience. Given these premises, the symbolism of the Party could replace the symbolism of the

Church as the nexus of ritual life. The fact that the Party has not succeeded in replacing the Church as the sponsor of rites of passage should, in this framework, be seen as a result of an organizational failure, linked to strategic considerations. The conciliatory posture of the Party toward the Church, in other words, has prevented the Party from making a convincing assault on the most zealously guarded domain of Church influence over the masses, the rites of passage. In support of this view, it could also be claimed that the time required for such a radical symbolic transformation is considerable, and the scarcely more than one generation that has passed since the advent of the PCI as a mass force has been too brief a period for such a transformation to occur.[12]

Doubts remain, though, such as those that arise from reports from the Soviet Union of continued strong ties to Church rites of passage and dissatisfaction with the rites of passage provided by the Communist state (Powell 1975). A theoretical justification for these doubts may be found in psychological interpretations of the ritual "impulse," such as those that link funerary ritual to a longing for immortality. Yet such attempts to find a universal psychological explanation for ritual have also run into difficulties, given the widely varying content of ritual activity cross-culturally (such as the extent to which any notion of life after death exists). In defense of the social perspective, moreover, the discontent with state-sponsored rites of passage in Communist nations could be attributed either to insufficient appreciation by the authorities of the importance of creating a satisfying symbol system for rites of passage or to dissatisfaction of the people with the symbolism of the Party.

Here we can do no more than raise these issues, issues that are not only of theoretical interest but that have considerable political implications for Italy. As indicated in

Chapter 6, the influence of the primary anti-Communist force in Albora, as in many other Italian communities, is dependent on continued monopoly of rites of passage.

Recent developments

Since 1972, when fieldwork was completed, Italy has experienced a succession of dramatic events. Although the most spectacular of these has been the outbreak of urban terrorism launched by small extremist groups,[13] the most substantial have been the series of political victories by the left. Separated from the DC by 11.6 percent of the popular vote in 1972, in the 1976 election the PCI, with over a third (34.4 percent) of all votes, rose to within 4.3 percent of the DC. Gaining forty-nine seats in the Lower House and twenty-five in the Upper, the PCI confronted a center that had lost thirty-five Lower and 8 Upper House seats, and a right that lost 21 Lower and 11 Upper House posts (Spreafico 1977:122, 136). When the Socialist party refused to form a government with the DC that would exclude the Communists, the DC found itself unable to form any government at all without Communist support. In the immediate aftermath of the 1976 election, a temporary solution was found when the PCI agreed to a *monocolore* DC government, with the Communists abstaining from the parliamentary vote of confidence on the condition that the Party would have influence in governmental policy formation. Inevitably a fragile formula, this solution crumbled by January of 1978, and one of the lengthiest governmental crises in Italian history ensued. The PCI demanded entrance into the governmental majority and the DC, holding firm to its anti-Communist guns, threatened to dissolve the parliament and call emergency national elections rather than allow Communists in the government. After several weeks of struggle, a compromise was reached allowing the

Communists explicitly to enter the parliamentary majority for the first time since the government of national unity dissolved in 1947, but retaining a *monocolore* DC government. The new government thus formed was hardly more stable than its predecessor, and by the beginning of 1979 it disintegrated because of the continued refusal of the Christian Democrats to give posts in the cabinet to the Communists. Against a festering terrorist background, emergency national elections were held in June of 1979, resulting in the first PCI electoral setback of the postwar period. Yet the Communists retained over 30 percent of the vote and the Christian Democrats remained at their historic electoral lowpoint, promising no more stable a political situation in the near future than had existed up to that point.

Church–Party relations were more directly affected in the past few years by two referenda, one on divorce and the other on abortion. Italy's first law providing for divorce was passed in 1970, despite DC opposition. In response, a petition calling for the repeal of the divorce law was organized by conservative clerical elements and other right-wing forces and was circulated nationally. In keeping with its national policy of conciliation, the PCI did all it could to avoid the referendum. The worry among Party leaders, reminiscent of the Constitutional Assembly vote on the Concordat over a quarter century earlier, was that the referendum would have a polarizing effect, driving a wedge between the PCI and the masses of those loyal to the Church. The Party had so often proclaimed that there was no conflict between being a Communist and being a Catholic that it was not eager to see a showdown take place in which the two competitors were so obviously in conflict. Meanwhile, many in the Church hierarchy were not eager for the referendum, afraid that in what would be seen as a plebiscite of popular support for the Church, the Church might lose. Yet, after much delay, in 1974 the referendum did take place. The PCI actively campaigned for a no vote (against repeal), whereas the Church, the MSI, and, to a lesser extent, the DC organized for repeal. The result was a resounding defeat for the Church, as 59 percent of the voters opposed repeal, just 41 percent siding with the Church (Marradi 1976; Parisi 1974; Galli 1974; Pedrazzi 1974).[14]

The PCI was more successful in heading off the scheduled referendum on abortion. Resulting from a petition drive organized by left-wing and civil libertarian forces outside the Party, the referendum called for the repeal of the national statute, of Fascist vintage, which criminalized abortion. Again the PCI worked furiously to avoid a plebiscite and, hence, to avoid any further confrontations with the Church. While devising compromise legislation that could pass Parliament and that would nullify the scheduled referendum, the Party came under heavy attack by militant proabortion forces. These supporters of the referendum saw the national vote as a means of showing the extent of popular support for their position and as the only way to abolish all governmental controls on abortion. This time, however, the DC eschewed obstructionist tactics (though of course voting against decriminalization), for fear of provoking the PCI into governmental opposition. Thus, much to the anger of the conservative elements of the Church, in 1978 Parliament proceeded to pass legislation allowing abortion on demand (though with some restrictions). Though the new law was among the most liberal in the Western world, champions of the referendum vociferously denounced the PCI for "selling out" women's civil rights to benefit the Party's strategic interests.

Reaction in the Church to the new abortion legislation was somewhat sidetracked by the preoccupation in the months that followed with the changing of papal regimes.

By Christmas of 1978, though, evidence mounted that the stridently antiabortion forces represented by the archbishop of Florence, who urged a new referendum to recriminalize abortion, were receiving the backing of the new pope, John Paul II. By early 1979 journalistic references to a "new crusade" and a new era of Church militancy under John Paul II proliferated.

In contrast with these substantial developments at the national level, the political-religious situation in Albora in these years has remained largely unchanged. The PCI vote, the rate of church attendance, the positions taken by Church and Party in the local context have remained the same. The storefront church, the hope of the "progressive" Church forces for the renaissance of the Catholic world in the *quartiere*, has not succeeded in altering the balance of forces. Indeed, unable to establish a core of local lay leaders and feeling isolated both from the community and from the Church hierarchy, don Francesco was working in a factory and considering leaving the priesthood. The party, meanwhile, has continued to flourish, adding a new section by splitting the territory of the overgrown Dovero section.

Yet changes are occurring in Albora, and they are being experienced by similar communities of the urban *periferia* in much of Italy. Expanses of undeveloped land are giving way to high-rise apartment complexes, and the population is growing via in-migration to the *quartiere* from other parts of the city, province, and nation. This expansion is bringing about not only an increase in population but a change in the socioeconomic composition of the *quartiere*, as many of the new apartments are selling for prices blue-collar workers cannot afford. It is just this development that has Albora's Party leaders most worried, for theirs has been a proletarian party organization, with a nucleus of proletarian section activists and a social nexus of proletarian unity. More important, from the point of view expressed in these pages, the new ecological setting – highrise apartment living – combined with an alteration in social class composition, may threaten the social basis of PCI hegemony in Albora if other social networks and social organizations, not connected with the Party, become more prominent. Against this assessment, though, it should be noted that the PCI has done well in Bologna in attracting the support of the middle class, and the Party-connected web of allied organizations includes several that are geared toward middle-class interests, though many of these have a downtown focus (see Hellman 1975).

The future of the PCI and the Church in Albora is also dependent on factors, both political and economic, originating outside the *quartiere*. Should, for example, there be a spectacular rise or fall in the fortunes of the PCI on the national level, it would have a substantial effect on the balance of power in the local PCI–Church struggle. Should the PCI enter the government, and should it solidify its position in the executive branch, we would expect an increase in the incentives to membership, through the federal spoils system (*sottogoverno*); at the same time the Church would lose much of its brokerage ability. The long-term effects of PCI participation in the government are more difficult to predict. Should the economic crises continue and, along with it, the political violence that has plagued many of Italy's cities, sharing governmental responsibility might prove to be a liability for the PCI. There are also those who predict that another economic boom in Italy would turn the tide of Communist success, moving the people to more conservative parties. Yet this frequently mentioned reason for decline in Communist appeal is questionable; it certainly fails to account for the rise of Party fortunes in Albora throughout the postwar years when percapita income was on the rise.[15]

The Communist–Church struggle in Albora is rich in apparent contradictions. Seen in traditional Marxist terms as the tool of the ruling class, the instrument used by the bourgeoisie to ensure the acquiescence of the lower classes, the Church in Italy is treated gingerly by the PCI. Avoiding all discussion of the history of Church collaboration with socially and politically conservative interests and expressing dismay at the steady output of denunciations of the PCI by the Church hierarchy, the Party continues its conciliatory campaign. The campaign has not been without its spectacular moments (such as the PCI alliance with the DC and the rightwing in voting for the inclusion of the Concordat in the Italian Constitution), nor has it been without its organizational innovations (such as the Party position that its ideology and program are separable). Yet, whatever else may be said about it, the Party's course has been an electoral success.

On the local level, in Albora, a more orthodox Marxist position has prevailed: Local activists recognize the Church as the Party's arch enemy and they see this as the natural state of affairs. Though constrained by national Party policy not to take any action directed against the Church, and undoubtedly ready to repeat the Party position of the compatibility of Catholicism and Communism to any wandering pollster,[16] the Communists of Albora have only to look as far as the lawn of the parish church to find the center of anti-Communist activity in the *quartiere*.

Envious of the position of the Church in the nation's white regions, where much of community life revolves around the church and where priests are typically among the most important local influence brokers (Evans 1976), the Church faithful in Albora find themselves outnumbered and isolated. Unable to evolve a viable strategy to counter Communist hegemony and tied to the middle-class minority in a working-class *quartiere*, the organizational web of the Church in Albora has been reduced to an embarrassing minimum. In Albora, the PCI has surpassed its goal of a "party section for every belltower . . . every section a community center." The Church is scorned, yet not abandoned. As for the future, the Catholic faithful take comfort in the thought that, though the Communists may continue to advance on the national scene, in Albora the Church's future can hardly be more bleak than its present.

Notes

1. Introduction

1. The division of Italy into two worlds – one Catholic and the other Communist – is dramatically expressed in Togliatti's (1954) famous appeal for the salvation of humanity.
2. For a penetrating analysis of Italian local-level political studies, see Catanzaro (1975).
3. Albora is a pseudonym, as are all other names of people and places within the *quartiere*.
4. The socioeconomic and political characteristics of Bologna's *periferia* are discussed in Ardigò (1963). The economic infrastructure of the *quartieri* is examined in Bellettini and Tassinari (1971).
5. Bologna's municipal decentralization, hailed by the PCI as a path-breaking step toward democratization of city government, has been the subject of numerous accounts and analyses. See Bologna (1963, 1970a, 1970b); Ardigò (1970); Assistenti (1968); Bellettini (1968); Castellucci (1970); Convegno Nazionale sul Decentramento (1970); Crocioni (1968).
6. The PCI's strength in Bologna is reflected in the fact that, in 1977, only three of Italy's twenty regions had more members than the Federation of Bologna, one of ten federations in Emilia-Romagna. These three regions are Emilia-Romagna, Toscana, and Lombardia (PCI 1978b:3–5).
7. The pitfalls and limitations of a survey approach to the question of Communist allegiance are evident in Evans's (1967) study of the PCI in Bologna. See also Almond and Verba's (1963) frequently cited study, in which just 10 percent of their Italian respondents admitted to voting PCI.
8. Parisi and Pasquino (1976) note a new trend in the electoral opinion surveys conducted previous to the national elections in 1976, in

which fewer respondents said they would vote DC than actually did vote DC (assuming the representativeness of the sample). They cite the comments of the president of one of the major Italian polling agencies: "until a few years ago people were afraid of saying that they were voting for the PCI, due to the intimidating climate of the time . . . today, instead, the opposite is happening: the Communist Party appears as legitimate to most people, while many people are ashamed to admit their vote for the DC." In addition, Parisi and Pasquino claim that a bias is introduced by people's perception of sociologists, intellectuals, and students – and, hence, pollsters – as part of the left, leading many respondents to hide their DC support (1976:346–7).

9. The two major regions of the Red Belt, Emilia-Romagna and Toscana, although having less than 14 percent of the national population, provided, in 1977, over 39 percent of the Party's national membership (Istituto Centrale di Statistica 1976:9; PCI 1978:4–5).

2. Communist world

1. Until 1979, the PCI had made steady electoral progress since the first postwar election in 1946, with its only stagnant period coming after the multiple crisis of 1956. Yet even in this period of the Soviet invasion of Hungary and the relevations about Stalin, the Party gained votes. The greatest electoral advance came in 1976, when the PCI received 12.6 million votes (PCI 1977:64–5).

2. By 1977 national PCI membership stood at 1.8 million (PCI 1978b:5).

3. By 1975 the PCI had become the major party in most of the nation's large cities. Of the ninety-five provincial capitals, twenty-one had Communists mayors in 1977. In smaller communities the PCI has been less successful, holding just 13.7 percent of the mayors' offices (PCI 1978b:37).

4. Among recent volumes dealing with the nature of PCI strength nationally, see the articles in *Sociologie du Communisme en Italie* (1974) and Blackmer and Tarrow (1975).

5. One of these cooperatives was closed down by the government in the early 1950s, leaving one of the sections without as associated *circolo*.

6. The Party *quartiere* coordinator, though a relatively recent position, is not a post unique to Bologna. Gori (1975:279) describes a similar organizational development in Florence.

7. According to a number of observers (see, especially, Weber 1977),

the difference between the vote of men (more to the left) and the vote of women (more conservative) has been dwindling. Parisi and Pasquino (1976:350) hypothesize, in the wake of the 1976 elections, that there is no longer any significant difference between the electoral behavior of men and women. Among earlier studies that found a sharp sexual differentiation in the vote, see Visentini (1974:197) and Dogan (1963).

8. See Chapter 9 for a full discussion of this incident.

9. Since the FGCI boom in the early postwar years, the organization has been numerically weak compared to its parent party. In 1977 the FGCI had 128,000 members, of whom the Bologna Federation provided 3,700 and Emilia-Romagna as a whole 24,000 (PCI 1978b:38–9). For a recent analysis of FGCI membership, see Barbagli and Corbetta (1978:20–2).

10. There is some evidence that since 1972 a number of PCI-allied organizations have acquired a greater autonomy, but at the local level this phenomenon has barely been studied (Pasquino 1978:10–11).

11. The politicization of recreational facilities can be illustrated by the following incident. One day an Albora Church activist and his wife invited my wife and me to play tennis. They drove us 15 miles to a church that had a tennis court. Later, I suggested that we play more often, proposing that we use the normally vacant tennis court of the municipal sports center in Albora. The churchgoer replied, *"non sono abituato ad andarci"* ("I'm not accustomed to going there") and suggested that we play again on the same court, 15 miles away.

12. A more precise figure cannot be given, for no data are available on the number of Alborese belonging to party sections based at their place of work (e.g., railroad workers, bus drivers). As of mid-1972, Albora's four sections had 1550 members. Party officials have estimated the number of Alborese belonging to sections at their place of work to be from 200 to 500. As the lower of these figures appears to be closer to the actual number, the somewhat arbitrary number of 250 has been used here.

13. In areas having a high PCI vote the ratio of Party members to Party voters also tends to be high, reflecting the local organizational strength and the nature of social pressures. Thus, whereas nationally well under 20 percent of PCI voters were Party members in 1972, in Albora over 40 percent were members. Nor is Albora exceptional in this regard. In the two Red Belt *comuni* studied by

Stern (1972:710), the ratio of PCI members to PCI voters was 48.4 and 57.4.

14. The size of Albora's PCI sections roughly reflects section size throughout the Bolognese Federation. Of the 368 Party sections in 1976, 16.6 percent had no more than 100 members, 25.3 percent had 101–200 members, 38.8 percent had 201–500 members, and 19.0 percent had over 500 members (data unavailable for one section). Compared to the national pattern, Bologna is characterized by large sections, the 1976 national figures showing sections of no more than 100 members to be much more common (53.7 percent) and sections of more than 500 uncommon (4.2 percent) (PCI 1977:28–9).

15. The data that follow are drawn from the official membership records of the Vapori section.

16. Data on sex were available for 389 of 420 members. Data on Federation membership by sex are for 1967. Of Albora's general population, 50.7 percent are female.

17. Related to the link between social identity and PCI membership is the fact that membership turnover in Albora is very low. The average annual proportion of new members of the Party in Albora through the period 1968–77 was 4.8 percent; for the city of Bologna in 1972 the proportion of new members was 5.2 percent (and 3.4 percent in 1977) (*Società* 1977:58–9). These figures do not include immigrants to the *quartiere* or to the city who had already been PCI members before their move. Recruitment is thus in good part a matter of young people replacing the deceased. The number of local people who join the Party in middle age is small, and it is rare for a middle-aged or older person to give up his or her Party membership. Gori (1974, 1975) has found the same pattern in Florence, and he has claimed that this is a characteristic of Party membership throughout the Red Belt. For national and regional data on rates of membership renewal and nonrenewal, see Barbagli and Corbetta (1978:9–12).

18. This reference is to the clause of the statute that states that membership in the Party is open to all regardless of "religious faith and philosophical convictions" (i.e., the Party is open to Catholics).

19. Barbagli and Corbetta (1978) have conducted a study of PCI section congresses held in 1977, which, as they note, is the only study of its kind. Of the five federations studied (Bologna, Brescia, Trento, Prato, and Napoli), Bologna showed the lowest proportion (13.2 percent) of members attending the annual congress, and Trento showed the highest (60.2 percent). Based on their data, they con-

cluded that the stronger the organizational force of the Party in a locality, the smaller the proportion of members attending the section congress. This they explain as follows:

> In other words, the weaker the party is organizationally, and the more hostile and foreign it finds the society in which it operates, the stronger the motivations must be of the people who decide to join, and the more significant and important in their eyes is the tie they have established with the party. Hence, in such circumstances we would expect greater participation of the membership in the life of the section. [1978:38–9]

20. The fact that lack of participation in Party affairs does not in any way signify a propensity to give up Party membership was also noted in Florence by Gori:

> While there appear to be few reasons to participate [in Party activities], there are virtually no reasons for people to abandon the Party in which for the most part they are no longer active. At the root of this phenomenon is the stable and deeply rooted identification of the masses of members with the Party; this seems to be the principal, if not the only reason for the survival of the mass membership of the Communist Party. [1975:273]

21. Gori, based on his study of the PCI in Florence, has noted a tendency for the section committees to increase in size. He attributes this development to the increasing limitation of activists to those who hold offices. In some cases, in fact, nonactive members are elected to office in the hope that their election will motivate them to start being active in section affairs (1975:244).

22. Although the PCI has the highest level of female participation in leadership positions of any of Italy's major parties, women are underrepresented relative to their number in the membership. Curiously, this imbalance is particularly great in the Federation of Bologna, where, despite the unusually high proportion of female members, just 19.1 percent of the federation committee members were women, not much above the national figure of 16.4 percent in 1977 (PCI 1978:13–14).

A study of the membership of section committees in Florence in 1970 found that 19.3 percent were women, though women constituted 28.3 percent of the general membership. More strikingly, of the women on section committees, 45.5 percent were under twenty-five years of age, compared to the general section committee membership figure of just 18.6 percent under twenty-five years old (Gori 1975:262). This provides one indication of the conflict between the roles of wife and mother and that of Party activist.

23. The following information on the Party leadership is based on data from questionnaires completed by thirty-three of the forty officeholders in Albora. It includes data from the coordinator, all nine *quartiere* councilors, and twenty-seven of the thirty-four committeemen.

24. These figures on the middle-class component of the office-holding group are somewat inflated by the absence of the seven officeholders for whom complete data were unavailable. My impression is that none of these seven is of middle-class status.

25. The relative youth of Albora section committee members is not a peculiarity of this *quartiere*, as is made evident in the data provided by Barbagli and Corbetta (1978:35) for five federations, including two in the Red Belt (Reggio Emilia and Ferrara). In 1976 over 38 percent of the section committee members of Reggio Emilia and Ferrara were composed of comrades aged thirty and under, and about two-thirds consisted of individuals no older than forty. Yet half of the members of these sections had joined the Party by 1950 and thus were at least in their mid-forties and older by 1976 (1978:34).

3. Catholic world

1. In 1971 a third parish was added to Albora. This church, which is the subject of Chapter 8, is not considered in the present discussion of local church organization.

2. The figure of twenty includes all those who attend the sessions with any regularity. Perhaps six of these may be regarded as core group members, rarely failing to attend.

3. Italian Catholic Action, as part of the Church's international Catholic Action movement, is a confessional association of laymen formally committed to furthering the religious aims of the Church in society, under the tutelage of the Church hierarchy.

4. Pasquino (1975:446) attributes the founding of the DC to three forces, in the following order: (a) the Church and the Catholic lay organizations, especially the leadership of Catholic Action; (b) the foremost industrialists and businessmen, bound together in the

Confindustria, together with the *piccola borghesia* of the South, as represented by the southern "notables"; and (c) the United States.

5. Although the support received from the Catholic organizations was a source of great strength for the DC, it was also, as Pasquino notes (1975:446–7), an organizational weakness.

6. Histories and analyses of the DC include Baget-Bozzo (1974), Caciagli (1977), Ardigò (1974), Manoukian (1968), Menapace (1974), Galli (1977), Orfei (1976), Pasquino (1975), Poggi (1968), Pansa (1975), Sivini Cavazzani (1968), and Tamburrano (1974).

7. That the practice of housing the local DC section in the parish church is not simply a reflection of the weakness of the Albora DC may be seen from Stern's comments:

> In fact, in the decaying farm areas of Veneto almost no effort is made to disguise the primacy of the Church over the party. The secretary of the DC zone committee sees his job as less the recruitment of party members and the sponsorship of party activities and more a matter of coordinating ties among parish priests. . . . The DC does not even bother to maintain distinct party headquarters, merely using the parish house when meetings are scheduled. [1975:237]

8. When I interviewed the executive director of the provincial DC organization, he immediately asked if I knew Tassi but did not recognize the name of the present section head.

9. The following data are based on observation of Sunday and holiday mass attendance at Camolia and Andara over a nine-month period.

10. The data of the 1969 Church survey were collected by parish priests, who estimated the number of people attending mass in their church on a particular Sunday. The percentage of parishioners attending, therefore, is almost certainly inflated.

11. These data come from the membership forms filled out by the members. Occupation is often left unclear, as when place of employment rather than particular position occupied is provided. I would like to thank Arturo Parisi for aiding me in deciphering these forms.

12. See especially Chapter 7.

4. The anti-Communist crusade

1. Recently the anti-Communist movement within the Church has been revivified through the formation of the organization *Comu-*

nione e Liberazione. This development has been of concern to the PCI (Pratesi 1977). The organization has also been the target of various violent attacks by extreme left-wing groups.

5. Communist policy toward the Church

1. A history of the PCI position toward the Church is provided in Riccamboni (1976). The positions of other groups on the left toward the Church is documented in Zunino (1975, 1977).
2. Though these writings were not published until much later, they were written in the period 1929–35 (Fiori 1970:295). The dates cited herein are indicative neither of the time in which the publications were written nor of the time at which they were first read by Party cadres.
3. Gramsci's conception of the nature of religion is examined in Portelli (1974).
4. As Marx (1844:42) wrote, "Religion is only the illusory sun which revolves round man as long as he does not revolve round himself."
5. Palmiro Togliatti was the head of the PCI for over thirty years, from the time of Gramsci's imprisonment until Togliatti's death in 1964.
6. Since 1947 there have been various attempts to change the Concordat, but it was only in 1976 that a commission was established, consisting of representatives from both the Italian government and the Vatican, charged with drafting an amended version of the pact. The draft produced was forwarded to parliament, where the Communists, in 1979, were still calling for alterations. Among the changes called for by the PCI were the disestablishment of the Roman Catholic Church as the official state religion, the recognition by the Church of civil weddings, and the repeal of the provision mandating the teaching of Catholicism in the public schools. Throughout these negotiations, the PCI retained its conciliatory posture and castigated those who took less accommodating positions. As an article in the PCI almanac of 1977 proclaimed:

   > It is obvious that making the question of the Concordat into a battleground and thus disturbing religious peace and tearing apart the life of the country can only serve the forces that want a battle and are trying to interfere with the unified movement of popular and democratic forces which is indispensable for the salvation and renovation of Italy. [Chiarante 1977:119]

7. A good idea of the stringent anti-Church rhetoric employed by the

PCI in the pre-Vatican Council years can be gleaned by reading the Bologna Party weekly publication of the period, *La Lotta*. See especially the following issues: August 27 and October 15 of 1948, January 12, 1951, March 20, March 27, April 24, and June 19 of 1958.

8. The same distinction is found today, with PCI officials discerning hopeful signs in the movement of the Church hierarchy out of the "political" realm. Instructive are the recent comments of one of the Party's leading intellectuals: "The Church is tending to better distinguish between the sphere of the sacred and that of the profane, between religion and politics. It is establishing a greater distance between its moral teachings, which ought to guide the social action of the Christian, and the way in which these are politically translated" (Gruppi 1977:11).

9. The theme of the PCI as the true repository of morality can be seen in Colombi's (1946:1) pointed comments: "In the heroic behavior of the communist proletariat and the communist intellectuals, there is more spiritual force, more idealism . . . than those who offer gratuitous moral lessons can ever dream of having."

10. The PCI has seized on all available means to enter into a public, high-level dialogue with Church officials in order to proclaim its openness to the Catholic world. When, in July of 1976, the Bishop of Ivrea wrote an open letter to Berlinguer in the weekly diocesan newspaper, the Party responded with a highly publicized reply on the part of the PCI leader. Berlinguer treated the Bishop's critical but fraternal letter as a sign of increasing openness of the Church hierarchy toward the Party. The two letters, along with relevant Vatican and PCI accounts, were published by the Party press (Tatò 1977), and the Party has also published an English translation (Berlinguer 1977). See also Baget-Bozzo (1978).

11. The ideological pluralism championed by the PCI is succinctly expressed by Longo (1966:68): "Just as we are against a confessional state, so we are against the atheism of the state. That is, we are contrary to the state granting any privilege to an ideology or to a religious faith or cultural or artistic current to the damage of others."

12. As part of its demonstration of the compatibility of being a Communist and being a Catholic, the PCI secured the candidacy of several prominent Catholics for the 1976 national elections. Among these were journalists from the Vatican press and a priest. Their candidacies were accompanied by national distribution of posters

entitled "Why We Entered the PCI List" and "On June 20 . . . Catholics Will Again Vote for the Parties of the Left." One of these read, in part: "Without denying the legitimacy of different choices for others, we affirm the profound compatibility of our choice with our faith in Jesus Christ. The DC, in the name of an abstract liberty and democracy, has utilized the votes of many Catholics for many years to benefit the interests of the rich and the powerful" (Pratesi 1978:89).

6. The battle for ritual supremacy

1. See, for example, Leach (1954:10–17).
2. See also Bonicelli (1965b).
3. The Italian sociology of religion literature has recently been reviewed by Burgalassi (1974), Cipriani (1975), and Prandi (1977). See especially the Prandi work for bibliographical references.
4. *Comunione e Liberazione* is the name of a national conservative lay Church organization of anti-Communist youths.
5. One of the more dramatic instances of the mixing of Communist symbolism with the Church funerary ritual is detailed in an article in the *Corriere della Sera* of March 1978 (Borgese 1978), entitled *"Rosse le Bandiere intorno alla Chiesa"* ("Red Flags Surround the Church"). Thousands of people – youngsters, mothers, factory workers – had gathered around the church for the funeral of two teen-agers sympathetic to the extraparliamentary left who had been assassinated, presumably by Fascists. It was a striking scene:

> But what was new about the atmosphere in that plain piazza of the Milanese periphery yesterday was the fact that the church was not towering over a parish festa but over a sea of red flags which circled the church and gave an unusual sensation to the scene: almost as if the church were confronted with the symbol of a new culture and of a new mode of participation.

6. A similar development in another part of Bologna is described in Tentori and Guidicini (1972:98).
7. The PCI no longer opposes Italy's continued membership in NATO.
8. Tarrow (1975:155) has recently referred to the "primordial anti-Fascist vocation of the PCI," going on to state: "When tension increases in Italy, the PCI instinctively calls up the symbol of interparty anti-Fascist resistance as a model for political action . . ."

7. The immigrants

1. For an analysis of the electoral geography of Bologna and Emilia-Romagna, see Leonardi and Pasquino (1975).
2. Data on immigration to Bologna may be found in two publications of the office of the deputy mayor for immigration (Bologna 1964, 1966).
3. For a study of the roles of the Church in a Southern community, see Anfossi (1967).
4. Voting is a legal obligation of all adults and 98 percent of Albora's qualified voters cast ballots in the 1972 election. It is likely that well over 90 percent of the Southerners officially resident in Albora voted. Some of the migrants in Albora, though, do not have official residency status, continuing to be legal residents of their *paesi* of origin. This involves primarily those lone men who have migrated temporarily to earn money.
5. Data on place of birth were obtained for 332 of the 420 members of the Vapori section. Lazio is here considered to be in the South. The 12.1 percent Southerner figure was obtained from an analysis of the voting districts encompassed in the Vapori jurisdiction.
6. The observations in this chapter on the political socialization of adult migrants are relevant to the controversy regarding the extent to which political socialization is a childhood phenomenon. For a discussion of this question in a similar context, see Cornelius's (1975) study of migrants to Mexico City.

8. Storefront church

1. On the left-wing Church movements, see Bedeschi (1974).

9. Catholic *gruppetto* and Communist power

1. The term *gruppetto* is used here for want of an equally suitable term in English. It refers, in Italian political parlance, to small, independent groups, primarily composed of young people, working for radical social change.
2. This discussion refers to the situation through 1972. Subsequently, most of Buca was demolished as part of an urban renewal project.
3. The public housing funds being applied for by the PSC come from obligatory contributions, automatically deducted from workers' paychecks.
4. Among those so warned was the author.

10. The social bases of political allegiance

1. The notion of political allegiance as being the product of participation in social networks identified with a particular party is incorporated in Parisi and Pasquino's (1977a) usage of the phrase *voto di
   appartenenza*, a vote determined by social group identification. See
   also Sani (1976).
2. Over a decade ago Tarrow (1967b) debunked one version of this
   Communist-as-fanatic thesis.
3. This is evident in his preface:

   > The findings of such a study may serve two useful purposes.
   > First, if we can throw light on the kinds of social situations and
   > attitudes which contribute to susceptibility to Communism, we
   > may increase our understanding of the vulnerability of the free
   > world to Communist penetration. Second, if we can discover
   > those aspects of the Communist experience which create dis-
   > affection . . .we may be in a position to suggest the kinds of
   > weaknesses and vulnerabilities which are to be found within
   > the Communist movement. Both of these contributions may
   > provide useful leads in appraising the various policy approaches
   > to the Communist problem. [Almond 1954:ix]

   Almond's work is by no means an extreme example of this anti-
   Communist bias producing gross distortions in cold war analyses of
   European communism. Indeed, Almond has been cited by Blackmer (1975a:8n) as something of a moderate exception to the anti-
   Communist hysteria of American social science in the 1950s.
4. One book alone, *Mondo Piccolo* (Guareschi 1948), has gone through
   dozens of printings.
5. A typical Guareschi story concerns the local Party chief who comes
   to the priest to have his baby baptized, while expressing his opposition to the Church by calling on the priest to baptize the child
   with the name of Lenin (Guareschi 1948).
6. Or, as Bonicelli (1965a:190) put it, only the intellectuals abandon
   religion, the "poor do not even succeed in being atheist!"
7. See Engels's essays on the Book of Revelations and "On the History
   of Early Christianity" (Marx and Engels 1964).
8. A recent electoral analysis, for example, distinguishes five *zone
   subculturali* in Italy: the Industrial Triangle, the White Zone, the
   Red Zone, the Center, and the South. The author states, "The
   Catholic subculture is predominantly localized in the White Zone,
   but is also strong in the Center–South; the Marxist subculture is,

conversely, concentrated in the Red Zone, but is also strong in the provinces of the Industrial Triangle." As the author attempts to relate the presence of the subcultures to the DC and PCI vote, the definition of the subcultures is apparently independent of the parties' electoral strength. Just what the subcultures consist of, though, is left undefined (Bartolini 1977). For another discussion of *la subcultura socialista* and *la subcultura cattolica*, see Sivini (1971).

9. A recent column by Alberto Ronchey (1978), one of Italy's most influential centrist political commentators, was entitled *Questa Parolaccia che è l'Egemonia* ("This Dirty Word – Hegemony").

10. An interesting discussion of Gramsci's conception of hegemony is found in Bobbio (1969).

11. Not long ago a book appeared, entitled *Gesù Socialista: una Tradizione Popolare Italiana* (Nesti 1974).

12. That the Church monopoly on rites of passage may finally be significantly eroding is indicated by the latest available statistics on civil marriages. Throughout the large urban centers of northern Italy, the proportion of non-Church weddings has been rising geometrically throughout the 1970s. Using Bologna by way of example, during the 1960s just 3 to 5 percent of all weddings between never married individuals took place outside of church. By 1977 this proportion had risen to 28.3 percent, a grim statistic for the faithful (Parisi and Senin-Artina 1979).

13. The most spectacular of these was the 1978 kidnapping and later execution by the Red Brigades of Aldo Moro, the leader of the DC.

14. For an analysis of the divorce referendum vote in Emilia-Romagna, see Leonardi (1974).

15. For a discussion of the relationship between economic change and PCI appeal in a different part of Italy, see Tarrow (1972).

16. See Visentini (1974:193) and Sani (1975:483).

Bibliography

Abbott, Walter M., ed. 1966. *The Documents of Vatican II*. Baltimore: Geoffrey Chapman.

Alberoni, Francesco, Vittorio Capecchi, et al. 1967. *L'Attivista di Partito*. Istituto di Studi e Ricerche Carlo Cattaneo. Ricerche sulla partecipazione politica in Italia III. Bologna: Il Mulino.

Alessandrini, Ada. 1948. "L'equivoco dell'interclassismo," *Rinascita* 5:6:202–3.

Almond, Gabriel A. 1954 (1965). *The Appeals of Communism*. Princeton: Princeton University Press.

Almond, Gabriel A., and Sidney Verba. 1963 (1965). *The Civic Culture: Political Attitudes and Democracy in Five Nations*. Boston: Little, Brown.

Anfossi, Anna. 1962. "L'immigrazione meridionale a Torino," pp. 169–83 in *Immigrazione ed Industria: Atti del Convegno su l'Inserimento degli Immigrati nelle Comunità Industriali*. Milano: Edizioni di Comunità.

1967. "Funzioni della parrocchia e partecipazione dei parrocchiani alla vita religiosa in comuni agricoli della Sardegna," *Quaderni di Sociologia* 16 (aprile–giugno):190–216.

Araldi, Vinicio. 1964. *Emilia Rossa*. Roma: Vito Bianco.

Arbizzani, Luigi. 1961. *Sguardi sull'Ultimo Secolo: Bologna e la sua Provincia 1859–1961*. Bologna: Editrice Galileo.

Ardigò, Achille. 1959. "Le trasformazioni interne nelle campagne settentrionali e l'esodo rurale," pp. 39–54 in *Aspetti e Problemi Sociali dello Sviluppo Economico in Italia*. Bari: Laterza.

1963. "Il volto elettorale di Bologna," pp. 801–49 in Alberto Spreafico and Joseph LaPalombara (eds.), *Elezioni e Comportamento Politico in Italia*. Milano: Edizioni di Comunità.

1970. "Intervento," pp. 157–65 in Convegno Nazionale sul Decentramento, *Comuni e Decentramento*. Roma: Editori Riuniti.

1974. "Evoluzione, crisi e prospettive della presenza politico-sociale dei cattolici in Italia," *Aggiornamenti Sociali* 25:557–82.

Assistenti Sociali di Quartiere. 1968. "Considerazioni ed esperienze del servizio sociale di quartiere," pp. 115–28 in Comune di Bologna, *Quartieri e Servizio Sociale*. Bologna.

Baget-Bozzo, Gianni. 1974. *Il Partito Cristiano al Potere, da Dossetti a De Gasperi 1949/1954*. 2 vols. Firenze: Vallecchi.

1978. *I Cattolici e la Lettera di Berlinguer*. Firenze: Vallecchi.

Balandier, Georges. 1970. *Political Anthropology*. New York: Pantheon Books.

Barbagli, Marzio, and Piergiorgio Corbetta. 1978. "Partito e movimento: aspetti del rinnovamento del PCI," *Inchiesta* 7:31:3–46.

Barbiana, the School of. 1970. *Letter to a Teacher*. Hammondsworth, Great Britain: Penguin Books.

Bartolini, Barbara. 1977. "Insediamento subculturale e distribuzione dei suffragi," pp. 103–44 in Arturo Parisi and Gianfranco Pasquino (eds.), *Continuità e Mutamento Elettorale in Italia*. Bologna: Il Mulino.

Bedeschi, Lorenzo. 1969. "Il comportamento religioso in Emilia-Romagna," *Studi Storici* 2:387–406.

1974. *Cattolici e Comunisti: dal Socialismo Cristiano ai Cristiani Marxisti*. Milano: Feltrinelli.

Bellettini, Athos. 1967. "La presenza dei quartieri nella politica di sviluppo economico della città," pp. 48–61 in Comune di Bologna, *Quartieri e Servizio Sociale*. Bologna.

Bellettini, Athos, and Luciano Mazzaferro. 1967. *Le Abitazioni nel Comune di Bologna*. Bologna: Istituto Autonomo per le Case Popolari della Provincia di Bologna.

Bellettini, Athos, and Franco Tassinari. 1971. *Dati sulle Caratteristiche Economico-Sociali dei Quartieri di Bologna*. Mimeo.

Berlinguer, Enrico. 1977. "Communists and Catholics: clarity of principles and bases for an understanding," *The Italian Communists* no. 4, pp. 23–39 (Roma: PCI).

Blackmer, Donald L. M. 1975a. "Introduction," pp. 3–17 in Blackmer and Tarrow (eds.), *Communism in Italy and France*.

1975b. "Continuity and change in postwar Italian Communism," pp. 21–68 in Blackmer and Tarrow (eds.), *Communism in Italy and France*.

Blackmer, Donald L. M., and Sidney Tarrow, eds. 1975. *Communism in Italy and France*. Princeton: Princeton University Press.

Bobbio, Norberto. 1969. "Gramsci e la concezione della società civile," pp. 75–100 in *Gramsci e la Cultura Contemporanea*. Roma: Editori Riuniti.

Boissevain, Jeremy F. 1969. *Saints and Fireworks: Religion and Politics in Rural Malta*. London: Athlone Press.

Bologna, Comune di. 1963 (1970). "Delibera consigliare per il regolamento degli organismi democratici di quartiere (29 marzo 1963)," pp. 28–29 in *La Politica del Decentramento* . . . Bologna.

1964. *L'Immigrazione a Bologna*. Assessorato ai Problemi Sociali del Lavoro e Immigrazione. Bologna.

1966. *Studio sull'Immigrazione a Bologna*. Assessorato ai Problemi Sociali del Lavoro e Immigrazione. Bologna.

1970a. "Regolamento degli organismi democratici di quartiere," pp. 30–36 in *La Politica del Decentramento* . . . Bologna.

1970b. *La Politica del Decentramento Democratico negli Atti Formali del Comune di Bologna*. Bologna. Mimeo.

1971. *Annuario Statistico 1970*. Bologna.

1972. *Dati per Quartiere: XI Censimento Generale della Popolazione, 24 Ottobre 1971*. Bologna.

Bonicelli, Gaetano. 1965a. "Il paradosso del comunismo italiano: note su un'inchiesta pastorale," *Studi Sociali* nos. 3–4, pp. 181–259.

1965b. "I comunisti italiani e la religione," *Studi Sociali* nos. 3–4.

Bonnet, Serge, Charles Santini, and Hubert Barthélémy. 1962. "Appartenance politique et attitude religieuse dans l'émigration italienne en Lorraine sidérurgique," *Archives de Sociologie des Religions* 13:45–72.

Borgese, Giulia. 1978. "Rosse le bandiere intorno alla chiesa," *Corriere della Sera* (23 March), p. 3.

Boschini, Aurelio. 1965. "Introduzione al numero speciale sul comunismo italiano," *Studi Sociali* nos. 3–4, pp. 177–80.

Brucci, P. Vincent. 1969. *Chiesa e Stato: Church–State Relations in Italy Within the Contemporary Constitutional Framework*. The Hague: Martinus Nijhoff.

Burgalassi, Silvano. 1968. *Il Comportamento Religioso degli Italiani*. Firenze: Vallecchi.

1970. *Le Cristianità Nascoste; Dove Va la Cristianità Italiana?* Bologna: Edizioni Dehoniane.

1974. "La sociologia della religione in Italia dal 1968 ad oggi," *Studi di Sociologia* 12:392–418.

Caciagli, Mario et al. 1977. *Democrazia Cristiana e Potere nel Mezzogiorno: il Sistema Democristiano a Catania*. Firenze: Guaraldi.

Cafaro, G., and G. Quarta. 1964. *Che Cos'è il P.C.I., Come si Combatte il P.C.I.* Roma: Editrice Presenza.

Candeloro, Giorgio. 1953. *Il Movimento Cattolico in Italia.* Roma: Edizioni Rinascita.

Cantril, Hadley. 1958. *The Politics of Despair.* New York: Basic Books.

Castellucci, Federico. 1970. "La relazione introduttiva," pp. 5–29 in Comune di Bologna, *Sviluppo della Politica del Decentramento Democratico.* Bologna.

Catanzaro, Raimondo. 1975. "Potere e politica locale in Italia," *Quaderni di Sociologia* 24:273–322.

Chapman, Charlotte Glover. 1971. *Milocca: A Sicilian Village.* Cambridge, Mass.: Schenkman.

Chiarante, Giuseppe. 1977. "La revisione del Concordato," pp. 114–19 in *Almanacco PCI '77.* Roma: PCI.

Cipriani, Roberto. 1975. "Riflessioni critiche sullo sviluppo delle ricerche italiane in sociologia della religione," *Sociologia* 9:2:49–73.

Colombi, Arturo. 1946. "Comunisti e Cattolici," *La Lotta* (7 marzo) 3:10:1.

Convegno Nazionale sul Decentramento. 1970. *Comuni e Decentramento: Atti del I Convegno Nazionale sul Decentramento Democratico dei Comuni.* Roma: Editori Riuniti.

Cornelius, Wayne A. 1975. *Politics and the Migrant Poor in Mexico City.* Stanford: Stanford University Press.

Cossutta, Armando. 1967. "Relazione all'Assemblea Nazionale dei Segretari di Sezione," *Vita di Sezione* no. 15 (aprile), pp. 5–7.

Crisafulli, A. 1948. "La politica del Vaticano nel momento presente," *Rinascita* 5:9–10, 339–43.

Crocioni, Pietro. 1968. "Quartieri e partecipazione pubblica," pp. 15–27 in Comune di Bologna, *Quartieri e Servizio Sociale.* Bologna.

Cronin, Constance. 1970. *The Sting of Change: Sicilians in Sicily and Australia.* Chicago: University of Chicago Press.

Daniels, Robert V. 1962. *The Nature of Communism.* New York: Random House.

Democrazia Cristiana. 1968. *Statuto del Partito.* Roma.

De Rosa, Gabriele. 1970. *Il Movimento Cattolico in Italia dalla Restaurazione all'Età Giolittiana.* Bari: Laterza.

De Rosa, Giuseppe. 1966. *Cattolici e Comunisti Oggi in Italia: Via Italiana al Socialismo e Dialogo con i Cattolici.* Roma: Edizioni La Civiltà Cattolica.

Dogan, Mattei. 1963. "Le donne italiane tra il cattolicesimo e il marxismo," pp. 475–94 in Alberto Spreafico and Joseph LaPalombara (eds.), *Elezioni e Comportamento Politico in Italia*. Milano: Edizioni di Comunità.

Donini, A. 1953. "Programma oscurantista e violazione del Concordato," *Rinascita* no. 5 (maggio), pp. 289-91.

Durkheim, Emile. 1915 (1947). *The Elementary Forms of the Religious Life*. New York: Free Press.

Duverger, Maurice. 1964. *Political Parties*. London: Methuen.

Engels, Friedrich. 1926. *The Peasant War in Germany*. New York: International Publishers.

Evans, Robert H. 1967. *Coexistence: Communism and Its Practice in Bologna, 1945-1965*. Notre Dame: University of Notre Dame Press.

  1976. *Life and Politics in a Venetian Community*. Notre Dame: University of Notre Dame Press.

Faenza, Liliano. 1959. *Comunismo e Cattolicesimo in una Parrocchia di Campagna*. Milano: Feltrinelli.

Federazione Giovanile Comunista Italiana. 1957. *Statuto della FGCI*. Roma: La Stampa Moderna.

Fiori, Giuseppe. 1970. *Antonio Gramsci: Life of a Revolutionary*. London: New Left Review.

Fondation Nationale des Sciences Politiques. 1974. *Sociologie du Communisme en Italie*. Paris: Armand Colin.

Friedrich, Paul. 1966. "Revolutionary politics and communal ritual," pp. 191-220 in Marc Swartz et al. (eds.), *Political Anthropology*. Chicago: Aldine.

Galli, Giorgio. 1958. *Storia del Partito Comunista Italiano*. Milano: Schwarz Editori

  1966. *Il Bipartitismo Imperfetto: Comunisti e Democristiani in Italia*. Bologna: Il Mulino.

  1974. "Referendum e sistema politico italiano," *Il Mulino* 23 (no. 233):396-409.

  1978. *Storia della DC*. Bari: Laterza.

Gluckman, Max. 1963. *Order and Rebellion in Tribal Africa*. New York: Free Press.

Gori, Neri. 1974. "L'organizzazione del PCI a Firenze (1945-1971)," *Rassegna Italiana di Sociologia* 15:3:381-412.

  1975. "Attivismo tradizionale e crisi della partecipazione nel PCI. Il caso di Firenze," *Rassegna Italiana di Sociologia* 16:243-91.

Gramsci, Antonio. 1967. *Il Vaticano e l'Italia*. Roma: Editori Riuniti.

  1971a. *Il Materialismo Storico e la Filosofia di Benedetto Croce*. Roma: Editori Riuniti.

  1971b. *Note sul Machiavelli, sulla Politica e sullo Stato Moderno*. Roma: Editori Riuniti.

Gruppi, Luciano. 1964. "Il rapporto con i cattolici nella storia del PCI," pp. 163–92 in Mario Gozzini (ed.), *Il Dialogo alla Prova: Cattolici e Comunisti Italiani*. Firenze: Vallecchi.

1972. *Il Concetto di Egemonia in Gramsci*. Roma: Editori Riuniti.

1977. "Introduzione," pp. 5–15 in Antonio Tatò (ed.), *Comunisti e Mondo Cattolico Oggi*. Roma: Editori Riuniti.

Guareschi, Giovannino. 1948. *Mondo Piccolo, Don Camillo*. Milano: Rizzoli.

Hellman, Stephen. 1975. "The PCI's alliance strategy and the case of the middle classes," pp. 373–412 in Blackmer and Tarrow (eds.), *Communism in Italy and France*.

Hoffer, Eric. 1951. *The True Believer*. New York: Harper & Row.

Istituto Centrale di Statistica. 1976. *Annuario Statistico Italiano, Edizione 1976*. Roma.

Jemolo, Arturo Carlo. 1965. *Chiesa e Stato in Italia dalla Unificazione a Giovanni XXIII*. Torino: Einaudi.

Kogan, Norman. 1966. *A Political History of Postwar Italy*. New York: Praeger.

Lange, Peter. 1975. "The PCI at the local level: a study of strategic performance," pp. 259–304 in Blackmer and Tarrow (eds.), *Communism in Italy and France*.

LaPalombara, Joseph. 1965. "Italy: fragmentation, isolation and alienation," pp. 282–329 in Lucian W. Pye and Sidney Verba (eds.), *Political Culture and Political Development*. Princeton, N.J.: Princeton University Press.

Leach, Edmund R. 1954 (1965). *Political Systems of Highland Burma*. Boston: Beacon Press.

Lenin, Vladimir. 1929. *What Is to Be Done?* New York: International Publishers.

Leonardi, Robert. 1974. "Fattori e prospettive di un voto. Un'analisi del 'si' in Emilia-Romagna," *Il Mulino* 23 (no. 233):453–68.

Leonardi, Robert, and Gianfranco Pasquino. 1975. "Le elezioni in Emilia-Romagna," *Il Mulino* no. 240, pp. 559–82.

Lombardo Radice, Lucio. 1964. "Un marxista di fronte a fatti nuovi nel pensiero e nella coscienza religiosa," pp. 81–111 in Mario Gozzini (ed.), *Il Dialogo alla Prova*. Firenze: Vallecchi.

1972. "La prova del dialogo," *Rinascita* no. 13 (31 marzo), pp. 18–19.

Longo, Luigi. 1946. "I comunisti e la religione," *La Lotta* (11 maggio) 3:20:3.

1966. "Relazione all'XI Congresso del PCI," in *XI Congresso del PCI: Atti e Risoluzioni*. Roma: Editori Riuniti.

Lopreato, Joseph. 1967. *Peasants No More: Social Class and Social Change in an Underdeveloped Society*. San Francisco: Chandler.

La Lotta: Organo della Federazione Provinciale Bolognese del PCI. 1945 (16 giugno). "Comunismo, religione e famiglia," *Lotta* 2:5:1.

1946 (7 marzo). "Comunisti e Cattolici," *Lotta* 3:10:2.

1948 (27 agosto). "L'anticomunismo è la maschera della reazione e della guerra," *Lotta* 5:38:1–2.

1948 (15 ottobre). "Per il migliore orientamento politico e per il rafforzamento ideologico: clericali e social-traditori al servizio dell'imperialismo," *Lotta* 5:46:3.

1951 (12 gennaio). "Un altro parroco ricatta i pionieri," *Lotta* 8:2:4.

1958 (20 marzo). "Una grande mobilitazione di popolo per sventare la minaccia clericale," *Lotta* 15:11:1.

1958 (27 marzo)."Una logica conclusione," *Lotta* 15:12:1.

1958 (24 aprile). "Per chi suonano le campane del Cardinale Lercaro," *Lotta* 15:16:2.

1958 (19 giugno). "Bologna culla di democrazia respinge l'attacco clericale," *Lotta* 15:24:1.

1958 (2 ottobre). "Se non sono matti non li vogliamo," *Lotta* 15:38:1.

Mack Smith, Dennis. 1969. *Italy: A Modern History*. Second edition. Ann Arbor: University of Michigan Press.

Manoukian, Agopik, ed. 1968. *La Presenza Sociale del PCI e della DC*. Istituto di Studi e Ricerche Carlo Cattaneo. Ricerche sulla partecipazione politica in Italia IV. Bologna: Il Mulino.

Marradi, Alberto. 1976. "Italy's referendum on divorce: survey and ecological evidence analyzed," *European Journal of Political Research* 4:115–39.

Marx, Karl. 1844 (1964). "Contribution to the critique of Hegel's philosophy of right," pp. 41–58 in Marx and Engels, *On Religion*.

Marx, Karl, and Friedrich Engels. 1964. *On Religion*. New York: Schocken Books.

Menapace, Lidia. 1974. *La Democrazia Cristiana: Natura, Struttura e Organizzazione*. Milano: Mazzotta.

Milani, Lorenzo. 1957 (1971). *Esperienze Pastorali*. Firenze: Editrice Fiorentina.

1970. *Lettere di don Lorenzo Milani, Priore di Barbiana*. Edited by Michele Gesualdi. Milano: Mondadori.

Natta, Alessandro. 1967. "Le conclusioni: la nostra forza punto di riferimento per una diversa prospettiva politica di progresso e di libertà," Relazione all'Assemblea Nazionale dei Segretari di Sezione. *Vita di Sezione* no. 5 (aprile), pp. 18–20.

1972. "Cattolici e comunisti: obiettivi dell'incontro," *Rinascita* no. 13 (31 marzo), pp. 13–16.

Nesti, Arnaldo. 1965. "Sul dialogo fra cattolici e comunisti," *Studi Sociali* nos. 3–4, pp. 277–344.

1969. *I Comunisti, l'Altra Italia*. Bologna: Edizioni Dehoniane.

1974. *Gesù Socialista: una Tradizione Popolare Italiana*. Torino: Claudiana.

Occhetto, Achille. 1972. "La funzione del sud nella lotta contrattuale," *Rinascita* no. 27 (7 luglio), pp. 3–4.

Ordine Nuovo. 1920 (1971). "La questione romana," *Ordine Nuovo* vol. 2, no. 16 (2 ottobre). Reprinted in PCI, *Comunisti e Cattolici, Stato e Chiesa 1920–1971*, pp. 7–10. Roma: PCI.

Orfei, Ruggero. 1976. *L'Occupazione del Potere: i Democristiani '45–'75*. Milano: Longanesi.

Pansa, Giampaolo. 1975. *Bisaglia, una Storia Democristiana*. Milano: Sugarco.

Parisi, Arturo. 1974. "Questione cattolica e referendum: l'inizio di una fine," *Il Mulino* 23 (no. 233):410–38.

Parisi, Arturo, and Gianfranco Pasquino. 1976. "20 giugno: struttura politica e comportamenti elettorali," *Il Mulino* 25 (no. 245):342–86.

1977. "Relazioni partiti-elettori e tipi di voto," pp. 215–49 in Parisi and Pasquino (eds.), *Continuità e Mutamento Elettorale in Italia*.

Parisi, Arturo, and Gianfranco Pasquino, eds. 1977. *Continuità e Mutamento Elettorale in Italia*. Bologna: Il Mulino.

Parisi, Arturo, and G. Senin-Artina. 1979. *Matrimoni e Secolarizzazione*. Firenze: Istituto di Storia delle Istituzioni Religiosi dell'Università di Firenze.

Partito Comunista Italiano. 1944. *Comunisti e Cattolici*. Piccola Biblioteca del P.C.I. Pamphlet.

1948. *Due Anni di Lotta dei Comunisti Italiani*. Relazione sull'attività del P.C.I. dal 5 al 6 Congresso. Roma.

1960. *Tesi Politiche del IX Congresso del Partito Comunista Italiano*. Roma.

1964. *Il Partito Comunista*. Sezione per l'educazione ideologica. Roma.

1968. *Dati sull'Organizzazione del PCI*. Sezione centrale di Organizzazione. Roma.

1970. *Il PCI e la Classe Operaia nella Lotta per il Socialismo*. Sezione scuola. Roma.

1972. *PCI '72*. Sezione centrale stampa e propaganda. Roma.

1975. *Statuto del Partito Comunista Italiano*. Roma.

1977. *Almanacco PCI '77*. Sezione centrale stampa e propaganda. Roma.

1978a. *Almanacco PCI '78*. Sezione centrale stampa e propaganda. Roma.

1978b. *Partito Comunista Italiano '78*. Booklet distributed with *Almanacco PCI '78*. Roma.

Partito Comunista Italiano, Federazione di Bologna. 1971. *Tesseramento e Proselitismo al P.C.I. e alla F.G.C.I.* Bologna.

Partito Comunista Italiano, Comitato Regionale Emiliano. 1950. *Le Organizzazioni Clericali in Emilia*. Bologna.

Partito Comunista Italiano, Segreteria Regionale Veneto. 1955. *Problemi della Propaganda fra le Masse Cattoliche del Veneto*. Mimeo.

Pasquino, Gianfranco. 1975. "Crisi della DC evoluzione del sistema politico," *Rivista Italiana di Scienza Politica* 5:443:72.

1978. *The P.C.I.: A Party with a Governmental Vocation*. The Johns Hopkins University Bologna Center Research Institute Occasional Paper no. 19. Bologna.

Pedrazzi, Luigi. 1974. "DC e Gerarchia prima e dopo il 12 maggio," *Il Mulino* 23 (no. 233):439–52.

Perego, Angelo. 1962. *Dottrina e Prassi del Partito Comunista Italiano*. Second edition. Roma: Sugraro.

1965. "Il P.C.I. di fronte alla religione," *Studi Sociali* nos. 3–4.

Pizzorno, Alessandro. 1966. "Introduzione allo studio della partecipazione politica," *Quaderni di Sociologia* 15:235–71.

1972. "Elementi di uno schema teorico con riferimento ai partiti politici in Italia," pp. 3–40 in Sivini (ed.), *Partiti e Partecipazione Politica in Italia*.

Poggi, Gianfranco. 1967. *Catholic Action in Italy. The Sociology of a Sponsored Organization*. Stanford: Stanford University Press.

1968. *L'Organizzazione Partitica del PCI e della DC*. Istituto di Studi e Ricerche Carlo Cattaneo. Ricerche sulla partecipazione politica in Italia II. Bologna: Il Mulino.

Portelli, Hugues. 1974. *Gramsci et la Question Religieuse*. Paris: Editions Anthropos.

Powell, David E. 1975. *Antireligious Propaganda in the Soviet Union*. Cambridge, Mass.: MIT Press.

Prandi, Alfonso. 1957. "La religiosità italiana tra il mito e la realtà," *Il Mulino* 6 (no. 68):383–403.

1968. *Chiesa e Politica: la Gerarchia e l'Impegno Politico dei Cattolici Italiani*. Bologna: Il Mulino.

Prandi, Carlo. 1977. "Religion et classes subalternes en Italie: trente années de recherches italiennes," *Archives de Sciences Sociales des Religions* 43:93–139.

Pratesi, Piero. 1977. "Il voto dei cattolici," pp. 90–92 in *Almanacco PCI* '77. Roma.

1978. "Il lungo viaggio di un cattolico," pp. 84–89 in *Almanacco PCI* '78. Roma.

Riccamboni, Giancarlo. 1976. "The Italian Communist Party and the Catholic World," *Social Compass* 23:141–69.

Ronchey, Alberto. 1978. "Questa Parolaccia che è l'Egemonia," *Corriere della Sera* (11 marzo), p. 1.

Rossi, Alberto Mario. 1963. "Il Partito Comunista in Emilia," *Il Mulino* 12 (no. 123):28–42.

Sani, Giacomo. 1975. "Mass-level response to party strategy: the Italian electorate and the Communist Party," pp. 456–503 in Blackmer and Tarrow (eds.), *Communism in Italy and France*.

1976. "Political traditions as contextual variables: partisanship in Italy," *American Journal of Political Science* 20:375–406.

Santini, Alceste. 1975. *Questione Cattolica, Questione Comunista*. Roma: Coines.

Sartori, Giovanni. 1965. *Partiti e Sistemi di Partito*. Firenze: Editrice Universitaria.

Sivini, Giordano. 1971. "Socialisti e cattolici in Italia dalla società allo stato," pp. 71–108 in Giordano Sivini (ed.), *Sociologia dei Partiti Politici*. Bologna: Il Mulino.

1972. "Struttura organizzativa e partecipazione di base nel Partito Comunista Italiano," pp. 141–67 in Sivini (ed.), *Partiti e Partecipazione Politica in Italia*.

Sivini, Giordano, ed. 1972. *Partiti e Partecipazione Politica in Italia: Studi e Ricerche di Sociologia Politica*. Milano: Giuffrè.

Sivini Cavazzani, Ada. 1968. "Partito, iscritti, elettori," pp. 161–79 in Umberto Segre (ed.), *La DC dopo il Primo Ventennio*. Padova: Marsilio Editori.

Smith, Waldemar R. 1977. *The Fiesta System and Economic Change*. New York: Columbia University Press.

La Società. 1977. "Gli iscritti al PCI negli ultimi dieci anni quartiere per quartiere, comune per comune," *La Società: Politica, Cultura, Economia* (mensile della Federazione Bolognese del PCI), no. 7 (novembre), pp. 58–61.

Spreafico, Alberto. 1977. "Analisi dei risultati elettorali del '76," *Quaderni dell'Osservatorio Elettorale* 1:119–53.

Stern, Alan J. 1972. "Organizzazione politica e sviluppo economico a livello locale," *Rassegna Italiana di Sociologia* 13:707–38.

1975. "Political legitimacy in local politics: the Communist Party in Northeastern Italy," pp. 221–58 in Blackmer and Tarrow (eds.), *Communism in Italy and France*.

Tamburrano, Giuseppe. 1974. *L'Iceberg Democristiano*. Second edition. Milano: Sugarco.

Tarrow, Sidney G. 1967a. *Peasant Communism in Southern Italy*, New Haven: Yale University Press.

1967b. "Political dualism and Italian Communism," *American Political Science Review* 61:39–53.

1972. "The political economy of stagnation – Communism in Southern Italy, 1960–1970," *Journal of Politics* 34:93–123.

1975. "Communism in Italy and France: Adaptation and Change," pp. 575–640 in Blackmer and Tarrow (eds.), *Communism in Italy and France*.

Tatò, Antonio, ed. 1977. *Comunisti e Mondo Cat; lico Oggi*. Roma: Editori Riuniti.

Tentori, Tullio, and Paolo Guidicini. 1972. *Borgo, Quartiere, Città: Indagine Socio-Antropologica sul Quartiere di S. Carlo nel Centro Storico di Bologna*. Milano: Franco Angeli.

Togliatti, Palmiro. 1929 (1971). "Fine della questione romana," pp. 15–21 in PCI, *Comunisti e Cattolici, Stato e Chiesa 1921–1971*. Roma.

1938 (1971). "Noi e i Cattolici," pp. 22–25 in PCI, *Comunisti e Cattolici*. Roma.

1944 (1964). "I compiti del partito nella situazione attuale," pp. 71–98 in PCI, *Il Partito*. Roma.

1947 (1971). "Discorso alla Costituente sull'articolo 7," pp. 30–41 in PCI, *Comunisti e Cattolici*. Roma.

1954 (1971). "Per un accordo tra Comunisti e Cattolici per salvare la civiltà umana," pp. 42–56 in PCI, *Comunisti e Cattolici*. Roma.

1956 (1975). "La via italiana al socialismo," dal rapporto al l'VIII Congresso del PCI, pp. 104–116 in Pietro Valenza (ed.), *Il Compromesso Storico*. Roma: Newton Compton Editori.

1965. *Comunisti e Cattolici*. Roma: Editori Riuniti.

Toldo, Antonio. 1960. *Risultati dell'Inchiesta sulla Frequenza alla Messa Festiva nel Comune di Bologna*. Bologna: ISAB.

1969. *Le Cento Parrocchie Urbane di Bologna*. centro Diocesano di Ricerche Socio-Religiose Bologna no. 14. Bologna: ISAB.

Toschi, Tommaso. 1964. "Di fronte al comunismo," in Archidiocesi di Bologna, *Il Cardinale Lercaro 50°*. Bologna: Casa della Carità.

Valentine, Charles. 1967. *Culture and Poverty*. Chicago: University of Chicago Press.

Visentini, Giorgio. 1974. "L'image du Parti comuniste," pp. 183–99 in

294 Bibliography

Fondation Nationale des Sciences Politiques, *Sociologie du Comunisme en Italie*. Paris: Armand Colin.

Viviani, Luciana. 1950. "Le feste popolari nel mezzogiorno," *Quaderno dell'Attivista* (1 maggio) 14:22.

Weber, Maria. 1977. *Il Voto delle Donne*. Torino: Centro di Ricerche e Documentazione Luigi Einaudi.

Wiatr, Jerzy J. 1970 (1967). "The hegemonic party system in Poland," pp. 312–321 in Erik Allardt and Stein Rokkan (eds.), *Mass Politics*. New York: Free Press.

Zaccone Derossi, Flavia. 1962. "L'inserimento nel lavoro degli immigrati meridionali a Torino," pp. 221–42 in *Immigrati ed Industria*. Milano: Edizioni di Comunità.

Zunino, Pier Giorgio. 1975. *La Questione Cattolica nella Sinistra Italiana (1919–1939)*. Bologna: Il Mulino.

   1977. *La Questione Cattolica nella Sinistra Italiana (1940–1945)*. Bologna: Il Mulino.

Index